Improving

What State NAEP Test Scores

Student

Tell Us

Achievement

DAVID GRISSMER · ANN FLANAGAN
JENNIFER KAWATA · STEPHANIE WILLIAMSON

Supported by the
ExxonMobil Foundation
Danforth Foundation
NAEP Secondary Analysis Program
Center for Research on Educational Diversity and Excellence

RAND
EDUCATION

the present system does not use additional resources effectively because of its bureaucratic structure and lack of appropriate internal incentives to change. According to this view, improving education requires structural reforms that introduce competition by providing more choice within the system and more alternatives outside the system. Additional resources without this kind of structural reform would simply be wasted.

The alternative position sees resource constraints as the key issue—particularly with respect to disadvantaged students. This view assumes that additional resources can be used effectively, but only if targeted to specific programs and types of students. This position has been slowly modified to include a different type of structural reform: standards-based accountability within the public education system through defined criteria and measurements of achievement outcomes. In this view, a structure of accountability is needed to focus resources on meeting achievement standards. This type of reform has been implemented primarily at the state level, beginning in a few states in the mid- to late 1980s and, with varying designs, gradually spreading across states. If this type of reform is successful, that success should primarily be reflected in differential score gains across states that cannot be accounted for by family characteristics or changing resources.

Another reason to focus on achievement outcomes by state is that about two-thirds of the variance in per-pupil spending is between states, while only one-third is within states. While the state courts can address within-state inequalities, federal legislation is the primary means of addressing between-state differences. Thus, to inform federal policymaking, it is important to determine whether the significant inequalities between states affect student outcomes—particularly those for disadvantaged students.

Empirical nonexperimental research has not definitively answered the question of whether additional educational resources affect educational outcomes. However, experimental research, in combination with new reviews and interpretations of the empirical literature, is pointing to a hypothesis that additional resources primarily affect disadvantaged students but may have little if any effect on more-advantaged students. Since there is a wide variance across states in the proportions of disadvantaged students and per-pupil expenditures, an analysis of state achievement scores can help test this hypothesis.

Finally, resources are spent differently across states, allowing estimates of the effectiveness of different uses of resources. Perhaps more important, the different ways that resources are used in states can provide measures of both the marginal cost and marginal achievement benefit of changing resource usage, allowing cost-effectiveness comparisons. Such measures can help answer the questions of what uses of resources are most cost-effective in boosting student achievement and how much resources can affect achievement of disadvantaged students.

Until 1990, achievement could not be validly compared across states because no test gave representative samples of students in each state the same tests. In 1990, the Department of Education began to use the National Assessment of Educational Progress (NAEP) test, which had previously been given to national samples of students, to test representative samples of students in participating states in reading and math at the 4th- and 8th-grade levels. Seven such tests were administered from 1990 to 1996. Successful reform initiatives are expected to take years to be fully reflected in achievement outcomes, so this period is probably too early to serve as a definitive test of whether reforms are successful. However, evidence of no achievement gains would certainly challenge current reform directions.

This report uses data from the NAEP to estimate score gains nationally and by state. It also uses these data to estimate the effects of varying levels and uses of per-pupil expenditures on student achievement. Finally, the report estimates the cost-effectiveness of the major alternatives for utilizing educational resources.

This report should be of interest to national and state executive branch policymakers and the state judiciary, all of whom are involved in setting educational policies. District superintendents and school principals, as well as teachers and parents, may also find parts of this analysis useful. This project was conducted under the auspices of RAND Education. The mission of RAND Education is to bring accurate data and careful objective analysis to the national debate on education policy.

CONTENTS

FIGURES

TABLES

This report presents results of a study that examined state-level achievement scores on the National Assessment of Educational Progress (NAEP) tests given in math and reading from 1990 through 1996. The report develops three measures that compare state performance: raw achievement scores, estimates of score differences for students with similar family characteristics, and estimated improvement trends. The analysis also focuses on measuring the effects on achievement of different levels of per-pupil expenditures and different policies that have significant resource implications and that have commonly been used in previous studies to explain achievement. The analysis also provides estimates of the cost-effectiveness of these resource-intensive policies. Finally, the report addresses whether there is evidence of score gains outside of resource-intensive variables that might indicate that diverse reform policies that have been widely implemented across states are raising achievement. The study represents a first step in understanding how various state policies, patterns of resource allocation, and reforms affect student outcomes and suggests directions for future research.

BACKGROUND AND MOTIVATION

States have always had significant influence over K–12 educational policies. That influence has increased even more during the latest wave of educational reform, dating from the mid-1980s. A broad and diverse range of new initiatives has been implemented, mainly at the state level. The initiatives include "systemic reform" efforts that establish and align standards with assessment, professional development, and some form of accountability for schools. Other initiatives include tightening certification and recertification standards for teachers, enhancing early education by subsidizing prekindergarten for lower-income families, and reducing class sizes in early grades. Many states also passed legislation authorizing charter schools, school choice, or contract schools. If reform policies are effective, these effects should appear in achievement gains and variations in trends in achievement gains across states.

States have a surprisingly wide degree of variation in the level of per-pupil expenditures and how they are utilized. Wide variation across states appears in nearly all educational measures, including

- Teacher-pupil ratios. In 1993, average pupil-teacher ratios for regular students varied from over 25 in California and Utah to under 15 in New Jersey, Vermont, and Connecticut.

- Spending per student. Levels of spending per student (adjusted for cost-of-living differences) varied from $9,000 in New Jersey and New York to $4,000 in Utah and Mississippi.

- Average teacher salary levels. Adjusted for cost-of-living differences, salaries ranged from over $40,000 in New York and Massachusetts to less than $30,000 in Mississippi.

- Teacher experience. The proportion of teachers with more than 20 years of experience varied from 11 percent in West Virginia to over 35 percent in Michigan, Pennsylvania, and Connecticut.

- Advanced degrees. The proportion of teachers with advanced degrees varied from over 80 percent in Indiana to less than 20 percent in North Dakota, Wyoming, and Idaho.

Such large variation in characteristics across states would offer a potential opportunity to measure their effectiveness if comparable measures of educational performance existed across states. Having 50 states take different approaches to education can provide a powerful advantage in the long run if research and evaluation can identify what works and what does not. Successful policies and practices can be adapted across states in a continual and ongoing process of improving education. Evaluating the effects of different and changing state policies then becomes an integral part of improving our schools and student outcomes.

Another reason to focus on states is that previous measurements of the effects of educational resources show quite different results if the measurements are done at the state level rather than the district, school, classroom, or individual level. Measurements at the state level have shown very consistent and robust positive effects of added resources on educational outcomes, while measurements at lower levels of aggregation show less-positive and more-inconsistent effects. The debate about the effectiveness of educational resources has primarily used measurements at lower levels of aggregation. More of such measurements are available, and researchers have presumed that less-biased measurements occur at lower levels of aggregation. The consistent and robust positive state-level measurements are generally viewed as biased upward.

The inconsistency of measurements at lower levels of aggregation has provided major support for a view that public education has been ineffective and inefficient in using additional resources. This inefficiency is hypothesized to be a result of poor incentives within the bureaucratic public school system, which is seen as "unreformable." In this view, providing more money to public schools is inefficient. A major focus of such reform efforts has been the attempt to circumvent existing public school structures by creating competition within the system or alternatives outside the system, including vouchers, charter schools, and outsource contracting for schools. A more-comprehensive assessment of student performance across states can help inform this debate by measuring whether different levels and allocations of resources across states affect achievement and the cost-effectiveness of various policy options. The results can also highlight states with different levels of unexplained performance on various measures related to achievement, thereby allowing more-intensive case studies to discover the source of these differences—particularly whether reform efforts are responsible.

STUDY OBJECTIVES

This study attempts to address these issues and has several specific objectives:

* to compare raw achievement scores across states and to determine which states have statistically significant improvements, taking account of all NAEP tests between 1990 and 1996

- to estimate NAEP scores for students with similar family characteristics across states to develop a better measure for the overall effects of educational policies and environments

- to determine whether trends and differences in scores across states for students from similar family backgrounds can be statistically linked to differences in state educational system characteristics that are resource intensive (including per-pupil expenditures, pupil-teacher ratios, public prekindergarten participation rates, teacher-reported adequacy of resources for teaching, teacher salary levels, teacher education, and teacher experience)

- to determine whether significant trends exist that are unaccounted for by these resource-intensive variables that might suggest effects from unobserved variables linked to reform efforts

- to estimate the costs of changing these resource-intensive policies and characteristics and to compare their cost-effectiveness in improving scores

- to propose a broader explanation for the pattern of achievement results reported here and in the empirical literature that also incorporates the new experimental class-size results and the historical pattern of spending and achievement in the nation

- to identify possible improvements in NAEP state data collection.

Given our results, we propose a broader explanation concerning the effectiveness of resources in the public school system that attempts to assess the pattern of previous nonexperimental results, the new results from experimental data, and the pattern of national score trends and resource growth from 1970 through 1996. This explanation states that additional resources provided to public schools mainly affect minority and less-advantaged students and that these effects can be large and significant if properly allocated and targeted. However, additional resources deployed in historical ways have had much less, if any, effect on more-advantaged students.

METHODOLOGY

Several issues have confounded attempts to assess student performance across states. Primarily, there have been no statistically valid measures of the achievement of representative samples of students across states until recently. While many states have collected achievement scores within their states for a number of years, these scores are not comparable across states. This absence severely restricted the type and likely success of evaluations of state policies. One result is that state-level research has focused on collecting data on what states are doing and how they are doing it, but rarely on how different state policies and practices affect educational outcomes.

Comparative state analysis became possible when the Department of Education gave the NAEP tests to representative samples of students across a voluntary sample of states in 1990, 1992, 1994, and 1996. Seven tests were given in reading and mathematics at either the 4th- or 8th-grade level. Each test was administered to approximately 2,500 students, with 44 states represented in the sample. These tests represent the first valid, comparable measures of achievement of representative samples of children in various states.

While these tests presented an opportunity to answer these questions, there were significant barriers to carrying out analysis with these data and obtaining the kind of reliable results policymakers need. First, previous research suggests that family variables would account for a substantial part of the variation of scores across states because of the wide variation in their demographic composition and family characteristics. The family variables collected with NAEP were limited, and those collected were reported by 4th- and 8th-grade students, making their quality problematic. Without accurate family control variables, the effects of school resource variables would be biased upward, since family characteristics are positively correlated with schooling characteristics. The analysis needed to address this issue.

The second issue is that the sample was small; the state scores lacked independence across tests; and states participated in an unequal number of tests. Our sample represented 44 states, with a total of 271 scores. Most states in the sample took either six or all seven tests, but some took only two. The scores from the same states are not independent, which effectively reduces the sample further. Results from small samples can be more vulnerable to statistical assumptions, estimation procedures, and the influence of a few extreme data points, so the analysis had to test the sensitivity of the results to these conditions.

The third issue is the credibility of results derived from models aggregated across states. Unlike the generally null effects previously measured at lower levels of aggregation, previous studies using state-level data have shown that educational resources have consistent positive, statistically significant effects on educational outcomes. The interpretation of this disagreement has generally been that measurements using less-aggregate data are more accurate and that state-level results are biased upward. So, an alternative explanation is required for this discrepancy to make state-level results credible.

The fourth issue also involves credibility. Models using nonexperimental data will be deemed more credible if they can predict results that agree with results using experimental data. The Tennessee Student-Teacher Achievement Ratio (STAR) class-size experiment showed that reducing class sizes in K–3 had positive and statistically significant effects through 8th grade. The effects are generally larger for minority and disadvantaged students. A more recent quasi-experiment with pupil-teacher reductions in Wisconsin also showed initial results similar to those of the Tennessee experiment. Models using nonexperimental data therefore need to test predictions against these results.

We attempted to address these issues in our study. First, instead of relying on NAEP-reported family variables, we used Census data and data from the National Educational Longitudinal Survey—the largest survey collecting both achievement scores *and parent-reported family characteristics*—to develop three sets of family variables that use different sources of data and methods of weighting the influence of family characteristics. We estimated both fixed- and random-effect models that make different, but plausible, assumptions about the statistical properties of the data. We used random-effect models with the general linear estimator with exchangeable correlation structure to address the issues of unequal variance and number of observations across states and the lack of independence of observations. We performed a variety of sensitivity analyses to determine how sensitive the results were to extreme data points and to alternative statistical estimation and modeling procedures.

Second, we used a model specification consistent with the results from the Tennessee class-size experiment. The experimental results from Tennessee seem robust to the inevitable flaws that occurred in the implementation of the experiment, and these results provide important lessons for specification of models with nonexperimental data, as well as important evidence about the effects of resources. The results of this experiment seem to indicate that including variables accounting for educational characteristics since school entry is important and that use of models incorporating pretests may be untenable. We also used our models to estimate a class-size effect for Tennessee and compared the results to the experimentally determined results from Tennessee. The results show agreement.

MAIN FINDINGS

Highlights of the Findings

Overall, the results paint a more positive picture of American public education than is commonly portrayed, especially with respect to effective allocation of resources. The following are some highlights of the findings:

- Public elementary students across states in our sample showed statistically significant gains (about 1 percentile point) in mathematics between 1990 and 1996.[1]

- Some states are making significantly more progress than others. The math gains across states showed that a few made gains of around 2 percentile points a year, while others had almost no gains.

- The group of more-rural northern states had the highest average achievement scores, and southern states were usually among the lowest. The more-urban northern states generally fell closer to the middle of the score distribution. This distribution is explained mainly by family rather than school characteristics.

- There were statistically significant differences—as large as 11 to 12 percentile points—among students with similar family characteristics across states. All regions of the country had states with both higher and lower student scores from similar families.

- Both the level of expenditure per pupil and, more importantly, its allocation affected student achievement—particularly for states

---

[1]The reading data are insufficient for analysis until the 1998 state NAEP reading data are included.

with disproportionately higher numbers of minority and less-advantaged students.

- Some educational expenditures are much more cost-effective than others. The difference in cost-effectiveness depends on how the expenditures are directed but can also vary markedly, depending on the SES level of the state, the current allocation of expenditures, and the grades targeted.

Evidence for the Effects of Reform

This analysis provides strong evidence that math scores from 1990 through 1996—controlling for population changes and participation rates—increased in most states for public school students by statistically significant amounts. Eighth-grade math scores increased more than 4th-grade scores. These math gains, which averaged about 1 percentile point a year, were far above the average gains experienced from 1973 through 1990. The small changes in resource-intensive variables during this period explain little of the improvement, so reform efforts would be the leading candidate to explain these gains. However, additional research, including case studies across states, is necessary to test adequately whether and which reform efforts may be linked to achievement gains.

Trends in reading scores cannot be assessed with the current data, since only two reading tests, given only two years apart, were available. The addition of the 1998 4th-grade reading test will provide a better assessment of national and state improvements in reading.

Some states had estimated math gains of approximately 2 percentile points per year, while some had little gain (see p. 62). Texas and North Carolina were among several states that made large, statistically significant gains, and state-administered tests also showed large gains during this period. The resource-intensive variables included in our analysis do not explain much of these gains over time. Therefore, reform efforts would be the leading candidates to explain the gains in these states.

Scores for Students from Similar Backgrounds

The scores of students with similar family and demographic characteristics varied by approximately 11 to 12 percentile points. Our analysis distinguishes three groups of states: those whose scores for students from similar families are significantly above the median state, those whose scores are below, and a broad middle group (see p.68). Adjoining states and states with similar family characteristics often have statistically significant differences for students with similar family characteristics.

In part, these score differences can be traced to several systemic features:

- lower pupil-teacher ratios

- higher public prekindergarten participation

- lower teacher turnover

- higher levels of teacher-reported adequacy of resources for teaching.

Texas was in the highest group of states and California in the lowest on scores for students from similar families. The difference is about 0.34 standard deviations, indicating that similar students in the two states would emerge from K–12 education with score differences of about 11 percentile points. The variables in our model explain two-thirds of the difference in these scores. The major contributions to the higher Texas scores are lower pupil-teacher ratios, a much larger percentage of children in public prekindergarten, and teachers who have more resources necessary to teach. However, in-depth analysis using these measures as guides will be necessary to reveal the more complex of the features of state educational systems that create differences.

The Effects and Cost-Effectiveness of Educational Resource Allocation

Other things being equal, NAEP scores are higher in states that have

- higher per-pupil expenditures

- lower pupil-teacher ratio in lower grades

- higher percentages of teachers reporting adequate resources for teaching

- more children in public prekindergarten programs

- lower teacher turnover.

Other things being equal, states with higher teacher salaries or a higher percentage of teachers with master's degrees do not have higher scores. The lack of effect from direct investment in salaries from this analysis may have four explanations, and further research should be undertaken to help identify the reason. One explanation is that interstate differences in salary may be less sensitive to achievement than are intrastate salary differences. The primary teacher labor markets may be within states in which interdistrict salary differentials may affect the supply and distribution of higher-quality teachers much more than do interstate differences. A similar analysis across school districts within a state might show stronger compensation effects.

A second explanation is that teacher salary is the schooling characteristic that correlates most highly with family SES variables, and part of the salary effect may appear as social capital. If teachers teach children who have SES levels similar to their own, it may be difficult to separate salary and social-capital effects. The other variables in our analysis show much less correlation with family characteristics.

A third explanation is that these measurements occurred during a period of an adequate supply—even surplus—of teachers across most regions and types of teachers. Lower salary sensitivity would be expected when supply is more readily available. However, labor-market conditions are changing markedly for teachers because of demand increases from rising retirements, lower class sizes, and rising attrition rates, partly because of a strong economy. The supply of teachers is not expanding much, because the job market outside teaching is strong. Sensitivity to teacher salaries would be expected to increase under these conditions.

Finally, the results could partly reflect the inefficient structure of the current teacher-compensation system. The current system rewards experience and education—but neither seems to be strongly related to producing higher achievement. If the system could distinguish and provide higher compensation for higher-quality teachers and those who are more effective with lower-scoring students, for whom there is more leverage for raising scores, one would expect a dollar of compensation to be more effective. However, in the current system, another dollar of compensation is used to reward experience and degrees and to raise all salaries—rewarding both high- and low-quality teachers—and teachers of both low- and high-scoring students. With such a compensation system, lower effects might be expected.

The effects of factors that influence achievement can vary markedly, depending on the type of students targeted and current program funding levels. For instance, lowering pupil-teacher ratios in states with high SES levels and current levels below the national average appears to have little effect. However, lowering pupil-teacher ratios for students in lower grades in states with low SES that have ratios above the national average has very large predicted effects. Prekindergarten also has much stronger effects in states with lower SES, while the adequacy of teacher resources appears to have significant effects for states regardless of family characteristics.

Taking into account both the costs and effects of policies, we found that the cost-effectiveness of resource expenditures could change by more than a factor of 25, depending on the program or policy, which types of students and grades are targeted, and the current program levels. The policies this analysis predicted to be most cost-effective include the following:

- providing teachers with more discretionary resources across all states

- in states with a disproportionate percentage of lower-SES students, lowering pupil-teacher ratios in the lower grades to below the national averages, expanding public prekindergarten, and providing teachers additional resources

- lowering pupil-teacher ratios in the lower grades to the national averages in states with average SES characteristics.

We also estimate that the use of in-classroom teacher aides is far less cost-effective than the policies cited above.

This analysis suggests that investing in better working conditions for teachers to make them more productive (lower pupil-teacher ratios, more discretionary resources, and improved readiness for school from prekindergarten) could produce significant gains in achievement scores. Conversely, efforts to increase the quality of teachers in the long run are important, but this analysis would suggest that significant productivity gains can be obtained with the current teaching force if their working conditions are improved.

THE BIGGER PICTURE: UNDERSTANDING EFFECTS OF INVESTMENTS IN PUBLIC SCHOOLS

Any general theory about the effects of public-school expenditures has to account for the following:

- the pattern of results in previous nonexperimental measurements

- the results of the Tennessee experiment and the Wisconsin quasi-experiment

- the pattern of national score gains and expenditure growth from 1970 through 1996.

One frequently advanced explanation holds that public schools have not demonstrated a consistent ability to use additional resources to improve educational outcomes. This explanation depends mainly on the inconsistency in nonexperimental measurements at levels of aggregation below the state level. It assumes that the inconsistency in measurements reflects inconsistency in the utilization of schooling resources rather than inconsistency in the measurement process. However, this explanation is not consistent with the experimental results from Tennessee or Wisconsin, with the large score gains for minority and disadvantaged students in the 1970s and 1980s, or with the positive and consistent nonexperimental results at the state level of aggregation.

We propose a different explanation that appears more consistent with the current experimental and nonexperimental evidence and historical expenditure and achievement trends. In our view, additional resources have been effective for minority and disadvantaged students, but resources directed toward more-advantaged students—the majority of students—have had only small, if any, effects. This explanation is consistent with the pattern of national score gains and expenditures from 1970 through 1996. Minority and lower-SES white students made significant score gains in the 1970s and 1980s, but more-advantaged students made much smaller, if any, gains. These gains for minority and lower-SES students followed the national effort to focus on inequalities in educational opportunity and southern desegregation, and modest levels of additional real resources were provided in the form of compensatory programs, reductions in pupil-teacher ratios, and more experienced and educated teachers. National pupil-teacher ratios declined during this period, and evidence from our model and from the Tennessee experiment would suggest that such reductions are consistent with explaining part of the black student gains in the 1970s and 1980s.

The results of the Tennessee experiment and Wisconsin quasi-experiment show positive, statistically significant long-term effects on achievement. The samples for these experiments were disproportionately drawn from the minority and disadvantaged student populations. Our state-level results also produced estimates for pupil-teacher ratio that are consistent with the size of the effects measured in the Tennessee experiment and also produced a similar pattern of larger effects for minority and lower-SES students found in the Tennessee experiment. This agreement suggests that aggregate-level measurements may provide more unbiased effects than less-aggregate models.

Our explanation cannot account for the lower, and inconsistent, pattern of previous measurements at levels of aggregation below the state level. Most independent literature reviews now conclude that the previous nonexperimental results show that the effects of additional resources on educational outcomes are generally positive. But these reviews have not yet explained the wide variance in previous results or why more-aggregate measurements show more positive and consistent effects than measurements at lower levels of aggregation. We hypothesize that the inconsistency reflects the measurement process itself rather than inconsistency in the use of resources.

Previous measurements used widely different specifications and assumptions that may account for the inconsistency. Previous measurements also did not focus much on measuring separate effects for high- and low-SES students. If most measurements contained typical student populations with large proportions of more-advantaged students, smaller effects might be expected, and effects would be "inconsistent" across studies if student characteristics changed.

Effects may also differ across grade levels, leading to "inconsistent" results across studies that focus on measuring different grade levels.

We also hypothesize that measurements at lower levels of aggregation made with available previous data sets may be biased downward. The Tennessee experimental data identified one source of such bias: missing variables for years of schooling since entry. Another is the use of pretest scores as controls in production-function specifications. However, other forms of bias, including selection effects and differential quality and specification of family variables across levels of aggregation, may plausibly introduce differential bias at lower levels of aggregation. Further research is needed that focuses on the direction and magnitude of differential bias across levels of aggregation. If the source of inconsistency in previous measurements at lower levels of aggregation can be found, whether from bias or different specifications or student characteristics, a broadly consistent picture could emerge of the effect of resources on educational outcomes.

IMPLICATIONS FOR POLICY: IMPROVING AMERICAN EDUCATION

As we have noted, one interpretation of the empirical evidence implies that, in the absence of fundamental reforms of incentives and organizational culture, additional resources for public education are not the answer to improving schools. Underlying this view is the idea that the public school system is too bureaucratic to reform itself and that it is necessary to create alternatives outside the current system or increased choice within the system to foster greater competition for public schools.

Our results show that resources can make significant differences for minority and lower-SES students in public schools and that between-state, rather than within-state, differences in resources are the main reason for inequitable resource levels for lower-SES students. Such between-state differences can only be addressed with federal programs. However, our results also suggest that significant gains that cannot be traced to changing resources are occurring in math scores across most states. Although much research is required to attribute these gains to specific reforms, a plausible explanation would suggest that ongoing systemic structural reform **within** public education might be responsible. These reforms may be linked to changing culture and/or incentives in public education or many other factors. But these results certainly challenge the traditional view of public education as "unreformable." Public education may be a unique type of public institution that can achieve significant reform because it consists of a large number of separate, but diverse, units whose output can be measured and compared, leading to the identification and diffusion of successful initiatives. But some caution is warranted until these student gains in elementary schools result in longer-term gains in secondary schools and lead to completion of more years of education and to greater success in the labor market.

There are reasons to believe that improvements in achievement may continue. The full effect of structural reform initiatives is not reflected in current achievement, and the identification of successful initiatives will likely result in diffusion across states. Better allocation of future resources can also raise achievement. A significant contribution may also come from improving educational research and development by relying more on experimentation, focusing on improving the methodologies and assumptions inherent in nonexperimental data, and pursuing a coherent research strategy focused on using experimental and nonexperimental results to build successful theories of educational processes within families and classrooms.

IMPLICATIONS FOR RESEARCH

Experimentation and Improving Nonexperimental Analysis

Expanded experimentation in education is critical to understanding educational processes and helping to determine the appropriate assumptions and specifications to use with nonexperimental data. Experimentation should be directed both toward measuring the effects of major resource variables and toward the critical assumptions used in nonexperimental analysis. In addition, research—both experimental and nonexperimental—is needed that seeks an understanding of what changes inside classrooms and in student development when resources changed. Research consensus is unlikely to emerge until we understand what causes the differences in experimental and nonexperimental measurements and the differences among nonexperimental measurements and until we have theories explaining how changing resource levels affect parent, teacher, and student behavior in the classroom and families and how these changes affect long-term student development in ways that result in higher long-term achievement.

Two hypotheses that arose from this analysis also need much more study. The first is the dynamic nature of achievement effects across grades, which the Tennessee experiment suggested. Schooling variables in one grade appear to be able to influence achievement at *all* later grades, so conditions during all previous years of schooling need to be present in specifications. It also appears that pretest scores may not adequately control for previous schooling character- istics. *The Tennessee results suggest that two students can have simi- lar pretest scores and similar schooling conditions during a grade and still emerge with different posttest grades that have been influenced by different earlier schooling conditions.* For instance, despite having similar schooling conditions in grades 4 through 8, relative changes in achievement occurred in grades 4 through 8 for students having one to two or three to four years in small classes in K–3. Thus, the answer to the question of whether a smaller class size in 2nd grade had an effect cannot be known until later grades, and that answer will depend on what the class sizes were in previous and higher grades.

Conceptually, this makes the effect of class-size reductions resemble a human "capital" input that can change outputs over all future peri- ods, and models that specify the effects of capital investments may be more appropriate. From the standpoint of child development, these results are consistent with the concepts of risk and resiliency in children. Children may carry different levels of risk and resiliency into a given grade that appear to interact with the schooling condi- tions in that grade to produce gains or losses. For instance, four years of small classes appear to provide resiliency against later larger class sizes, whereas one or two years do not.

A second key hypothesis underlying this analysis is that resource substitutions can occur between families and schools that can affect achievement. High family resources may often substitute for and supplement school resources in indirect and unmeasured ways that affect the accurate measurement of policy variables. Families may apply more of their own resources of time and money when school resources are lowered but apply less when schools are devoting more resources to students. Thus, students with higher levels of family resources may be more immune to changing school resources than are students with lower levels of family resources. This could help explain the weaker schooling effects for students in higher-resource families. Students from families with few resources show the most sensitivity to levels of school resources. However, the results of this analysis would imply that more school resources can substitute for lower family resources. These substitutions need to be the focus of much more research.

Improving NAEP Data

If NAEP would collect a *school district* sample rather than a *school* sample, historical data from school districts (not available at the school level of aggregation) and Census data could be used to obtain decidedly superior family and schooling variables for models. Census data can provide good family characteristics for school districts but not generally for schools. The necessity of including variables since school entry into specifications makes district-level samples necessary for developing analytical models below the state level of aggregation.

One additional advantage of moving to a district sample is that more scores could be compared for major urban school districts. The urban school systems pose a large challenge to improving student achievement, and being able to develop models of NAEP scores across the major urban school districts could provide critical information for evaluating effective policies across urban districts. The sample sizes would be much larger than at the state level and could be expected to provide more-reliable results than for states.

If NAEP does not move toward a district-level sample, collecting a very limited set of data from parents should be considered. The critical parental information could be obtained with no more than ten questions.

ASSUMPTIONS AND CAVEATS FOR INTERPRETING THE STUDY RESULTS

Achievement is only one of many desirable outcomes expected from our schools. Until other comparable measures of outcomes are available, test scores probably will receive a disproportionate share of attention. It is certainly possible to overemphasize achievement at the expense of other outcomes. It is also possible to have good schools that satisfy parents that may not be among the highest achieving. However, achievement is one important outcome expected of schools, and we should try to understand the policies that contribute cost-effectively to increase achievement and, at the same time, begin collecting a broader range of measures of school outcomes to achieve balance.

No test is a perfect indicator of what students have learned. Achievement scores reflect particular test items, and these items can emphasize more basic skills than critical-thinking skills. The NAEP state tests were redesigned in 1990 and reflect a mix of items testing more basic skills and some more-advanced, critical-thinking skills. Composite scores can mask important differences in kinds of achievement and knowledge, and more detailed analysis of sub-groups of questions is certainly needed to explore these differences.

Although NAEP strives to reflect a broad range of items so that some items reflect skills learned at earlier grades and some at later grades, the scores can reflect the timing of when students learn skills. Because of differences in curricula, students in different states do not learn particular skills in the same sequence or at the same grade level. The types of state assessments done and whether these assessments are more or less similar to NAEP tests may also influence scores. States that have standards and assessment systems that reflect NAEP might be expected to score higher because the curriculum is aligned with NAEP items.

"Teaching to the test" is often cited as a concern in assessments. Such a term carries three connotations. One is a temporary inflation of achievement: Teachers are doing something that can result in a short-term achievement gain, but the student's achievement will not benefit in the long term. In this case, achievement scores can be misleading indicators, and testing can provide perverse incentives. A second connotation of "teaching to a test" is more positive and suggests that tests reflect accepted standards for what children should know and that review and repetition are necessary to achieve both short- and long-term gains in achievement. This connotation should be of less, if any, concern. A third connotation is that an imbalance occurs in the time spent and priority placed on tested rather than untested subjects or on educational goals related to achievement rather than those not related directly to achievement. If achievement gains occur at the expense of untested subjects or other socially desired objectives, some concern is warranted. In this case, broader measures are needed, and priorities should be set across objectives.

These concerns are more prevalent for "high stakes" tests, those for which there are consequences for students, teachers, or administrators. These concerns are minor for the NAEP, since students and teachers receive no feedback or consequences for NAEP tests. However, high-stakes state assessments could certainly be reflected in NAEP assessments to the extent that the tests are similar.

The effects measured should be seen primarily as long-term effects of differences in policies. States should not necessarily expect to see the full effects measured in the first few years. The state differences measured here have, for the most part, existed over long periods, allowing students, teachers, parents, and curricula to make longer-term adjustments.

Our estimated differences in scores for students from similar families can reflect a variety of factors both related and unrelated to the education system. We have identified several factors related to the characteristics of the state educational systems that do account for part of the differences. However, these factors explain less than one-half of the differences. The remaining variance can arise from unmeasured family characteristics; unmeasured characteristics of the educational system; characteristics of other social-support systems for families and children; or particular factors creating social capital in states, such as foundations. The estimates made here are a first step to identifying further the factors within each state that contribute to achievement.

The effects and rankings presented here all have ranges of uncertainty associated with them that need to be taken into account in using these results for policy guidance. The effectiveness of certain policies measured across states can also hide certain context-sensitive factors that can make a factor either more or less effective. Implementation of similar policies can differ across states and local school districts; therefore, the particular effects predicted here may vary depending on the local or state context. The effects cited here represent estimates given the current contexts and implementation existing broadly across states.

Finally, these results are meant to identify effective policies and states whose students from similar backgrounds are performing at different levels. This information is a first step toward further identification of policies and practices that contribute to higher achievement and to understanding the reasons constraining broader implementation of successful policies.

The tendency for policymakers to blame or to take credit for these achievement results should be tempered by at least three factors. First, the achievement results from 1990 through 1996 can reflect policies and practices from the early 1980s through 1996. Eighth graders tested in 1990 entered school in 1982, and their scores reflect the quality of education throughout their schooling. The 1996 4th-grade scores reflect more-recent policies. Second, many of the reforms initiated since the mid-1980s require significant organizational adjustments and affect schools, teachers, and students only gradually. So, the full effects of policies initiated since the mid-1980s will not be reflected in these scores. Third, the research and development community in education has been unable to provide consensus results or pilot-tested policies and practices that could guide policymakers and educators to more effective practices. Without a critical mass of high-quality research, policymakers lack the key process required to improve education systematically. Without good research and development, progress in education or any other area will be slow, uncertain, and inefficient.

ACKNOWLEDGMENTS

Every RAND report reflects the influence of the technical reviewers, but the authors are unusually indebted to the technical reviewers of this report: Lionel Galway, Laura Hamilton, Lynn Karoly, and Stephen Klein. Their guidance and perseverance through several drafts was instrumental in improving the statistical methodology, the positioning of the research within the existing literature, the policy implications that could be drawn from the analysis, and the needed caveats associated with the analysis. The report also benefited from support, informal reviews, and comments by Dominic Brewer, Thomas Glennan, Steven Gorman, Cathleen Stasz, and Mike Timpane. David Adamson provided a more clearly written executive summary, and Phyllis Gilmore, in her role as editor, produced a final version much improved from the author's version.

We are also indebted for financial support and encouragement from Ed Ahnert of the ExxonMobil Foundation, Robert Koff of the Danforth Foundation, Alex Sedlacek, Program Director of the NAEP Secondary Analysis Program and Roland Tharp, Director of the Center for Research on Education, Diversity & Excellence (CREDE).

ABBREVIATIONS

COL   Cost of living

HLM   hierarchical linear modeling

IEP   Individualized Education Plan

IEP/DS   Individualized education plan and/or learning dis-
                abled student

K   Kindergarten

LEP   Limited English proficiency

NAEP   National Assessment of Educational Progress

NCES   National Center for Educational Statistics

NELS   National Education Longitudinal Study

OLS   Ordinary least squares

R&D   research and development

SAGE   Student Achievement Guarantee in Education

SAS   A statistical computer package

SASS   School and Staffing Survey

SAT   Scholastic Aptitude Test

SES   Socioeconomic status

SES-FE   Socioeconomic status—fixed effect

STAR   Student-Teacher Achievement Ratio

STATA   A statistical computer package

Chapter One

INTRODUCTION

RATIONALE FOR FOCUSING ON STATE ACHIEVEMENT RESULTS

States are the primary policymakers in several important areas of K–12 education. They are instrumental in determining how much is spent on education and how that money is used to reduce inequity in funding among school districts. States' policies include setting teacher certification standards; establishing maximum class sizes and minimum graduation requirements; setting educational standards in subjects; and establishing methods of assessing student performance and methods of accountability for teachers, schools, and school districts.

States have been the primary initiators of the latest wave of educational reform, starting in the mid-1980s, and a broad and diverse range of new policies has been implemented (Elmore, 1990; Finn and Reharber, 1992; Massell and Furhman, 1994). Many have followed a "systemic reform" movement that includes defining educational standards, aligning curriculum and teacher professional development to the standards, and having some form of assessment and accountability with respect to the standards (Smith and O'Day, 1990; O'Day and Smith, 1993).[1] While simple in concept, the design and implementation process is arduous, and states have made varying

---

[1]The phrase "systemic reform" is used to refer to an imprecisely defined set of reform initiatives. See Vinovskis (1996) for an excellent discussion of the origin of the concept, its use, and a critique.

1

amounts of progress toward these goals (Goertz et al., 1995; Cohen, 1996; Elmore et al., 1996; Massell et al., 1997).

Recent reform initiatives also include tightening certification and recertification standards for teachers either through more demanding college curriculum and professional development or passing entrance or recertification tests. Some states focus more on early education by subsidizing prekindergarten for lower income families or lowering class sizes in early grades. Many states passed legislation authorizing charter schools, school choice, or contract schools.

Another source of state variation in educational policies comes from state court decisions. Starting with the constitutional challenge in California in 1971 to the inequity across school districts in per-pupil expenditures, finance reform litigation has occurred in 43 states (Evans et al., 1999). Courts have overturned systems in 19 states and upheld systems in 20 states, with four still pending. Some states have made significant changes in the way education is financed by decreasing or eliminating reliance on the property tax to reduce inequality in per-pupil expenditures. Such reforms seem to result in modest reductions in inequality within states, but with diverse results across states (Evans et al., 1999). Only a few states have substantially eliminated variation in per-pupil expenditures across districts.

Having 50 states taking different approaches to education can provide a powerful advantage in the long run if research and evaluation can identify successful and unsuccessful approaches. If this occurs, successful policies and practices can be identified, refined, and appropriately adapted across states in a continual and ongoing process of improving education. Evaluating the effects of different and changing state policies then becomes a critical function in improving our schools and student outcomes.

If states adopted fairly uniform policies and implemented similar reform initiatives at the same time, evaluation would be more difficult, and its potential usefulness would be significantly weakened. However, the states have a surprisingly wide degree of variation in their educational policies and practices, making between-state variation a significant part of total variation. For instance, two-thirds of the variance in district per-pupil expenditures is between rather than within states (Evans et al., 1997). Thus, state-level analysis can be important in analyzing the effects of differential resources. Reform initiatives across states have also varied widely both in substance and timing of implementation. If reform policies are effective, it should be possible to see variations in trends in achievement scores across states.

The wide variation across states appears in nearly all educational measures. In 1993, average pupil-teacher ratios for regular students varied from over 25 in California and Utah to under 15 in New Jersey, Vermont, and Connecticut. Levels of spending per student (adjusted for cost-of-living [COL] differences) varied from $9,000 in New Jersey and New York to $4,000 in Utah and Mississippi. Average teacher salary levels (adjusted for COL differences) range from over $40,000 in New York and Massachusetts to less than $30,000 in Mississippi, while a measure of the experience of the teaching force—the proportion of teachers with over 20 years of experience—varies from 11 percent in West Virginia to over 35 percent in Michigan, Pennsylvania, and Connecticut. The proportion of teachers with advanced degrees varies from over 80 percent in Indiana to less than 20 percent in North Dakota, Wyoming, and Idaho. Such large variation in characteristics across states would offer a potential opportunity to measure their effectiveness if comparable measures of educational performance existed across states.

POTENTIAL BARRIERS TO ANALYZING STATE ACHIEVEMENT

Until recently, there were no statistically valid measures of the achievement of representative samples of students across states.[2] While many states have collected achievement scores within their states for a number of years, these are not currently comparable

---

[2]Average Scholastic Aptitude Test (SAT) scores are sometimes used to compare state outcomes. Research has shown that differences in average SAT scores at the state level primarily reflect different participation rates among students in the state (Powell and Steelman, 1996). State participation rates vary from less than 5 percent to over 80 percent of seniors. These differences in participation do not reflect only differing abilities to succeed in college, since some of the states with the highest National Assessment of Educational Progress (NAEP) scores have the lowest SAT participation. The states of Iowa, North Dakota, South Dakota, Minnesota, Nebraska, Wisconsin, and Oklahoma score above state averages on NAEP tests but have among the lowest SAT participation rates, at less than 10 percent.

across states, and there is significant doubt whether they ever will be (Feuer et al., 1999). This absence severely restricted the type and likely success of evaluations of state policies. One result is that state-level research has focused on collecting data on what states are doing, and how they are doing it, but rarely on how educational outcomes are affected by different state policies and practices.[3]

Comparative state analysis became possible when the Department of Education gave the NAEP tests to representative samples of students across a voluntary sample of states in 1990, 1992, 1994, and 1996. Seven tests were given in reading and mathematics at either the 4th- or 8th-grade level. Each test was administered to approximately 2,500 students with 44 states represented in the sample. These tests represent the first valid, comparable measures of achievement of representative samples of children in various states. These data are unique for assessing comparative trends in state achievement, whether students from similar families score differently across states and whether differences in state education policies and characteristics are linked to higher achievement.

While these tests present an opportunity to answer these questions, there are significant barriers to carrying out analysis with these data and obtaining the kind of reliable results policymakers need. First, previous research would suggest that family variables would account for a substantial part of the variation of scores across states because of the wide variation in demographic composition and family characteristics. The family variables collected with NAEP are limited, and those collected are reported by 4th- and 8th-grade students, making their quality poor. Without accurate family control variables, the effects of school resource variables would be biased upward, since family characteristics are positively correlated with schooling characteristics. The analysis needs to address this issue.

The second set of issues that the methodology must address is the small sample, the lack of independence of the state scores across

---

[3]Powell and Steelman (1996) used state SAT scores controlling for participation rates to assess the effects of some state policies. Hanushek and Taylor (1990) explored how model specification and missing variables affect the estimates of the net effect of state characteristics on achievement using the High School and Beyond surveys. But no specific policies were included. Card and Krueger (1996) attempt to link wages to the characteristics of state school systems, but significant unresolved methodological issues are present (Heckman et al., 1996).

tests, and the unequal number of tests in which states participated. There have been five math tests—8th-grade tests in 1990, 1992, and 1996 and 4th-grade tests in 1992 and 1996—and two reading tests at 4th grade in 1992 and 1994. Our sample represents 44 states, with a total of 271 scores. Most states in the sample took either six or all seven tests, but some took only two. The scores from the same states are not independent, which effectively reduces the sample further. Results from small samples can be more vulnerable to statistical assumptions, estimation procedures, and the influence of a few, extreme data points, so the analysis must test the sensitivity of the results to these conditions.

The third issue is the credibility of results derived from models aggregated across states. Unlike the generally null effects previously measured at lower levels of aggregation, previous studies using state-level data have shown consistent positive, statistically significant effects of educational resources on educational outcomes (Hanushek et al., 1996). The interpretation of this disagreement has generally been that measurements using less aggregate data are more accurate and that state-level results are biased upward. So, an alternate explanation is required for this discrepancy to make state-level results credible.

The fourth issue also involves credibility. Models using nonexperimental data will be deemed more credible if they can predict results that agree with results using experimental data. The Tennessee Student-Teacher Achievement Ratio (STAR) class-size experiment has so far withstood analytical scrutiny (Grissmer, 1999). The results show positive and statistically significant class-size effects through 8th grade from lower class sizes in K–3 (Finn and Achilles, 1999; Nye et al., 1999a; Nye et al., 1999b; Krueger, 1999a). These effects are generally larger for minority and disadvantaged students (Krueger, 1999a; Finn and Achilles, 1999). A new quasi-experiment in Wisconsin of pupil-teacher reductions also shows initial results similar to the Tennessee experiment (Molnar et al., 1999). So, models using nonexperimental data need to test predictions against these results.

The fifth issue is not analytic, but political. If evaluations are successful, some state educational systems will be identified as more successful than others. Inevitably, such results are reported by the press and enter the political debate. So, the reporting of results should place the results in the context of other research; reflect the uncertainties inherent in any analysis of this kind; and address, as far as possible, the potential misinterpretations, although misuse and misinterpretation will inevitably occur.

A particular problem is that state achievement results reflect policies and practices over at least the past 10 to 15 years, but current policy-makers and educators are likely to receive credit or blame.   Any credit or blame should be tempered not only by the long lead time required to develop and implement successful educational policies, but also by the absence of a productive research and development system that was able to provide guidance to policymakers and educators (Saranson, 1990; Wilson and Davis, 1994; Vinovskis, 1999; Cook, 1999; Grissmer and Flanagan, 2000).   With little useful guidance from research and development, it is difficult to hold policymakers and educators responsible for lack of progress.

Finally, setting sound policies requires not only credible measurement of the effects of different programs and policies but also corresponding estimates of the costs of each.   It is the relative cost-effectiveness of different programs and resource utilization that is needed to improve educational outcomes efficiently, yet there has been little work comparing cost-effectiveness of major policies and program alternatives. The importance of such estimates is illustrated by recent estimates that national class-size reductions in grades 1–3 to 20, 18, and 15 of at least $2, 5, and 11 billion, respectively (Brewer et al., 1999).   The opportunity costs of such expenditures can be high if later research shows more cost-effective approaches.

STUDY OBJECTIVES

We have tried to address each of these issues in this study. The study has the following objectives:

- to determine whether states are making significant achievement gains taking into account all NAEP tests between 1990 and 1996, and to estimate the annual trend and statistical significance for each state, controlling for changing demographics, exclusions and school-level participation rates

- to determine the size and statistical significance of differences in scores for students from similar families across states to develop a measure more closely connected to the effectiveness of K–12 schools and other nonfamily state characteristics

- to determine whether the trends in scores and the differences in scores across states for students from similar family backgrounds can be statistically linked to differences in resource-intensive state policies and educational-system characteristics

- to determine whether significant trends exist that are unaccounted for by these resource-intensive variables that might suggest effects from unobserved variables linked to reform efforts

- to estimate the costs of changing these resource-intensive policies and characteristics and compare their cost-effectiveness in improving scores

- to place the results in the context of previous experimental and nonexperimental studies and to suggest a hypothesis that might reconcile the current differences among nonexperimental studies and between experimental and nonexperimental studies

- to identify ways that the NAEP state data collections and research can be improved so that, as more state scores accumulate over time, even better results will become available.

This analysis serves only as an initial step toward understanding how state policies and education characteristics affect student outcomes and which are cost-effective. We focus in this report on measuring the effect of policies and characteristics that have significant resource implications and have been used commonly in previous studies. The combined set of resource variables accounts for over 90 percent of the variance in per-pupil spending across states and so captures much of how states are using resources differently. The variables include per-pupil expenditure, teacher salary levels, teacher experience and education, pupil-teacher ratio, public prekindergarten participation, and the teacher-reported adequacy of resources for teaching. There are many other variables that can affect education outcomes that need to be included in future models.

We measure the possible effects of reform only indirectly. Eventually, variables will need to be included that track specific reform efforts by state. However, we include trendlike variables in the analysis to account for any score increases that cannot be accounted for by changes in the resource-intensive variables listed above. The strong positive significance of the trend variables would provide some evidence for the presence of unobserved variables over time that affect achievement—a necessary, but not sufficient, condition if reform efforts are working.

A primary objective of the analysis is to guide more in-depth case studies of state education systems and reform initiatives. While our analysis identifies some important policies and characteristics that partially account for the different trends and scores across states, it leaves as much or more of the variance that can be linked to states unexplained as it explains.

Undiscovered variables or the more complex, interactive character-istics not easily captured in current statistical analysis may account for much of what creates the best educational outcomes. Only case studies can identify these characteristics. But simply doing case studies for states without knowing which states are performing better can be wasted effort. It is comparative case studies of states performing well and poorly that can best identify the undiscovered variables and the more-complex characteristics. This analysis can provide the needed guidance for such case studies.

REPORT ORGANIZATION

Chapter Two describes the state test results, the differing demo-graphic and family characteristics in states, and the policies and characteristics of state K–12 education used in this analysis. Chapter Three presents a literature review. Chapter Four provides the methodology. Chapter Five presents the results of the analysis esti-mating trends by state. Chapter Six provides estimates of scores by state for students from similar family backgrounds. Chapter Seven provides estimates of the effects of state policies and characteristics on state achievement scores. Chapter Eight provides cost estimates for changing policies and characteristics and compares the cost-effectiveness of various policies and characteristics. Chapter Nine summarizes the results, focusing on their policy and research impli-cations; places the results in context of previous experimental and nonexperimental studies; and provides a discussion of the strengths and weaknesses of the analysis.

Appendix A contains achievement results by state for each test and the characteristics of families and schools in each state. Appendix B provides exclusion and participation rates by state. Appendix C discusses potential sources of bias in measurements made at different levels of aggregation. Appendix D discusses the results of the Tennessee experiment and predicted results using our model. Appendix E presents the methods used to develop family control variables. Appendix F provides variable definitions. Appendixes G, H, I, J, and L provide the full regression results. Appendix K provides cost-effectiveness results for class size and teacher aides, based on the Tennessee experiment.

Chapter Two
THE STATE NAEP ACHIEVEMENT RESULTS AND STATE FAMILY AND EDUCATIONAL CHARACTERISTICS

This chapter first describes the NAEP achievement tests and their results by state. Achievement scores partially reflect the characteristics of families in states, and we discuss the two components of family influence: family and social capital. We also contrast the differing family characteristics by state. Achievement scores also reflect the characteristics of educational systems, and we contrast the differing educational system characteristics by state.

NAEP ACHIEVEMENT TESTS

The NAEP tests are the only tests using nationally representative samples of U.S. students that can be used to track long-term national trends and accurately measure differences between states. The tests have been given to national samples of 9-, 13-, and 17-year-old students beginning in 1969. The early tests were in science, math, and reading and were administered approximately every four years through 1988 and more frequently after 1988. Writing tests that could be compared over years were started in 1984, and geography, history, civics, and the arts have been tested more recently. State samples of students began in 1990, and seven state tests have been given in 4th-grade reading and math and 8th-grade math through 1996.

NAEP data collection takes students approximately 90 minutes to complete for a given subject. Matrix sampling of questions is used to allow testing a broad range of knowledge while limiting the time each student is tested. Bib spiraling of questions ensures that effects from the placement of questions within booklets and grouping of questions are minimized. The NAEP state tests are not simply multiple-choice tests measuring basic skills. The tests have constructed response items requiring responses from a few sentences to a few paragraphs, thereby testing more critical thinking skills.

Table 2.1 shows descriptive characteristics of the seven state reading and math tests given from 1990 to 1996 (Shaughnessy et al., 1998; Miller et al., 1995; Reese et al., 1997; Campbell et al., 1996). 8th-grade math tests were given in 1990, 1992, and 1996. Fourth-grade math tests were given in 1992 and 1996, and 4th-grade reading tests were given in 1992 and 1994. The four tests in the 1990-to-1992 period sampled only public school students. The 1994 reading and the 1996 4th and 8th-grade math tests also sampled representative groups of private-school students in states. Our analysis is focused only on public school scores.

Schools in each state serve as the sample frame, and stratification occurs within each state based on the state's unique characteristics. Stratification is aimed at increasing representation of minority students and adequate samples in rural, suburban, and urban areas. The samples ranged from approximately 2,000 to 3,000 students per state and from 30 to 150 schools within states.

Since participation was voluntary, the sample of states changes from test to test. Thirty-six states in our analysis participated in either six

Table 2.1

Description of Seven State NAEP Reading and
Math Tests Given Between 1990 and 1996

Year	Subject	Grade Level	States Tested	Range of Student Samples	Range of School Samples
1990	Math	8	38	1,900–2,900	30–108
1992	Math	8	42	2,000–2,800	28–112
1992	Math	4	42	1,900–2,900	44–143
1992	Reading	4	42	1,800–2,800	44–148
1994	Reading	4	39	2,000–2,800	51–117
1996	Math	4	44	1,800–2,700	51–132
1996	Math	8	41	1,800–2,700	30–116

or seven tests, and a total of 44 states participated in at least two tests.[1] Appendix A shows the states that took each test.

Two types of exclusions from testing are allowed: limited English proficiency (LEP) and individualized education plan and/or disabled student (IEP/DS). Approximately 1–2 percent of students nationally is excluded for LEP and about 4–6 percent for IEP/DS. Appendix B describes the exclusion criteria and shows the percentage exclusions by state for LEP and IEP/DS for each test. The range of variation across states for the average IEP/DS exclusion rate across tests is from 2.6 in North Dakota to 6.7 percent in Florida. The similar range for LEP exclusion is from 0.0 percent in Wyoming to 8.3 percent in California.

States show a fairly stable pattern across tests in exclusion rates, indicating uniformity in application of criteria over time. The cross-sectional variation in exclusion rates across states appears to arise mainly from differences in actual incidence of LEP and IEP/DS students. For instance, the variation in LEP rates is mainly accounted for by recent Hispanic immigration. In Appendix B, we address possible issues of bias caused by exclusion rates, and see little evidence that would indicate any significant bias arising from differential exclusion rates.

Nonparticipation also has the potential to bias results if nonrandom and significant differences exist across states. Both entire schools and individual students can choose not to participate. A high proportion of the nonparticipation comes from school nonparticipation. Substitution is attempted in the case of nonparticipation. Nationally, participation rates after substitution are approximately 85 percent. The range of variation across states for average participation

---

[1] Our methodology requires that a nationally representative sample of each racial and/or ethnic group be spread throughout at least several states. We eliminated Alaska and Hawaii because each contains significant proportions of unique racial and/or ethnic groups that do not have corresponding groups in other states. We eliminated the District of Columbia because it more closely resembles an urban school system and also because of the uniqueness in governance structure that involves both federal and district governments. It also has a unique mix of public and private school participation, in that most white students attend private school, while almost all other students attend public schools. We also eliminated Nevada, since it participated in only one test.

across tests is from 74 to 100 percent (see Appendix B for participation by state by test and the discussion of bias).

There is some evidence that participation tends to be lower for schools with lower socioeconomic status (SES), resulting in a correlation across tests in participation rates. States with lower participation on one test also tend to have lower participation in other tests. We correct for the effects of participation differences by including the participation rate in the regressions and also by weighting our family variables by the **actual** participation by race for each test.

STATE ACHIEVEMENT RESULTS

The state scores are highly correlated across tests (at least 0.77 and usually above 0.85). So, we summarize the achievement scores in Figure 2.1 using the average across all tests in which each state participated. Appendix A provides the ranked scores for each test and the correlation matrix across tests. The pattern of scores shows that

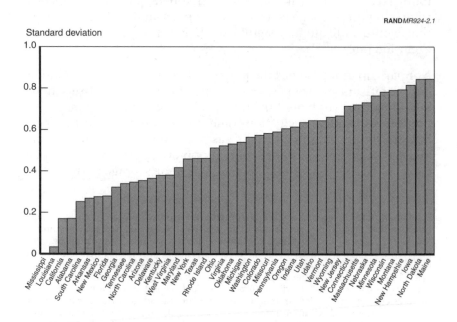

RAND*MR924-2.1*

Figure 2.1—Average State NAEP Scores Across Seven Tests

smaller, more rural northern states are disproportionately in the upper part of the distribution, while southern states disproportionately appear in the lower part of the rankings. Highly urban eastern, midwestern, and western states tend to be closer to the middle of the distribution. However, exceptions are present in nearly all categories. The difference between the scores for the highest and lowest state is three-quarters to one standard deviation across tests. Average scores in the highest ranked state would be approximately between the 62nd and 67th percentile nationally, while average scores from the lowest state would be around the 33rd to 38th percentile. This represents a significant variation in test scores among students from different states.

DIFFERENCES IN FAMILY AND DEMOGRAPHIC COMPOSITION AMONG STATES

Research that attempts to explain the variance in test scores across populations of diverse groups of students shows that family and demographic variables explain the largest part of total explained variance. Among commonly collected family characteristics, the strongest associations with test scores are parental educational levels, family income, and race and/or ethnicity. Secondary predictors are family size, the age of the mother at the child's birth, and family mobility. Other variables, such as being in a single-parent family and having a working mother, are sometimes significant after controlling for other variables.[2] The states differ significantly in the racial or ethnic composition of students and in the characteristics of the families of students, so it would be expected that a significant part of the differences in the NAEP test scores might be accounted for by these differences.

Table 2.2 summarizes the differences among states in our sample for eight family and demographic measures for families with children 8

---

[2]See Grissmer et al. (1994) and Appendix E for estimates of the relationships between national achievement scores and family characteristics for a national sample of 8th graders of almost 25,000 students. The family characteristics commonly available for analysis are often proxies for other variables that actually measure different behavior within families. When such variables as reading time with children, home environment, parenting styles, and measures of the characteristics of the relationships within families are available, they usually replace part of the effects from the more commonly available variables.

to 10 years old. Appendix A provides these measures by state. The racial and demographic composition of states varies dramatically, with less than 1 percent of students being black in many small northern states to almost 50 percent in Mississippi. The Hispanic student population is less than 5 percent in most states, but rises to almost 50 percent in New Mexico.

States also vary considerably in the average levels of parental education. For instance, the highest educational level of parents being college graduates varies from less than 20 percent in Mississippi, Arkansas, Louisiana, Kentucky, and West Virginia to over 36 percent in New Hampshire, New Jersey, Vermont, Utah, and Connecticut. The percentage having no high school diploma varies from about 20 percent in Texas, California, and Mississippi to less than 5 percent in Utah, Nebraska, North Dakota, and Minnesota. Family income varies significantly, from less than $28,000 in Mississippi and Arkansas to over $48,000 in Connecticut and New Jersey. States differ in the proportion of births to teen mothers—a proxy for the

Table 2.2

Range of Variation in Family Characteristics
Across States in Our Analysis

| Characteristic | Mean Value | Range of Variation | |
		Minimum	Maximum
Black[a] (%)	12.5	0.2	48.4
Hispanic[a] (%)	9.6	1.7	49.8
College graduate[a] (%)	25.9	17.5	40.0
No HS Diploma[a] (%)	14.5	5.9	25.9
Family income[a] ($000)	35.0	25.1	49.0
Teen births[b] (%)	12.8	7.2	21.3
Single parent[a] (%)	18.9	10.1	31.6
Working mothers[a] (%)	69.4	53.9	78.5
Family mobility[c]	64.8	50.0	75.9

[a]SOURCE: 1990 Census; characteristics are for families with children 8–10 years old.

[b]SOURCE: Statistical Abstract, 1993, Table 102.

[c]Family did not move in last two years. SOURCE: 1992 4th grade NAEP tests.

mother's age at a child's birth—from less than 8 percent in New Hampshire, Massachusetts, North Dakota, and Minnesota to over 18 percent in Arkansas and Mississippi. The percentage of single-parent families varies from under 12 percent in Idaho, Minnesota, and Utah to over 25 percent in South Carolina, Louisiana, and Mississippi. The percentage of working mothers varies from less than 60 percent in West Virginia, Kentucky, and Louisiana to almost 80 percent in Iowa, New Hampshire, and Nebraska. Finally, a measure of family mobility—the percentage of families who did not move in the last two years—varies from less than 55 percent in Texas, Arizona, California, and Florida to over 74 percent in Vermont, New Hampshire, and North Dakota.

It is clear that the states start with very different student populations to educate, and state test scores may largely reflect the difference in the ways that families and racial and/or ethnic groups are distributed among the states. For instance, a cursory review of the NAEP results shows that the states that score highest—small northern rural states—typically have among the highest levels of family income and parental education, while the lowest-scoring southern states have among the lowest levels of income and education.

FAMILY CAPITAL AND SOCIAL CAPITAL

The variance in scores explained by family characteristics arises from two sources: family human capital and social capital. Family capital refers to the characteristics within families that create higher achievement that would stay with families as they relocate. Family capital reflects innate characteristics passed from parent to child, the different quality and quantity of resources within families, and the different allocation of these resources toward education and each child (Becker, 1981, 1993).

Social capital usually refers to long-term capacities existing within communities and school districts or states, outside of individual family capital, that affect achievement but are outside of explicit control of the educational system (Coleman, 1988, 1990). Differences in social capital can arise partly from the long-term differences in joint characteristics of the families in geographical areas but can also arise from the different economic and social institutions present. Social capital influences achievement through such things as peer effects, quality of communication and trust among families in communities, the safety of neighborhoods, and the presence of community institutions that support achievement.

If families and economic and social institutions were randomly distributed across communities and states, few differences in social capital would arise, but there would still be significant differences between individual scores because of family-capital differences. However, families and social and economic institutions are not randomly distributed but tend to be grouped together by level of family capital in communities and states creating social capital. More social capital arises in communities and states having higher income and more educated families. Thus, the achievement scores across schools, communities, and states differ partly because their families differ in their internal capacity to produce achievement and partly because families with similar characteristics are grouped in communities or states creating different levels of social capital that can change the average achievement for their children.

Accounting for these differences due to family and social capital is critical before the contributions of the educational system can be assessed. It can be difficult to determine, empirically or even conceptually, where the effects of family capital end and those of social capital begin, or where those of social capital end and those of schooling begin. This is because families with higher family capital tend to seek, have better access to, and create areas of high social capital, and part of the expression of social capital is to influence the educational policies and practices of schools. Thus, communities with higher income and more educated families usually have higher per-pupil spending and smaller class sizes.

However, there are also significant nonfamily influences that create different educational policies and characteristics in school districts and states. The correlation between the key characteristics of educational systems and family characteristics across states shows the expected positive correlation of per-pupil expenditures, pupil-teacher ratio, and teacher salary with family income and parental education (see Appendix A). However, the correlation is usually less than 0.5. For instance, pupil-teacher ratio is correlated at less than 0.3 with any family variable. Thus, a significant amount of variation exists in state educational characteristics independent of social-capital effects.

DIFFERENCES IN STATE EDUCATION CHARACTERISTICS

There are several sources of nonfamily influence on state education policies and characteristics. Since educational funding and policymaking are inherently political processes, differences in political persuasion and leadership at all levels of policymaking can produce differences that do not reflect the characteristics of families. The courts have also influenced school policies through enforcement of policies designed to produce equity and adequacy in educational opportunity. The states also differ widely in their historical reliance on various sources of taxation for education and in their reliance on local, state, and national sources of funding. Thus, states and communities will have different vulnerabilities to economic cycles that can influence educational spending in states and communities.

Simple differences in population density also produce significant differences in average class and school sizes in more rural and urban states.[3] The relative influence of teacher unions and other stakeholders can also vary by state. For instance, some states prohibit collective bargaining contracts for teachers. The quite different distribution of teachers with different experience levels across states is partly caused by the dynamics of the baby-boom and -bust enrollments in the 1960s and 1970s and partly by the different population growth rates in states in the 1980s and 1990s (Grissmer and Kirby, 1997).

Another reason states have not followed similar policies is that little consensus existed from educational research and development about which policies are successful. So, states have tried a wide variety of different approaches to improving their educational systems. The net result of both family and nonfamily influences is a significant variance in educational policies among states. We illustrate the differences using six common measures: per-pupil spending, pupil-teacher ratio, teacher salary, teacher degree levels, teacher experience, and proportion of children in public prekindergarten.

---

[3]Schools that have only enough pupils for one or two classes per grade will generally have smaller class sizes if there is a maximum class size, above which classes must be divided. The average class size will approach uniformity as the number of students increases to fill more and more classes per grade.

Table 2.3 summarizes the range of these measures for states in our analysis during the period of schooling for our NAEP sample. Appendix A has measures for each state. Estimates of pupil-teacher ratio for regular students vary, with the largest ratios—over 25 in Utah and California—to the smallest—under 15 in New Jersey, Connecticut, and Vermont. Estimates for per-pupil spending for regular students (adjusted for COL differences) show less than $4,400 per pupil in Utah, Mississippi, and Alabama to almost $9,000 in New Jersey and New York. Average teacher salary levels (adjusted for COL differences) vary from less than $31,000 in Mississippi, Alabama, and New Mexico to over $40,000 in New York, Connecticut, and Massachusetts. These salary differences reflect variance in levels of teacher experience and education, as well as real differences in pay for teachers with similar experience and education (Chambers, 1996).

The educational levels of teachers vary considerably, from less than 20 percent with advanced degrees in North Dakota and Idaho to over

Table 2.3

Range of Variation in State Educational Characteristics
Among States in Our Analysis

| Characteristic | Mean Value | Range of Variation | |
		Minimum	Maximum
Pupil-teacher ratio[a]	18.1	14.2	26.4
Per-pupil expenditure[a, b]	5,957	4,000	9,200
Teacher salary[a, b]	34,360	28,320	44,020
Teachers without advanced degree[a] (%)	57.3	15.0	88.0
0–3 years of experience[a] (%)	9.6	3.3	14.0
20 or more years of experience[a] (%)	24.0	15.2	37.9
Students in public prekindergarten[a] (%)	6.8	0.2	30.8
Teachers reporting inade-quate resources[c] (%)	40.1	17.0	57.0

[a]SOURCE: The Digests of Educational Statistics (1980–1998). See Appendix F for more specific sources.

[b]Constant 1993–1994 dollars adjusted for cost-of-living differences across states.

[c]NAEP teacher survey for 4th-grade teachers in 1992.

80 percent in Connecticut and Indiana. The percentage of teachers with 25 or more years of teaching experience varies from over 30 percent in Michigan and Connecticut to less than 11 percent in West Virginia, Texas, and New Mexico. The percentage of children attending public prekindergarten programs varies from over 15 percent in Texas, Wisconsin, and Maryland to less than 2 percent in Mississippi, Indiana, North Carolina, and New Hampshire. Finally, the percentage of teachers that indicated the lowest categorical level for the adequacy of teaching resources varied from less than 25 percent in Nebraska, Wyoming, Iowa, and Montana to over 54 percent in Utah, Louisiana, Alabama, and Rhode Island. Such large variance in key variables improves the chances that analysis of state scores can measure their effects.

Chapter Three

REVIEW OF THE LITERATURE

Our literature review traces the changing debate about the effectiveness of additional resources in education and the effects of specific uses of resources on educational outcomes. Two-thirds of the total variation in per-pupil spending is between states, with only one-third within states. Besides the wide variation in average spending by state, the states also differ markedly in how the resources are spent. Surprisingly, almost all of the variance in the expenditure patterns between states can be captured by a few variables. Educational systems can hire more teachers to lower class size or support instruction, provide teachers higher salaries, provide teachers with more resources for teaching, or add an additional year of school at the preschool level. These four categories of expenditures (together with a per-pupil transportation and incidence of special education and LEP) account for 95 percent of the variance in per-pupil expenditures across states. So, these categories capture the major differences in the ways resources are used across states.

The schooling variables in our analysis correspond to these strategies: pupil-teacher ratio, teacher salary, teacher-reported adequacy of resources for teaching, and public prekindergarten participation. Two major sources of variance in teacher salary arise from differing experience and education of teachers. Our review of the previous literature will focus on these resource-intensive variables.

The debate about the effectiveness of total and specific resource uses mainly revolves around different interpretations from literature reviews and different conclusions about how educational resources have changed nationally from 1970 to 1996 and whether these changes are reflected in achievement scores. We address the latter debate first.

EVIDENCE FROM NATIONAL EDUCATIONAL RESOURCE GROWTH AND ACHIEVEMENT TRENDS

Measured in constant dollars using the standard Consumer Price Index to adjust for inflation, expenditures per pupil doubled between the late 1960s and the early 1990s. Hanushek (1994, 1996, 1999) cites an apparent lack of achievement gains in this period as support for the ineffectiveness of additional resources. The most visible measure of achievement—SAT scores—declined in this period. While the SAT scores can be easily discounted as valid measures of school achievement trends because of self-selection, Hanushek also cites the NAEP scores of representative samples of 9-, 13- and 17-year-old students as showing no clear positive trends.[1]

Other studies, however, provide a different interpretation of this evidence. Rothstein and Miles (1995) suggest that using the Consumer Price Index to adjust educational expenditures overstates the growth, since education is highly labor intensive. Use of more-appropriate indices for adjustment of educational expenditures provides much lower estimates of real growth—approximately 60 percent rather than 100 percent (Rothstein and Miles, 1995; Ladd, 1996a).

Even this smaller increase appears to overestimate the additional resources available to boost achievement scores. A significant part of the smaller estimated increase went for students with learning disabilities, many of whom are not tested.[2] A significant part also went for other socially desirable objectives that are only indirectly related

---

[1] See Grissmer et al. (1994) and Grissmer (forthcoming) for comparisons of SAT and NAEP scores and discussions of the flaws in the SAT scores.

[2] There is agreement that a disproportionate portion of the expenditure increase during the NAEP period was directed toward special education (Lankford and Wyckoff, 1996; Hanushek and Rivkin, 1997). Hanushek and Rivkin estimate that about a third of the increase between 1980 and 1990 was related to special education. NAEP typically excludes about 5 percent of students who have serious learning disabilities. However, special education counts increased from about 8 percent of all students in 1976 to 1977 to about 12 percent in 1993 to 1994. These figures imply that 7 percent of students taking the NAEP tests were receiving special education resources in 1994, compared to 3 percent in 1976 to 1977. This percentage is too small to have much effect on NAEP trends, but it should in principle have had a small positive effect.

to academic achievement. Taking into account better cost indices and including only spending judged to have been directed at increasing achievement scores for tested students, Rothstein and Miles (1995) concluded that the real increase in per-pupil spending for achievement of tested students was approximately 35 percent, rather than 100 percent.

This increase was disproportionately spent on compensatory programs directed toward minority and lower-income students or toward programs that might have disproportionate effects on their scores. Pupil-teacher ratios were significantly reduced nationwide in this period, and experimental evidence now suggests that minority and low-income students have much larger effects on achievement from such reductions (Finn and Achilles, 1999; Krueger, 1999a). If resources matter, the effects should be disproportionately seen in the scores of minority and lower-income students.

Overall NAEP scores show small to modest gains. Gains occurred in all three subjects (math, reading, and science) for 9- and 13-year-old students and in math and reading for 17-year-old students from the early 1970s to 1992 (Digest of Educational Statistics, 1995). The gains in science and reading were small—approximately 0.10 standard deviation (3 percentile points) or less for all age groups. However, math gains were larger for 9- and 13-year-old students—between 0.15 and 0.30 standard deviation. However, these aggregate results mask important differences for racial and/or ethnic groups.

During this period, substantial gains occurred for both Hispanic and black students and for lower-scoring white students (Hauser, 1998; Grissmer et al., 1994; Grissmer et al., 1998a; Grissmer et al., 1998b; Hedges and Nowell, 1998). For instance, black gains between 0.30 and 0.80 standard deviation occurred for almost all subjects for each age group. Hispanic gains were also much larger than white gains. NAEP scores show flat or minor gains only for white students not classified as disadvantaged—the majority of students.

Analysis of the cause of these gains suggests that changes in family characteristics could explain the smaller white score gains but could not explain most of the large minority gains (Grissmer et al., 1994; Cook and Evans, 1997; Grissmer et al., 1998b; Hedges and Nowell, 1998). Grissmer et al. (1998b) suggest that the timing and regional pattern of black score gains in the 1970s and 1980s are consistent with two explanations: changes in schooling and changing attitudes and motivations of black parents and students and their teachers.[3]

Pupil-teacher ratio fell nationally in this period of rising minority NAEP scores by approximately eight students per teacher—similar to reductions in the Tennessee experiment.[4] The national black score gains that would be predicted by the Tennessee experimental results are not inconsistent with explaining part of these national gains (Krueger, 1998; Grissmer et al., 1998b; Ferguson, 1998a).[5]

This evidence suggests an alternative explanation to Hanushek's: that additional resources matter most for minority and disadvantaged students but may matter much less, if at all, for more advantaged families—probably the majority of students (Grissmer et al., 1998b; Grissmer et al., 1998c).

PREVIOUS STUDIES

Reviews of Nonexperimental Studies

Until the early 1990s, the empirical evidence was widely interpreted as showing that providing schools additional resources would have little effect on student achievement—the so-called "money doesn't matter" thesis. This counterintuitive view dated from the "Coleman Report," which found family influences strong and school resources weak in explaining achievement differences across schools (Coleman et al., 1966).

Influential reviews by Eric Hanushek (1986, 1989, 1994) argued that evidence from the literature published prior to approximately 1990

---

[3]The shift in motivation and attitudes of black parents and students and their teachers would be expected with the expanding economic and educational opportunity for blacks arising from the implementation of civil rights, affirmative action programs, and war-on-poverty programs. Such a shift may have significantly altered the schooling experience of black students.

[4]There is some evidence, however, that actual class size may not have declined in proportion with pupil-teacher ratio (Boozer et al., 1992). We also do not know whether class size differentially changed for black and white students.

[5]Further research is needed on the NAEP trends to determine better the role of reduced class size and other changing factors that could have affected minority and white scores. For instance, the Tennessee results seem to predict higher white gains than can be attributed to nonfamily factors (Grissmer et al., 1998b).

provided no strong or systematic relationship between school expenditures and student performance. The reviews found that only a small proportion of previous studies had statistically significant results indicating a positive effect of resources, and a significant number of negative coefficients. It was suggested that a reason for this was the lack of appropriate incentives within the public education system to use resources effectively and efficiently (Hanushek and Jorgenson, 1996; Hanushek, 1994). This conclusion implied that the measurements reflected real differences in the effectiveness of resources across schools and school districts rather than bias from the measurement process itself.

Subsequent literature reviews questioned the criteria used in these reviews to choose studies for inclusion and questioned the assignment of equal weight to all measurements from the included studies. Two subsequent literature reviews used the same studies included in Hanushek's reviews but came to different conclusions. One study used meta-analytic statistical techniques for combining the measurements that do not weigh each measurement equally (Hedges et al., 1994). Explicit statistical tests were made for several variables for the hypotheses that the results support a mean positive coefficient and reject a mean negative coefficient. The researchers concluded that, for most resource variables, the results supported a positive relationship between resources and outcomes. In particular, per-pupil expenditures and teacher experience provided the most consistent positive effects, with pupil-teacher ratio, teacher salary, and teacher education having much weaker effects.

A more recent literature review using the same studies included in Hanushek's reviews also concluded that a positive relationship exists between resources and outcomes (Krueger, 1999b). This review criticized the inclusion and equal weighting of multiple measurements from single published studies. Some studies provided as many as 24 separate measurements because sets of results were presented for many subgroups. Since the average sample size will decline as subgroups increase, many of the measurements lacked the statistical power to detect policy-significant effects; thus, many insignificant coefficients might be expected. Since the presentation of results for subgroups is not done uniformly across studies, and may even be dependent on the results obtained, Krueger (1999b) reanalyzed the data to determine whether the inclusion of multiple measurements significantly affects the conclusions reached. His analysis concluded that the inclusion of multiple measurements is a significant factor in explaining the original conclusions and that placing less weight on these multiple measurements would lead to support for a positive relationship between higher per-pupil expenditures and lower pupil-teacher ratios and outcomes.

A more-comprehensive review of the literature prior to 1990 used meta-analytic statistical comparison techniques but searched a wider literature and imposed different quality controls. Greenwald et al. (1996) included studies that all used achievement as the dependent variable and measurements at the individual or school level only. The resulting set of measurements used in the study included many not included in Hanushek's studies, and about two-thirds of the measurements included in Hanushek's reviews were rejected.

The conclusions analyzing the set of coefficients from six variables (per-pupil expenditure, teacher ability, teacher education, teacher experience, teacher-pupil ratio, and school size) supported statistically the hypothesis that the median coefficients from previous studies showed positive relationships between resource variables and achievement. However, the variance in coefficients for each variable across studies was very large. Extreme outliers appeared to be a problem for some variables, and the coefficients across studies appeared to have little central tendency, indicating the presence of nonrandom errors.

This review also reported results for measurements using different model specifications (longitudinal, quasi-longitudinal, and cross-sectional).[6] The results showed that median coefficients changed dramatically for most variables across specifications, with no recognizable pattern. Although few studies were considered to have had superior specification (longitudinal studies), the median coefficients for these models were negative for per-pupil expenditure, teacher education, teacher-pupil ratio, and school size. When the median coefficients of studies having quasi-longitudinal studies were compared to coefficients from the entire sample, results were similar for

---

[6]*Longitudinal* studies were defined as those having a pretest control score, and *quasi-longitudinal* studies were defined as having some earlier performance-based measure as a control. *Cross-sectional* studies merely included SES-type variables included as controls.

four variables, but differed for the remaining two variables by factors ranging from 2 to 20. In the case of teacher salary, these studies provided a median coefficient indicating that a $1,000 salary increase could boost achievement by over one-half standard deviation.

This review used better screening criteria and better statistical tests to conclude that the overall evidence supported positive effects from additional resources. However, the large variance in coefficients and sensitivity of the median coefficients to which studies were included provided little confidence that the literature could be used to estimate reliable coefficients. In particular, models thought to have superior specifications provided no more consistent results and sometimes provided noncredible estimates. So, Hanushek's conclusion that results show inconsistency remains valid.

Two books published in 1996 addressed the questions of the effect of school resources on both short-term educational outcomes and longer-term labor force outcomes and were unable to reconcile the apparent diverse results from the literature (Ladd, 1996b; Burtless, 1996). While unable to explain the diverse results, the summaries focused attention on more-specific and testable questions (which uses of money matter) and on the critical methodological assumptions underlying much of the literature. In particular, Heckman et al. (1996) empirically tested a set of assumptions used in one study and found little support for many of the assumptions.

Some newer studies after 1990 that used better and more-recent data did show positive effects from resources (Ferguson, 1991; Ferguson and Ladd, 1996; Raudenbush et al., 1998). More-recent reviews by Hanushek (1996, 1999) included more-recent studies (over 90 studies and about 300 measurements) and showed similarly inconsistent results when results are equally weighted.

Hanushek's newer reviews also attempted to determine whether results differed when studies were grouped according to achievement outcomes, model specifications, grade level, and level of aggregation. Studies focusing on achievement showed no evidence of consistent effect whether focused on secondary or elementary levels or when they used the "best" specification (production function with pre- and post-test). However, the level of aggregation did show a marked difference in the pattern of results.

Table 3.1 summarizes the results of previous measurements by level of aggregation for the two reported variables: per-pupil expenditures and teacher-pupil ratio (Hanushek et al., 1996). The data show that the percentage of both the positive and the positive and significant coefficients increase with level of aggregation but shift dramatically upward at the state level. Almost all coefficients are positive at the state level, and about two-thirds are positive and statistically significant compared to less than 20 percent at the school and classroom level. These data are particularly surprising, since samples sizes of studies are probably much smaller at the state level.

The presumption among researchers has usually been that data at lower levels of aggregation provide superior estimates, but results at higher levels of aggregation are more prone to bias (Bryk and Raudenbush, 1988; Greenwald et al., 1996; Hanushek et al., 1996). So, the explanation of these results has generally been that aggregate measurements have an unidentified, upward bias. One analysis has suggested that the source of this bias is unobserved variables at the state level that are positively correlated with observed state-level variables (Hanushek et al., 1996). The unobserved variables suggested involve regulation of schools and teachers, but no empirical support was provided that these variables have significant effects.[7]

Goldhaber and Brewer (1997) provided empirical evidence suggesting that unobservables do not bias the measured effects of teacher characteristics at the *individual and school levels.* Using the National Education Longitudinal Study (NELS), they estimated achievement models using random and fixed effects at the teacher and school levels to account for unobservables. They concluded that, while unobserved teacher and school effects influence achievement, they introduce no bias in the measured effect, implying that there is no

---

[7]This analysis maintains on the one hand that resource variables at the state level have little effect but that positively correlated regulatory variables have strong, significant effects. Given that both state resource and regulatory policies arise from a somewhat similar political process, it is hard to see how one set of policies could be effective and the other not. There is also little empirical evidence to suggest a strong effect for regulatory policies in effect during the period of previous measurements. Recent research has suggested that one area of state regulation—teacher certification—has no effect on achievement, leading some to suggest a deregulation of teacher certification (Goldhaber and Brewer, 1999; Kanstoroom and Finn, 1999).

Table 3.1

Percentage of Coefficients from Previous Studies with Positive
or Positive and Statistically Significant Signs

	All Educational Outcomes				Achievement Only	
	Per-Pupil Expenditures		Teacher-Pupil Ratio		Per-Pupil Expenditures	
Aggregation Level	Positive	Pos. and Signif.	Positive	Pos. and Signif.	Positive	Pos. and Signif.
School/class	63.4	16.2	45.2	10.8	61.0	17.8
District	65.1	25.1	61.6	19.3	61.4	24.7
State	96.0	64.0	91.0	64.0	88.0	75.0

SOURCE: Hanushek et al. (1996).

correlation between the unobservables and included teacher characteristics. However, the result cannot be generalized beyond the current data set.

While reviews of past studies would now support a conclusion that a
generally positive relationship exists between resources and
achievement, the results are so inconsistent and unstable that no
reliable estimates are available to guide policy. The source of this
instability may be in the actual differences in effects across schools
and school districts or in bias arising from the measurement process.
Ferguson and Ladd (1996) and Heckman et al. (1996) directed attention to the number and fragility of assumptions underlying model
specification and estimation. These studies implied that a key source
of variation across previous studies might come from the measurement process itself (different model specifications and assumptions)
rather than real differences in resource effectiveness.

Previous studies have had widely different specifications and
assumptions that essentially make them impossible to compare.
Rarely is the same set of variables found in models, and the moderate
correlations between family and school variables and among school
variables make coefficients sensitive to missing and included variables. It is impossible to determine from previous measurements
whether the differences arise from real effects or differences in the
measurement process. The question needing an answer is how
results compare if previous studies used similar specifications and
assumptions while focusing analysis on similar types of students at

similar grade levels. It would not be surprising to see more consistent results emerge from past measurements if such a study could be carried out. However, this still leaves the question of what specification should be used in such an exercise.

There is no consensus among researchers for specification and estimation methods. Production function approaches have received much support, especially when used at lower levels of aggregation (Greenwald et al., 1996; Meyer, 1996; Hanushek, 1996). Others have suggested that hierarchical linear modeling (HLM) incorporating data from several levels of aggregation (individual, class, school, district) comes closest to producing unbiased results (Bryk and Raudenbush, 1988). Use of longitudinal data that would support modeling of achievement growth rather than depend on cross-sectional differences has also been suggested (Murnane, 1982). Singer (1998) has suggested that there may be far less difference between these approaches than commonly believed.

One consensus that seems to exist is that—regardless of the specific specification and estimation techniques used—measurements at lower levels of aggregation always dominate measurements at higher levels of aggregation. Partly, this preference arises because individual-level data are usually collected with special surveys allowing a more-diverse set of variables, and individual-level data usually have much larger sample sizes and wider variance in both independent and dependent variables. But this preference does not address the possibility that some forms of bias may be greater for less-aggregate measurements. The larger sample sizes usually present with data at lower levels of aggregation cannot compensate for bias. Thus, it is possible that more-aggregate measurements, even with significantly smaller sample sizes, may produce more-accurate measurements than analysis with individual-level data with significantly larger sample sizes.

We propose below that a possible consistent explanation of the non-experimental literature is that measurements at lower levels of aggregation are biased downward rather than that more-aggregate measurements are biased upward. However, distinguishing between these hypotheses requires a "benchmark" measurement that establishes whether more- or less-aggregate measurements are accurate. Such benchmark measurements can only come from experimental or quasi-experimental data.

Experimental Data on Class Size

Well-designed, implemented, and analyzed experimental data that are replicated remain as close as we can come to causal evidence in social science. The basic premise of experimentation—choosing two groups of subjects through randomization or preselection such that the only difference between them is the variable of interest—remains the ideal method of building social science knowledge. While experiments are potentially capable of providing the most compelling evidence, they often fall far short of achieving this objective because of the inevitable deviations from the ideal design (Boruch, 1994; Heckman and Smith, 1995; Manski, 1996). So, experimental data need to be analytically tested to determine whether the flaws undermine the results.

The main value of good experimental data is generally seen as providing a benchmark measurement for a given variable. However, experimental data can serve a far broader, and perhaps more important, purpose: testing assumptions and specifications used with nonexperimental data. The Tennessee experimental data have provided much information to guide model specifications.

The first experimental evidence on the effect of major educational variables came from a Tennessee study on the effects of class size (Word et al., 1990; Finn and Achilles, 1990; Mosteller, 1995). About 79 schools in Tennessee randomly assigned about 6,000 kindergarten students to class sizes of approximately either 15 or 23 students, and the design called for maintaining their class size through 3rd grade. Additional students entering each school at 1st, 2nd, and 3rd grades were also randomly assigned to these classes, making the entire experimental sample approximately 12,000. After 3rd grade, all students were returned to standard, large classes through 8th grade. The students in the experiment were disproportionately minority and disadvantaged—33 percent were minorities and over 50 percent were eligible for free lunches.

Analysis of the experimental data shows statistically significant, positive effects from smaller classes at the end of each grade from K–8 in every subject tested (Finn and Achilles, 1999; Krueger, 1999a; Nye et al., 1999a; Nye et al., 1999b). The magnitude of results varies depending on student characteristics and the number of grades in small classes. Measurements of the effect of spending four years in small classes at 3rd grade varies from 0.25 to 0.4 standard deviation (Krueger, 1999a, Nye et al., 1999). The current measurement of long-term effects at 8th grade show sustained effects of approximately 0.4 standard deviation for those in small classes all four years, but little sustained effect for those in smaller classes for one or two years (Nye et al., 1999a). Short-term effects are significantly larger for black students and somewhat larger for those receiving free lunches.[8]

Questions were raised about whether the inevitable departures from experimental design that occur in implementing the experiment biased the results (Krueger, 1999a; Hanushek, 1999). These problems included attrition from the samples, leakage of students between small and large classes, possible nonrandomness of teacher assignments, and schooling effects. Recent analysis has addressed these problems without finding any significant bias in the results (Krueger, 1999a; Nye et al., 1999a; Nye et al., 1999b). It is possible that further analysis would find a flaw in the experiment that significantly affects the results, but extensive analysis to date has eliminated most of the potential problems.

The Wisconsin Student Achievement Guarantee in Education (SAGE) quasi-experimental study differed in several important ways from the Tennessee STAR experiment (Molnar et al., 1999). In the SAGE study, only schools with very high proportions of free-lunch students were eligible for inclusion. Assignments were not randomized within schools; rather, a preselected control group of students from different schools was matched as a group to the students in treatment schools. The treatment is more accurately characterized as pupil-teacher ratio reduction, since a significant number of schools chose two teachers in a large class rather than one teacher in a small class. The size of the reduction in pupil-teacher ratio was slightly larger than class-size reductions in Tennessee.

There were about 1,600 students in the small pupil-teacher treatment group in Wisconsin, compared to approximately 2,000 students

---

[8]Long-term effects have not been reported by student characteristics. Following the experiment, Tennessee also cut class sizes to about 14 students per class in 17 school districts with the lowest family income. Comparisons with other districts and within districts before and after the change showed even larger gains of 0.35 to 0.5 standard deviations (Word et al., 1994; Mosteller, 1995). Thus, the evidence here suggests that class-size effects may grow for the most disadvantaged students.

in small classes in Tennessee. However, the size of control groups differed markedly—around 1,300 students in Wisconsin and around 4,000 in Tennessee, if both regular and regular-with-aide classes are combined. The SAGE sample had approximately 50 percent minority students, with almost 70 percent eligible for free or reduced-price lunches.

The results from the Wisconsin study for two consecutive 1st-grade classes show statistically significant effects on achievement in all subjects (Molnar et al., 1999). The effect sizes in the 1st grade are in the range of 0.1 to 0.3 standard deviations. The lower estimates between 0.1 to 0.2 occur in regression estimates, while the raw effects and HLM estimates are in the 0.2-to-0.3 range. While the estimates seem consistent with the Tennessee study at 1st grade, more analysis is needed before the results can be compared.

Evidence on Prekindergarten Effects

While little experimentation has been done with school resources, some quasi-experimentation has been done with respect to prekindergarten programs. The evidence from the best-designed and most-intensive small-scale "model" preschool programs showed significant short-term effects on achievement and IQ for disadvantaged minority children of 0.5 standard deviation or even higher (Karoly et al., 1998; Barnett, 1995). Ten of twelve model programs that had control groups showed gains between 0.3 and 0.7 standard deviation at age five (Barnett, 1995). Eleven of these programs measured achievement and IQ at 3rd grade or older, and only approximately one-half showed significant positive effects at these ages. The effects generally grew even smaller at older ages, although two studies showed significant achievement results at 14 or older.

However, these model programs focused on small samples of disadvantaged children with intensive interventions. Some interventions started at birth, while others were directed toward 3- to 4-year-olds, and almost all combined other services in addition to preschool programs. These programs generally had higher-quality staff, higher teacher-child ratios, and more funding than large-scale programs. So, the effects generated by these programs would be unlikely in large-scale public preschool programs (Barnett, 1995).

The evidence on the effects of pre-elementary school participation in large-scale programs points to significant effects for early grades that decline for later grades. Short-term effects are commonly measured in large-scale programs, such as HEADSTART (Barnett, 1995). Of the 21 programs Barnett reviewed, 17 had positive and statistically significant achievement effects in early grades. By the end of 3rd grade, only 12 had significant effects and only six had significant effects at the oldest age measured. The short-term effects for successful large-scale programs are much smaller than those for intensive, small-scale programs, which average 0.5 standard deviation (Barnett, 1995). So, short-term gains of around 0.1 to 0.3 might be expected.

However, the effects of early intervention for measures other than achievement (grade retention, special education placement, graduation rate, criminal activity, welfare utilization) were generally stronger and longer term (Karoly et al., 1998). This study did a cost-effectiveness analysis that showed positive long-term savings from investments in two early interventions when the interventions were targeted toward the more disadvantaged population. However, programs targeted toward less-disadvantaged populations showed no net cost savings. So, this analysis points as well to the need to match programs to particular populations. It is possible that a differently designed program could have been more effective for the more advantaged population.

The Effects of Teacher Characteristics

Since there are no experiments associated with teacher characteristics, their effects are more uncertain than for class size or prekindergarten programs. Recent literature reviews covering the nonexperimental studies on teacher characteristics suggest that teacher cognitive and verbal ability, teaching style, and expectations matter more than teacher education and experience (Ferguson, 1998a; Ferguson, 1998b; Darling-Hammond, 1997). Previous literature reviews and empirical evidence have generally shown stronger effects from teacher experience than teacher education (Greenwald et al., 1996; Ferguson, 1991; Ferguson and Ladd, 1996; Ehrenberg and Brewer, 1994; Ehrenberg and Brewer, 1995). Measurements of the effects of teacher salary have generally shown quite inconsistent effects (Greenwald et al., 1996).

SPECIFICATION IMPLICATIONS FROM EXPERIMENTAL STUDIES

The results from experimental data on class size are more consistent with nonexperimental studies at the state level than are the studies using less-aggregate data. This consistency at the state level may suggest that state-level measurements are not biased and that measurements at less-aggregate levels are biased downward. We suggest below that the Tennessee experimental data point to flaws in model specification that would introduce more bias into individual-level than state-level measurements with nonexperimental data. We also discuss in Appendix C other forms of bias known to be present in educational data that can plausibly produce greater bias in less-aggregate measurements.

The Tennessee results suggest several specification implications. First, schooling variables in one grade can influence achievement at **all** later grades, so conditions in all previous years of schooling need to be present in specifications. Second, a pretest score cannot control for previous schooling characteristics. *The Tennessee results suggest that two students can have similar pretest scores and similar schooling conditions during a grade and still emerge with different posttest scores influenced by different earlier schooling conditions.* For instance, despite having similar schooling conditions in grades 4–8, relative changes in achievement occurred in grades 4–8 for those having one to two or three to four years in small classes in K–3. Another way of stating this analytically is that effect sizes at a given grade can depend on interactions between this year's schooling characteristics and those of all previous years.

The production-function framework using pretest controls assumes that any differences in pre- and posttests are captured by changed inputs during the period. The Tennessee results suggest that coefficients of such specifications are **uninterpretable from a policy perspective**, since the effect of a change in resources during a period cannot fully be known until past and future schooling conditions are specified. Thus, the answer to the question of whether a smaller class size in 2nd grade had an effect cannot be known until later grades, and the answer will depend on what the class sizes were in previous and higher grades.

Conceptually, this makes the effect of class-size reductions resemble a human "capital" input that can change output over all future periods, and models specifying the effects of capital investments may be more appropriate.[9] Production functions generally assume constant levels of capital, but children's human "capital" is probably constantly changing and growing.

From the standpoint of child development, these results are consistent with the concepts of risk and resiliency in children (Masten, 1994; Rutter, 1988). Children carry different levels of risk and resiliency into a given grade that appear to interact with the schooling conditions in that grade to produce gains or losses. For instance, four years of small classes appear to provide resiliency against later larger class sizes, whereas one or two years do not.

Among commonly used model specifications, cross-sectional models that incorporate the schooling characteristics of all previous years come closest to being able to estimate the Tennessee results at each grade. Using a simple average class size in all previous years would provide a fairly accurate estimate of the Tennessee effects at 4th and 8th grade for students with different numbers of years in small classes.

Few, if any, previous studies have included variables for prior years' school characteristics from elementary school. At the individual level, virtually no longitudinal data from kindergarten were available. At more-aggregate district and state levels, data are usually available describing average characteristics for earlier years but were probably seldom used. We provide evidence from our data set in Appendix C that using only a single year of pupil-teacher ratio instead of an average over previous grades changes results significantly. Coefficients have appropriate signs and are highly significant when previous are years are included but are insignificant and have varying signs when only current-year pupil-teacher variables are used.[10]

---

[9]Production functions are typically used to model complete growth cycles in agriculture or other areas. We have tried to apply the production function to the much smaller increments of growth in children by using pre- and posttest results. Production functions may have done less well in earlier studies at predicting weekly plant growth than at predicting the complete cycle of growth over a season.

[10]These results can certainly be peculiar to this data set, and much wider empirical testing will be required.

RECONCILING EXPERIMENTAL AND NONEXPERIMENTAL RESULTS

Grissmer and Flanagan (2000) and Grissmer (1999) suggested that the issue of model specification and estimation for nonexperimental studies must be addressed through three approaches that could eventually generate scientific consensus and the "gold standard" model:

- focusing on empirical research that can validate or invalidate the assumptions underlying model specifications using nonexperimental data

- using experimentation and the resulting data to test specifications and assumptions used with nonexperimental data

- directing research toward understanding **why** changes in resources affect achievement and developing theories of educational processes.

Heckman et al. (1996) provided an example of testing assumptions underlying model specifications. It is possible to undertake a wide range of research directed toward verifying assumptions made in nonexperimental educational analysis. Why do students in large and small classes have different characteristics? How important are parent and teacher selection processes in determining class size? Do more-senior teachers choose smaller classes? Are assumptions more valid in some kinds of schools? Are class sizes in rural areas mainly randomly determined, whereas more selection occurs in cities? There are many empirical approaches to addressing these kinds of questions that would give us a better idea whether assumptions made in specifications are reasonable.

The second approach is to examine the assumptions made in nonexperimental specifications, such as production functions, concerning the nature of the mechanism inside the classroom that produces achievement effects. Previous studies have generally treated the classroom as a black box and the transforming processes inside as unnecessary to understand to measure accurate effects. Grissmer (1999) suggested that an understanding of these processes may guide the search for better specifications and assumptions to obtain accurate measurements.

We need to understand why changes in variables, such as class size, cause achievement gains. An understanding of what changes inside classrooms when class size is reduced and how these changes cause short- and long-term achievement gains can inform the model specification process. Some studies have suggested that teachers have more instructional time in small classes because they spend less time in discipline and administrative tasks and that teachers shift to more individualized instruction in small classes (Molnar et al., 1999; Betts and Shkolnik, 1999; Shkolnik and Betts, 1998; Rice, 1999). Students also exhibit more on-task behavior in such classes, even after being returned to larger classes in later grades (Finn and Achilles, 1999). Such shifts appear to be more dramatic in classes with more disadvantaged students.

Such research can lead to development of theories that explain why achievement might increase in small classes based on changed teacher and student behavior and the developmental path of students. For instance, Betts and Shkolnik (1999) and Shkolnik and Betts (1998) developed an economic framework for teacher time allocation in classes and its relationship with achievement. Grissmer (1999) suggested an expanded theory that includes the substitution of parental individual time for teacher individual time in the classroom, leading to different time allocation and styles of teaching in classes in which students have high or low levels of parental support. This type of analysis can suggest what variables should be in specifications, how they should be specified, and the interactions that need to be present in specifications.

Finally, experimental data can be designed to test the assumptions inherent in nonexperimental analysis. The Tennessee experiment— although not by design—has provided such information. In the long run, confidence in nonexperimental analysis is needed for policy guidance, since only a limited number of experiments will be possible. Also, contextual effects will be important influences in education because they limit the generalizability of experimental results.

SUMMARY: A NEW INTERPRETATION OF THE EMPIRICAL EVIDENCE

Any general theory about the effects of expenditures has to account for the following:

- the pattern of results in previous nonexperimental measurements

- the results of experimental data

- the pattern of national score gains and expenditure growth from 1970 to 1996.

One explanation advanced is that public schools have not shown any consistency in being able to use additional expenditures to improve educational outcomes. This explanation relies mainly on the inconsistency in nonexperimental measurements at levels of aggregation below the state level. It assumes that the inconsistency in measurements reflects the inconsistency in utilization of schooling resources. However, this explanation cannot account for the experimental results from Tennessee, for the large score gains for minority and disadvantaged students in the 1970s and 1980s, or for the previous nonexperimental results at the state level of aggregation. In the last case, it has been assumed that state-level measurements are biased upward, but no credible source of bias has been identified.

The explanation proposed here is that additional resources have been most effectively used for minority and disadvantaged students and that resources directed toward more-advantaged students have had only small, if any, effects. This explanation is consistent with the pattern of national score gains and expenditures from 1970 to 1996, the results of the Tennessee experiment and the Wisconsin quasi-experiment, and the results of previous nonexperimental measurements at the state level of aggregation. Both experiments had positive, statistically significant results and had samples that were disproportionately drawn from the minority and disadvantaged student populations.

This explanation cannot account for the inconsistent pattern of previous measurements at levels of aggregation below the state. We hypothesize that the inconsistency reflects the measurement process itself rather than inconsistency in the use of resources. The measurements have used widely different specifications and assumptions that may account for the inconsistency. We also hypothesize that measurements at lower levels of aggregation made with available previous data sets are generally biased downward. One source of such bias was identified by the Tennessee experimental data:

missing variables for years of schooling since entry. Another is the use of pretest scores as controls in production-function specifications. However, other forms of bias, including selection effects and differential quality and specification of family variables across levels of aggregation, may plausibly introduce differential bias at lower levels of aggregation. Further research is needed focusing on differential bias across levels of aggregation.

It should be noted that these conclusions are based on the characteristics of the data available to previous researchers. Few, if any, longitudinal data used in measurements prior to 1990 included data starting at kindergarten. Few, if any, measurements made prior to 1990 were able to use variables from school entry. Individual-level data that follow children from kindergarten and collect the important schooling characteristics—especially if the data can also be aggregated to the class, school, and district levels—still represent the ideal nonexperimental data set, and these data are now becoming available. Such longitudinal data can be used to test many of the hypotheses raised here and to assess whether individual-level data are more vulnerable to bias than more-aggregate–level data. Recently reported results with one such data set showed very large effects due to teacher quality (Sanders and Horn, 1998; Wright et al., 1997). But significant questions remain about the model specifications used in these studies.

Previous state-level studies did not have available achievement scores from representative samples of students across states. These studies either used nonachievement measures (high school graduation rates, etc.), the badly flawed SAT scores, or possibly results from a common set of tests used across a few states. One purpose of our study is to determine whether state-level aggregate results can be obtained that are broadly positive and significant when valid measures of achievement are used.

Chapter Four

METHODOLOGY

IMPLICATIONS OF THE LITERATURE FOR THIS ANALYSIS

The above evidence suggests that specifying aggregate models of state scores that take account of all educational characteristics from previous years is consistent with the Tennessee experiment. In fact, such aggregate analysis may be preferable to using the NAEP data at the individual or school level, since no previous-year data are available either for students or schools and since the quality of family data is decidedly inferior to that available at the state level.

The previous studies also suggest that the estimated model should compare its prediction of pupil-teacher ratio with the results from Tennessee using population parameters similar to those of the experimental sample. The Tennessee results also suggest the need to test whether effect sizes are different for disadvantaged and advantaged students.

Several other analytical issues arise that must be addressed by the methodology:

- the questionable quality of family data collected with NAEP tests

- the panel data with few observations over time and much stronger cross-sectional than time-series variation for scores and independent variables

- the nonindependence of the scores for each state

- the unequal number of observations per state

- the possible sensitivity of results to a few, extreme data points.

DEVELOPING FAMILY CONTROL VARIABLES

The scope and accuracy of NAEP family data are limited because 4th- and 8th-grade students reported them. The NAEP collects from students the family type (one or two parents), highest parental educational level, a measure of family mobility, and race and/or ethnicity. In addition, it collects from administrative records the percentage of students receiving free lunches or eligible for Title I, as proxies for family income. To supplement and check the accuracy of the NAEP variables, we derived five family variables for each state from the 1990 Census for families with students at the NAEP ages. Not surprisingly, Census and student-reported NAEP data on race and/or ethnicity and on family type show strong agreement (correlation of 0.95 and above). However, we found major differences between student-reported parental education and parent-reported education from the Census. For instance, data on parental education were missing for 36 percent of 4th-grade students. For those responding, about 57 percent reported that at least one parent was a college graduate, compared to about 25 percent from Census data for similar families.[1]

We used the 1990 Census data and NELS to develop alternative family control variables. The latter is the largest nationally representative data collection containing both achievement and family data. The NELS tested over 25,000 8th-grade students and collected data from their **parents** on family characteristics.

We developed three distinct sets of family control variables to determine whether the results are sensitive to the source of family data and the methods used to weight the effects from different family characteristics. The first set combines data from the 1990 Census and NAEP to provide parental educational levels, family income, race and/or ethnicity, family type, and family mobility. We also developed two composite SES-like variables using the NELS sample. We describe these variables briefly below. Appendix E describes the development of these three sets of family control variables in more detail.

---

[1]See Appendix E for comparison of Census and NAEP data and a discussion, and see Grissmer et al. (no date) for an analysis of differences.

The Census-NAEP Family Variables

Census data for families with children of ages similar to those of NAEP test-takers can provide better estimates for some family variables that are inaccurately reported by students. However, Census data still do not reflect the family characteristics of actual NAEP test-takers. NAEP excludes private-school, disabled, and LEP students and nonparticipants—all of whom are represented in Census files. In addition, the NAEP sample will reflect normal sampling variation and changes in population characteristics from 1990 to 1996. The Census can provide estimates only for the 1990 Census year.

If NAEP family variables are reported accurately, they will describe the NAEP test-taking population better than Census data will. Our analysis of these differences shows that the small differences in race and/or ethnicity and in family type primarily arise from differences in the NAEP and Census samples, while the differences in parental education are primarily due to inaccuracy in student reporting and bias in missing data (Grissmer et al., no date).

The most accurate set of family variables can be obtained by using a combination of NAEP and Census variables. NAEP variables appear to be accurately reported for race and/or ethnicity, family type, and family mobility. Census data appear to be better for parental education and family income. However, the Census variables can also be made to reflect the actual NAEP sample more closely by taking into account the actual racial and/or ethnic composition of the NAEP test-takers for each test.

We first used Census data for families having children either 8 to 10 years of age (4th graders) or 12 to 14 years of age (8th graders) to generate data on their parental education and family income **by racial and/or ethnic group** within each state. We then used the racial and/or ethnic composition of each NAEP test by state as weights to develop an estimate of the parental education and income of the families of NAEP test-takers.

For instance, the Census data may show that 35 percent of non-Hispanic white parents in Indiana with children 8 to 10 are college graduates, 15 percent for similar black parents, and 10 percent for similar Hispanic parents. If 80 percent of NAEP test-takers in Indiana for the 1990 test were white, 12 percent black, and 8 percent Hispanic, the estimates for NAEP families in the state would be (0.35) x (0.80) + (0.15) x (0.12) + (0.10) x (0.08) = 0.306. The estimated percentage of NAEP test-takers in Indiana who have a college-graduate parent is 30.6.

This method provides family variables that partially reflect changes in the characteristics of NAEP test-takers that are due to changes in private-school participation, exclusion rates, participation rates, population shifts over time, and normal sampling variation. To the extent that these factors shift the race and/or ethnicity of students taking NAEP, our variables will reflect such changes. However, these variables will not reflect that part of changing family characteristics that affects within-race and/or -ethnicity changes.

We have used this composite set of family variables from NAEP and Census for one set of family controls (called Census-NAEP in the rest of the report). These variables are race and/or ethnicity (NAEP), single parent (NAEP), highest parental education (Census adjusted by NAEP race and/or ethnicity), family income (Census adjusted by NAEP race and/or ethnicity), and family mobility (NAEP).

Composite SES Family Control Variables

Entering the above-defined Census-NAEP variables in the achievement regressions will generate coefficients for the family variables that essentially provide estimates for how much of the score differences should be attributable to family characteristics. The weakness of this approach is that these coefficients are estimated using only the 271 data points from state scores. Besides being a small sample, these data have much less variation in family characteristics than is available at the individual level. We developed a second approach to derive family control variables that uses the much larger sample of individual-level data from NELS to develop SES-like variables that weight the influence of each family characteristic.

We developed equations from NELS that relate reading and math achievement to eight family characteristics: highest educational level of each parent, family income, family size, family type, age of mother at child's birth, mother's labor-force status, and race and/or ethnicity (see Appendix E for the equations). These equations also essentially develop weights for the influence of each family characteristic and estimate how much of the difference in scores can be attributable to family influence.

We then used these equations to predict a score for each child in our Census sample in each state based on family characteristics alone. We then obtained the mean predicted score for three racial and/or ethnic groups in each state. We next used the actual race and/or ethnic composition taking each NAEP test to weight the race and/or ethnic mean predicted scores to obtain a state-level predicted score based on the family characteristics of NAEP test-takers. This SES variable may actually contain more accurate information about family influence than the Census-NAEP variables because the larger individual-level sample was used in its development. We refer to this composite family control variable as SES.

We want the family control variables to reflect the influence of family only. However, the NELS equations containing family variables only may still reflect some influence of school variables because of the correlation between family and school variables. To address this, we developed a third SES-like variable that used NELS achievement equations with family variables and added school fixed effects. This equation introduces a dummy variable for the approximately 1,000 schools in NELS that further reduces any influence of school variables in the family coefficients. The family coefficients from these equations are then used similarly to the way they are in SES to develop a "score" for each Census student with an age similar to those in NAEP. We refer to this family control variable as SES-fixed effect (SES-FE). When using the SES variables, we also include the measure of family mobility from NAEP, since this variable is not included in the SES composite.

MODEL SPECIFICATION AND ESTIMATION

We made estimates for the following:

- national and individual state gains on the three different tests (4th math, 8th math, and 4th reading) by state, and a composite annualized gain across all tests for the nation and by state while controlling for changes in family characteristics of the NAEP samples and NAEP participation rates

- differences in scores by state for students from similar families

- the effects of state education policies and characteristics on achievement scores

- the differential cost of changing state education policies and characteristics.

We estimated all models as a panel data set using both random- and fixed-effect specifications. Forty-four states are included, with up to seven tests per state. We used a generalized estimator with an exchangeable correlation structure for estimating the random-effect models. This estimator is recommended for panels with short time-series variation, accounts for the unbalanced panel, and provides robust standard errors that account both for the lack of independence of observations within states and heteroskedascity.[2] We used ordinary least squares (OLS) to estimate fixed-effect models with robust standard errors.

Using both random- and fixed-effect estimates allowed us to determine whether results change with different specifications. Random- and fixed-effect models apply different, but plausible, sets of assumptions to the data. The random-effect models assume no correlation between the set of independent variables and the state-specific error terms. The fixed-effect estimates allow a correlation to exist. Both specifications produce a state-specific residual that can be interpreted as the joint influence of state-specific factors not reflected in the independent variables in each analysis.

The Pagan-Breusch tests for the existence of state-specific effects were always highly significant across models. In the appendixes, we report on the Hausman test for systematic differences in fixed- and random-effect coefficients.

Annualized Score Gains by State

We modeled the average state scores as a function of state family and demographic characteristics and dummy variables for a score gain

---

[2]We have also fit the models using generalized least squares and maximum likelihood with nearly identical results. All estimation, except for the score differences for similar students, was done in STATA using the GEE estimator with exchangeable correlation structure. However, this procedure does not produce the random effects and estimates of standard errors for the random effects. We used the SAS Mixed procedure to estimate these models. This uses the maximum likelihood estimator and produces "estimates" of standard errors for the state-specific random effects. The results were virtually identical using any of the three correlation structure options in SAS.

on each repeated test. Because of the similarity between random- and fixed-effect models, we present the random-effect equations only:

$$y_{ij} = a + \sum b_k \, F_{ijk} + \sum g1_i \, d928th_i + \sum g2_i \, d968th_i$$
$$+ \sum g3_i \, d944th_i + \sum g4_i \, d964th_i + h1 \, d8th \qquad (4.1)$$
$$+ h2 \, d4rth + r1 \, p_{ij} + u_i + e_{ij} \, ,$$

where y_{ij} is the normalized test score (see detailed definition of how scores are normalized on page 52) for the ith state (i = 1,44) in the jth test (j = 1,7); F_{ijk} is a set of k family characteristics for the ith state at the time of the jth test; $d928th_i$ is a gain score dummy variable for improvement between the 1990 and 1992 8th-grade math test for the ith state; $d968th_i$ is a gain score dummy variable for improvement from the 1990 to the 1996 8th-grade math test for the ith state; $d944th_i$ is a gain score dummy variable for the improvement from the 1992 to 1994 4th-grade reading test for the ith state; $d964th_i$ is a gain score dummy variable for the improvement from the 1992 to 1996 4th-grade math test for the ith state; d8th and d4rth are dummy variables for the 8th-grade tests and 4th-grade reading tests, respectively; p_{ij} is the participation rate for the ith state in the jth test; u_i is the random effect for state i; e_{ij} is the usual identical and independently distributed error term; and a, b_k, $g1_i$, $g2_i$, $g3_i$, $g4_i$, h1, h, and r1 are coefficients in the regression.

We also included interaction terms between family variables and the 8th-grade math and 4th-grade reading dummies. This allows for the possibility of different family effects for 4th- and 8th-grade students and for reading and math.[3] The participation rate is included in the regressions to correct for changing participation rates of states. Using dummies for the 8th-grade and 4th-grade reading tests simply allows for differences in scaling or other differences between the three different tests.

To develop a single composite annualized gain measure across all tests, we substituted for the individual gain dummies a single vari-

---

[3]The NELS equations in Appendix E shows different family coefficients for reading and math. Reading is generally more influenced by family variables than math. We found that the family effects for 8th-grade math are generally stronger than they are for 4th-grade math.

able for each state that contains the number of years between each repeated test.[4] This variable, which reflects systemic gains across all grades and subjects from 1990 to 1996, will be a better indicator of the existence of successful state policies than simple two-way test comparisons.

Score Differences by State for Students from Similar Families

Meyer (1996), Raudenbush (1994), and Raudenbush and Wilms (1995) described the methodology to estimate value-added measures. These approaches usually assume that data are available at multiple levels of aggregation rather than just one level. In our case, the state-specific effects that both the random- and fixed-effect models estimate cannot be interpreted as estimates of "state value-added" in the sense that state factors alone are reflected. These parameters also reflect the net effects of district- and school-level policies. However, a more straightforward interpretation is that they reflect estimates of the differences in scores for students from similar families that can reflect influence across all levels of aggregation. The state-specific u's from random- and fixed-effect aggregate models can also reflect family factors not picked up by family variables in the equation, as well as influences of educational systems, social-service systems, and other factors specific to a state that influence achievement.

For each state, we estimated the predicted score difference for students with similar family backgrounds by estimating random- and fixed-effect models using family characteristics, participation rate, and national gain variables:

$$y_{ij} = a + \sum b_k \ F_{ijk} + g1 \ d928th + g2 \ d968th + g3 \ d944th$$
$$+ g4 \ d964th + h1 \ d8th + h2 \ d4rth + r1 p_{ij} + u_j + e_{ij} \ , \tag{4.2}$$

---

[4]We developed a single variable whose value is zero for the first application of each test and is the number of years between the first application and each subsequent application for remaining values. The order of our j tests is as follows: 1990 8th math, 1992 8th math, 1992 4th math, 1992 4th reading, 1994 4th reading, 1996 8th math, and 1996 4th math. So, the annualized gain variable entries for each state would be (0, 2, 0, 0, 2, 6, 4). The regression coefficient for this variable is the annualized gain across all tests.

where the variables are as defined above, and u_j is the estimate of score differences for students from similar families. We also include interaction terms between family variables and the 4th- and 8th-grade dummies.

The Effects of Educational Policy and State Characteristics

We estimated the effects of state policies and characteristics by introducing the variables corresponding to the state policies and characteristics (E_{ijl}) into equation 4.2, along with regional dummies (reg_m) and the urban and rural percentages (pd_n). The regional and urban-or-rural variables are recommended when modeling state-specific policy effects to ensure that the effects do not arise from factors connected to regional, rather than state, factors or population density.

The general model is:

$$y_{ij} = a + \sum b_k\, F_{ijk} + \sum c_l\, E_{ijl} + \sum r_m\, reg_m + \sum s_n\, pd_n$$
$$+ g1\, d928th + g2\, d968th + g3\, d44th + g4\, 964th \qquad (4.3)$$
$$+ h1\, d_{8th} + h2\, d_{4rth} + r1\, p_{ij} + u_i + e_{ij}\,,$$

where E_{ijl} is a set of l educational resource variables for the ith state averaged for the time in school before the jth test. In our estimation, we first included only one educational characteristic: per-pupil expenditure. We then estimated using variables that account for almost all the variance in per-pupil expenditures: pupil-teacher ratio, teacher salary, teacher-reported resource levels, and public prekindergarten participation. Finally, instead of teacher salary, we used two variables that explain much of the variance in teacher salary: teacher advanced degrees and teacher experience. The estimation also includes a full set of interactions between family variables and grade level and subject.

All of our resource variables are estimates of the average school characteristics during the period test-takers were in school, except the teacher-reported adequacy of resources, for which historical data were not available before 1990. For pupil-teacher ratio, we included the average from grades 1 through 4 and 5 through 8 separately, to reflect the possible stronger influence of early grades.

Cost Estimations

We estimated the cost of changing state policies and characteristics by regressing the per-pupil expenditure against the policy and characteristics variables and a per-pupil transportation cost, proportion IEP, and proportion LEP. The last two variables serve to control for differences in costs across states because of different transportation costs and differences in special education and LEP populations:

$$c_{ij} = a + \sum c_1\, E_{ijl} + q1\, ds_{ij} + q2\, le_{ij} + q3\, tr_i + u_i + e_{ij}\,, \qquad (4.4)$$

where c_{ij} is the per-pupil expenditure for the ith state for students taking the jth test; ds_{ij} is the proportion of IEP students in state i at the time of test j; le_{ij} is the percentage of LEP students in state i at the time of the jth test; and tr_I is the per-pupil transportation cost in the ith state.

Sensitivity to Outliers

In Appendix J, we present robust regression results to check for the sensitivity of results to outliers. We also ran other diagnostic analyses to test the sensitivity to outliers and multicollinearity. We did not find significant sensitivity to these factors in our equations.

VARIABLE DEFINITIONS

Appendix F contains detailed definitions for the variables. We briefly describe them below.

Achievement Scores

The data set contains 271 state achievement scores. The earliest state scores in each test category (1990, 8th-grade math; 1992, 4th-grade math; and 1992, 4th-grade reading) are converted to variables with a mean of zero and are divided by the standard deviation of national scores. The later tests in each category are subtracted from the mean of the earlier test and are divided by the same national standard deviation. This technique maintains the test gains within each category and allows the results to be interpreted in terms of changes with respect to national scores.

Family Variables

We described our family variables earlier in this chapter and in Appendix E. Three family variable sets were constructed. The first set (Census-NAEP) was constructed from 1990 Census data and NAEP family data from each test. The second and third sets (SES and SES-FE) were constructed using the NELS, Census, and NAEP data, for family mobility.

Educational Measures

Our educational variables focus mainly on the major variables that account for differences in resource expenditures in the state. We used per-pupil expenditures (adjusted for COL differences), pupil-teacher ratio, teacher salary (adjusted for COL differences), teacher education (percentage without advanced degrees), teacher experience (0 to 3 years, 4 to 9 years, 10 to 20 years, and greater than 20), teacher-reported adequacy of resources (some or none, most, all), and the percentage of children in public prekindergarten.

We defined our education measures as averages over the time in school prior to the NAEP test. So, the per-pupil expenditure is the state average for the years the student has attended school before the NAEP test. For instance, for the 1990 8th-grade test, we averaged per-pupil expenditures for 1983 through 1990. The public prekindergarten variable corresponds to the state participation in the year in which the tested group was four years old. The only variable not defined during the time in school is the NAEP-reported level of teacher resources that is recorded at the time of each test, so this may be biased downward. Appendix F contains more detailed definitions, means, and standard deviations for the variables in the analysis.

Chapter Five

TRENDS IN STATE SCORES

TESTING FOR EVIDENCE OF THE EFFECTS OF REFORM

The current wave of educational reform started in the late 1980s, and changes continue. It is too early to expect to see the full effects of such reforms but not too early to expect some effects. Some educational reforms require significant changes in the behavior of organizations and large groups of individuals—a process that requires years, not months. Other reforms operate gradually because they effectively "grandfather" current students and teachers. For instance, changes in entrance standards for teachers will take 10 years or more to affect a sizable portion of teachers, and new graduation requirements for students are usually scheduled to start at least five years into the future to give students and teachers time to adapt.

Another reason for expecting gradual effects is that student scores are likely dependent on all previous grades, so students need to experience reforms from the 1st grade before their full effects on scores at later grades are seen. If so, reform effects will be seen first in early grades. All of these considerations point to gradual, rather than dramatic, changes in scores from changing policies—a conclusion Murnane and Levy (1996) reached.

The 8th graders taking the 1990 math state test entered kindergarten in 1982, while the 1996 8th-grade group entered in 1988. Thus, the former group would have spent most of their years of schooling before much of the reform began, and the latter group would have experienced some reform during most of their school career. However, they would experience little reform over their entire school career.

The 4th graders taking the math test in 1992 would have experienced some early reforms during their schooling, while the 1996 group would have experienced the reforms implemented between 1988 and 1992 over their entire schooling. The reading tests should probably show the smallest difference from reforms, simply because the tests were given only two years apart, in 1992 and 1994.

The official state NAEP reports contain an indication of gain for each state from the previous similar test and an indication of the statistical significance based on the sampling standard errors (Shaughnessy et al., 1998; Miller et al., 1995, Reese et al., 1997; Campbell et al., 1996). These measures do not take into account changes in student populations that are due to migration, exclusions, participation rates, or sampling variations. They also do not reflect whether states are making systematic gains across all tests.

For instance, states in the southeast and southwest had significant increases in the population of Hispanic children from 1990 to 1996, while many northern states showed no increases. Unless these changes are accounted for in assessing trends, we cannot tell whether the educational system is causing changes in scores or whether population shifts are changing scores. Besides population shifts, the participation rates change for each state across tests, which can affect scores. Variations in the characteristics of students that are due to normal sampling variations also need to be taken into account. Our estimates take these factors either partially or wholly into account.

RESULTS

Estimated Gains Across All Participating States

We present estimates for five models consistently throughout the report.[1] To ensure that trends were robust across at least two of the

---

[1]The five reported models all have family coefficients with expected signs. The fixed-effect model using the Census-NAEP variables is the only model showing some perverse signs for family variables. These results imply that families with better-educated parents—other things being equal—would have lower scores. This model specification (fixed effect with Census-NAEP family variables) has the fewest degrees of freedom among the six models estimated. It contains five family variables fully interacted with 4th- and 8th-grade dummies. Given our limited sample size, this model seems to be unable to accurately estimate all family variables. For the gain results reported in

three repeated tests, our trend estimates include only states that participated in six or seven tests. We will focus on the nonfamily effects in the main body of this report. The full regression estimates for the trend analysis are contained in Appendix G.

Table 5.1 shows the estimated national gains for each repeated test, controlling for the changing family characteristics of the NAEP samples and participation changes. The results show statistically significant differences for each test, with little difference across models. The largest gains occurred for 8th-grade math tests, where composite gains from 1990 to 1996 are about one-quarter of a standard deviation, or 8 to 9 percentile points. Smaller gains of approximately 0.10 standard deviation or 3 percentile points occurred in 4th-grade math from 1992 to 1996. Reading scores show declines of about 0.10 standard deviation from 1992 to 1994. Such declines over such a short period for practically all states could reflect imperfect equating of successive tests.[2]

Table 5.1

Estimated Score Gains for Each Repeated Test
(standard deviation units)

	1990–1992 8th-Grade Math	1990–1996 8th-Grade Math	1992–1996 4th-Grade Math	1992–1994 4th-Grade Reading
Random—SES	0.104[a]	0.229[a]	0.096[a]	−0.092[a]
Random—SES-FE	0.104[a]	0.230[a]	0.095[a]	−0.097[a]
Random—Census-NAEP	0.126[a]	0.242[a]	0.094[a]	−0.073[a]
Fixed—SES	0.104[a]	0.227[a]	0.095[a]	−0.094[a]
Fixed—SES-FE	0.104[a]	0.226[a]	0.092[a]	−0.099[a]

[a]The data are statistically significant at the 1-percent level. Equation (4.2) was used for estimation, controlling for differences in student populations and state participation rates. Full regression results are given in Appendix G (Tables G.1, G.2, and G.3).

---

this chapter, there are virtually no differences between this model and the other five estimates. The model estimates differ more for the policy and score differences for similar students. We report the results of all six models in the appendixes.

[2]The 1998 4th-grade state reading NAEP results show a slight gain over 1992 results that may indicate a possible slight downward bias in the 1994 test.

There are sufficient math scores to make separate estimates for math gains alone. Table 5.2 converts the separate gains from each test to an estimated **annualized** gain in math scores. The results in the first row indicate statistically significant average annual gains in math scores (regardless of grade) of about 0.03 standard deviation or about 1 percentile point a year from 1990 to 1996.

The educational variables included in later analyses do not explain much of the trend in scores. When these variables are also included in the regression (row 2 of Table 5.2), the trend coefficients are only slightly reduced. Thus, much of the math increases have to be explained by factors outside our resource variables. Reform efforts of various kinds unrelated to per-pupil expenditure, pupil-teacher ratio, teacher characteristics, and teaching resources would be the leading candidates to explain these gains. The pattern of gains across states can provide further evidence about the source of these gains.

Estimated Annual Gains by State

The estimated annualized gains for individual states are summarized in Tables 5.3 and 5.4; Table 5.3 includes all seven tests, while Table 5.4 includes only math tests. We summarize the state results by presenting the average and range of coefficients across models and the statistical significance for each model.

About one-half of states show consistent, statistically significant annual gains when all seven tests are included, and about three-

Table 5.2

Estimated Annualized National Gains in Math Scores With and Without Policy Variables (standard deviation units)

| | Random Model | | | Fixed Model | |
	SES	SES-FE	Census-NAEP	SES	SES-FE
Annual gain (no policy variables)	0.032	0.032	0.032	0.031	0.031
Annual gain (policy variables included)	0.029	0.028	0.025	0.027	0.028

NOTE: The data are statistically significant at the 1-percent level.

quarters of states show consistent, statistically significant annual gains when only the five math tests are included. However, the rate of gains varies markedly across states, from being flat to as much as 0.06 to 0.07 standard deviation per year. The sizes of the latter gains are remarkable—far above what was experienced over the NAEP period from 1971 to 1990, where annual gains are around 0.01 standard deviation per year or less. Thus, there is significant evidence that many states are experiencing math score gains far above historical averages, and some states are producing gains far above those of other states.

Texas and North Carolina—the states showing the highest rate of improvement—were the subject of a case study to determine whether their state-administered test scores showed similar gains and to try to identify plausible reasons for such large gains (Grissmer and Flanagan, 1998). The state-administered tests given to all students statewide showed similarly large gains in math scores in both states, providing an independent verification of the NAEP trends.[3]

The case study concluded that the small changes in key resource variables and teacher characteristics could not explain any significant part of the gains. The study identified a set of similar systemic reform policies implemented in both states in the late 1980s and early 1990s as being the **most plausible reason** for the gains.[4] These policies included developing state standards by grade, assessment tests linked to these standards, good systems for providing feedback to teachers and principals, some accountability measures, and deregulation of the teaching environment. However, research across all states is needed before any conclusions about the cause of these gains can become compelling.

---

[3]The state-administered reading tests show somewhat smaller gains than the math tests, but the reading gains are still large. The reading gains for the state-administered tests are not reflected in the two NAEP reading tests from 1992 to 1994. However, the 1998 reading tests do show gains over 1992, and this evidence may support the hypothesis that equating the 1994 NAEP test with the 1992 test may have been problematic.

[4]These policies seemed to have originated in the business community in each state, which was instrumental in generating the agenda for reform and its passage in the legislature, and in the systemic reform ideas generated in the educational research community (Smith and O'Day, 1990; O'Day and Smith, 1993).

Table 5.3

**The Range, Mean, and Statistical Significance of Estimated
Annual Score Gains, Including All Seven Tests**

	Range		Average	Significance Level				
				Random Effect			Fixed Effect	
				SES	SES-FE	C-N	SES	SES-FE
North Carolina	0.056	0.058	0.057	1	1	1	1	1
Texas	0.047	0.055	0.052	1	1	1	1	1
Michigan	0.048	0.051	0.049	1	1	1	1	1
Minnesota	0.038	0.042	0.040	1	1	1	1	1
Indiana	0.036	0.043	0.040	1	1	1	1	1
Maryland	0.037	0.042	0.039	1	1	1	1	5
Florida	0.033	0.038	0.035	1	5	1	1	5
Connecticut	0.033	0.039	0.035	1	1	1	5	5
Kentucky	0.030	0.042	0.035	5	5	1	1	5
Nebraska	0.033	0.036	0.034	1	1	1	5	5
California	0.029	0.039	0.034	5	5	1	1	5
New York	0.032	0.035	0.033	5	1	1	5	5
Wisconsin	0.025	0.033	0.030	5	5	5	10	10
West Virginia	0.027	0.037	0.030	5	5	1	5	10
Colorado	0.026	0.029	0.027	5	10	5	5	10
Rhode Island	0.021	0.032	0.026	10		1	5	5
South Carolina	0.023	0.029	0.026	5	10	10	10	
New Jersey	0.014	0.026	0.023					
Maine	0.017	0.028	0.023	10	10	5		
Arizona	0.021	0.023	0.022			10	10	
Alabama	0.019	0.024	0.022			5	10	
New Mexico	0.015	0.025	0.021	10	10			
Louisiana	0.019	0.022	0.021			10		
Iowa	0.016	0.023	0.020	10	10	10		
Tennessee	0.016	0.027	0.019			5		
North Dakota	0.013	0.021	0.017					
Mississippi	0.014	0.020	0.017					
Virginia	0.011	0.018	0.014					
Delaware	0.012	0.018	0.014					
Arkansas	0.009	0.019	0.014					
Wyoming	0.011	0.015	0.013					

Table 5.3—Continued

	Range		Average	Random Effect SES	SES-FE	C-N	Fixed Effect SES	SES-FE
				Significance Level				
Massachusetts	0.008	0.019	0.012					
Missouri	0.007	0.015	0.011					
Pennsylvania	0.009	0.014	0.011					
Utah	0.003	0.016	0.008					
Georgia	0.001	0.010	0.006					

NOTE: Equation (4.1) was used for estimation. The full regression results are given in Appendix G (Tables G.4, G.5, and G.6).

It should be noted that, while the results clearly show that many states in the top portion of the ranking show statistically significant differences from those near the bottom, groups of states more closely ranked cannot be distinguished with any precision. In Table 5.3, states below South Carolina cannot be distinguished from each other with any precision. In the top part of the ranking, the first ten states also cannot be distinguished statistically. So, while Texas and North Carolina show the largest gains, their gains cannot be distinguished with any precision from states ranked in the next five to ten positions.

In Table 5.4, the results show about 12 states at the bottom that cannot be distinguished. States near the top cannot be distinguished well from those ranking between 10 and 12. Six additional state NAEP tests will be added in the next two years, which will likely allow greater precision.

Table 5.4

The Range, Mean, and Statistical Significance of Estimated Annual Score Gains, Math Tests Only

	Range		Average	Significance level				
				Random Effect			Fixed Effect	
				SES	SES-FE	C-N	SES	SES-FE
North Carolina	0.070	0.073	0.072	1	1	1	1	1
Texas	0.056	0.062	0.059	1	1	1	1	1
Michigan	0.057	0.060	0.058	1	1	1	1	1
Indiana	0.048	0.050	0.049	1	1	1	1	1
Maryland	0.046	0.052	0.048	1	1	1	1	1
West Virginia	0.041	0.044	0.043	1	1	1	1	1
Kentucky	0.038	0.042	0.040	1	1	1	1	1
Rhode Island	0.037	0.043	0.040	1	1	1	1	1
Minnesota	0.040	0.041	0.040	1	1	1	1	1
Colorado	0.039	0.040	0.040	1	1	1	1	1
Connecticut	0.038	0.042	0.040	1	1	1	1	1
Florida	0.038	0.040	0.039	1	1	1	1	1
New Jersey	0.034	0.044	0.038	5		5		5
California	0.037	0.040	0.038	1	1	1	1	1
Wisconsin	0.036	0.038	0.037	1	1	1	1	1
New York	0.036	0.038	0.037	1	1	1	1	1
South Carolina	0.031	0.038	0.034	1	5	1	5	1
Tennessee	0.030	0.038	0.033	5	5	5	5	1
Nebraska	0.031	0.036	0.033	1	5	1	5	1
Arizona	0.032	0.035	0.033	1	1	1	1	1
Arkansas	0.028	0.036	0.032	5	5	5	5	5
Louisiana	0.031	0.032	0.031	1	1	1	1	1
Alabama	0.029	0.032	0.031	1	1	1	5	1
New Mexico	0.026	0.032	0.029	1	5	1	5	5
Mississippi	0.025	0.029	0.027	5	10	5	10	5
Virginia	0.025	0.029	0.026	5	5	5	5	1
Pennsylvania	0.022	0.026	0.024					
Massachusetts	0.022	0.027	0.023	10		10		5
Iowa	0.021	0.024	0.022	5	10	5	10	10
Missouri	0.018	0.023	0.021	10		10		10
Maine	0.014	0.024	0.020	10		10		10
North Dakota	0.017	0.021	0.018	10		10		10

Table 5.4—Continued

				Significance level				
				Random Effect			Fixed Effect	
	Range		Average	SES	SES-FE	C-N	SES	SES-FE
Utah	0.016	0.021	0.018					
Delaware	0.015	0.019	0.016					10
Georgia	0.009	0.016	0.012					
Wyoming	–0.008	–0.004	–0.006					

NOTE: Equation (4.1) was used for estimation using math tests only. The full regression results are given in Appendix G (Tables G.8, G.9, and G.10).

Chapter Six

ESTIMATING SCORES ACROSS STATES FOR STUDENTS FROM SIMILAR FAMILIES

BACKGROUND AND RATIONALE

The family variables in our equations account for about 75 percent of the variance in average state achievement scores.[1] So, the raw NAEP scores mainly reflect the family characteristics of students in the state and not the particular policies and characteristics of the educational systems. Raw scores are perhaps the important measure for parents and students, since they will partially determine future admission to colleges and labor force opportunities. However, the

---

[1]Explaining 75 percent of the variance with family variables at the state level does not imply that family variables explain 75 percent of the variance in achievement scores. The total variance consists of both within- and between-state variance, and the within-state variance is larger than the between-state variance. There are three major sources of within-state variation. The first source is the same type of differences in interfamily characteristics used in the state-level model. Another component can be explained by variables outside the family. The third component arises from the random and nonrandom intrafamily variation that is "unexplainable" through the family characteristic variables usually collected. This variation is the source of differences between siblings from the same parents and is caused by both the random genetic-selection process at birth and the within-family environmental differences siblings experience (Dunn and Plomin, 1990). These two factors are major contributors to individual-level variation as evidenced by the significant differences between siblings (Plomin and Daniels, 1987). At levels of aggregation above individual-level data, much of the intrafamily variance disappears, leaving only the portion of the variance explained by different interfamily characteristics and variables outside the family. While interfamily characteristics, rather than variables outside the family, typically explain the largest portion of variance in aggregated data sets, a large amount of individual-level variance remains that cannot be explained. An indication of this is that models of achievement at the individual level typically have R-squared of much less than 0.5, whereas models at higher levels of aggregation can have R-squared above 0.8. The difference is due to the disappearance (averaging out) of the intrafamily variance when results are aggregated across many children.

use of such raw scores in evaluating school systems or teachers has been heavily criticized, and the development of "value-added" indicators has been recommended (Meyer, 1996; Raudenbush and Wilms, 1995; Consortium on Educational Productivity, 1995; Porter, 1993; Monk, 1992).

Two conceptually different types of value-added measures have been identified (Meyer, 1996; Raudenbush and Wilms, 1995). The first corresponds to the combined effect of social capital and schools. Since both schools and social capital can boost achievement scores for children, parents consider both factors in choosing neighborhoods and schools. So, a first value-added measure would be what parents would like to know to help them choose schools for their children—effective schools in communities with high social capital.

Since family and social-capital influences are outside the influence of school systems, another measure is needed that attempts to isolate the value added by discretionary school policies and personnel. Not eliminating the effects on scores from family and social capital is inherently unfair in evaluating school systems, schools, and their personnel.

Few studies in the educational literature develop value-added measures explicitly (Sanders and Horn, 1998; Wright et al., 1997; Raudenbush and Wilms, 1995; Clotfelter and Ladd, 1996). None have tried to develop measures at the state level. However, new emphasis on testing at the state level and developing accountability methods for schools is placing a new emphasis on developing reliable state-level value-added measures. Methods to estimate such measures have been outlined (Meyer, 1996; Raudenbush and Wilms, 1995).

To estimate "state" value-added indicators, one needs to separate not only the effects of family and social capital but also the effects from local school districts. High state scores may be partially caused by effective school-district policies that may not be directly linked to state policies. Achievement may also be affected by policies outside the school system—social welfare and health policies. Until we can identify the factors that underlie "value-added" indicators specifically, it is premature to refer to present estimates as state "value-added" indicators. We prefer to refer to them as state-specific residuals or estimates of differences in scores for students from similar families across states.

These estimates of how much differences in scores occur for students with similar family backgrounds will be most useful for guiding in-depth case studies of states. The estimates will tell us whether the score differences for similar students among states are statistically significant and, if so, will identify states at each extreme. Focusing case studies on states at either extreme will be more likely to identify the likely sources of "value-added" variables and combinations of variables that produce effective educational systems.

Random- and fixed-effect models each provide a set of state-specific residuals under different assumptions.[2] Although these residuals cannot be interpreted as solely associated with the educational system, they almost certainly provide a better indicator than raw scores of the contribution of the educational system.

RESULTS

Table 6.1 summarizes the results across the five random- and fixed-effect models. The mean coefficients and their range across the models are given, together with the statistical significance in each model.[3] Appendix G shows the regression results for all models (excluding the results for the state-specific random and fixed effects). Appendix H summarizes the values of the state-specific random and fixed effects and also contains the correlation matrix across the six estimates of the state-specific residuals. The three random-effect estimates of residuals using different family variables are correlated at 0.93 or higher, and the two fixed-effect models correlate at above 0.95. The correlation is lower when comparing random- and fixed-effect results, but the lowest correlation among the results excluding the Census-NAEP fixed-effect model is 0.67. It is the difference

---

[2]The primary difference is that the random-effect models assume that there is no correlation between the state-specific effects and the set of family variables, while fixed-effect models allow that correlation. However, fixed-effect models need long-time-series data to obtain accurate estimates, since they effectively remove the cross-sectional variation from the equation and also reduce the degrees of freedom in estimation. This makes the results of the fixed effect models understandably less robust and more fragile than the random-effect models.

[3]The "standard errors" of the state-specific effects in random-effect models are the standard error of the predictions. See the SAS Mixed Procedure, pp. 576–577 of SAS Institute (1999).

Table 6.1

Estimates of Score Differences for Students from Similar Families

	Range		Average	Significance Level				
				Random Effect			Fixed Effect	
				SES	SES–FE	C-N	SES	SES–FE
Texas	0.088	0.212	0.166	1	1	1		
Wisconsin	0.105	0.163	0.142	1	1	1	1	1
Montana	0.095	0.158	0.122	1	1	5	1	1
Iowa	0.071	0.151	0.113	1	1	5	5	1
Maine	0.060	0.143	0.099	10	5	10	5	5
North Dakota	0.037	0.124	0.081	10		5	10	10
Indiana	0.055	0.084	0.074	5	1	10	10	5
New Jersey	0.037	0.079	0.061	10	1		10	5
Nebraska	0.037	0.085	0.056	10			10	10
Missouri	0.044	0.065	0.055	5	5			
Connecticut	0.024	0.091	0.052		10			5
Oklahoma	0.018	0.055	0.040	10				
Georgia	−0.041	0.085	0.039	10	1	5		
Virginia	0.020	0.060	0.037		10	5		
Wyoming	−0.001	0.064	0.034					
Minnesota	−0.003	0.080	0.031					
Massachusetts	−0.013	0.047	0.020					
Michigan	0.000	0.025	0.014					
Pennsylvania	−0.023	0.020	0.005					
Arizona	−0.053	0.039	0.003					
New Hampshire	−0.035	0.063	−0.001					
Colorado	−0.018	0.015	−0.006					
North Carolina	−0.079	0.041	−0.010					
Washington	−0.027	0.008	−0.014					
Idaho	−0.035	0.012	−0.015					
Ohio	−0.031	−0.004	−0.016					
New Mexico	−0.095	0.039	−0.019					10
South Carolina	−0.133	0.033	−0.026					10
Florida	−0.091	0.002	−0.034					10
Oregon	−0.057	−0.018	−0.038					
New York	−0.080	0.005	−0.038					5
Maryland	−0.074	−0.026	−0.055				5	5
Delaware	−0.095	−0.037	−0.064	10			10	5

Table 6.1—Continued

	Range		Average	Significance Level				
				Random Effect			Fixed Effect	
				SES	SES–FE	C-N	SES	SES–FE
Utah	–0.115	–0.021	–0.074	1	1	1		
Tennessee	–0.135	–0.043	–0.077	10	10		10	1
Kentucky	–0.129	–0.063	–0.086		5	10	5	1
Arkansas	–0.162	–0.039	–0.087		10	5		1
Vermont	–0.121	–0.085	–0.106	1	1	5		
Rhode Island	–0.131	–0.084	–0.117	1	1	5	1	5
Alabama	–0.229	–0.075	–0.133	5	1	5	5	1
West Virginia	–0.167	–0.108	–0.135	1	1	1	5	1
Mississippi	–0.319	0.006	–0.137		5		10	1
Louisiana	–0.289	–0.089	–0.156	10	1	5	5	1
California	–0.238	–0.117	–0.174	1	1	1	1	1

NOTE: Equation (4.2) was used for estimation. The full regression results are given in Appendixes G and H (Tables G.1, G.2, G.3, and H.1).

between random- and fixed-effect results that primarily accounts for the range of estimates for each state.

The results in Table 6.1 show that the estimated range of score differences for students from similar families is, at most, about one-third standard deviation or 11 to 12 percentile points on a national scale. However, this only indicates the range for present policies and does not limit the potential variance that future policies could create.

Generally, the results show three bands of states within which differences cannot be statistically distinguished with present scores. The results show that 8 to 12 states have statistically significant, higher residuals than average states, while 10 to 12 states have statistically significant, lower residuals than the average state. There is a broad range of states near the middle that cannot be statistically distinguished.

Unlike raw scores, the results show some southern states in the top ranks and some northern states in the lower ranks. States with high family income and education appear throughout the table, as do states with high and low percentages of minorities. Some states, such as Montana, Iowa, North Dakota, and Maine, have high raw scores as well as high value-added scores.

States with similar raw scores in the same regions can appear with wide separations. In particular, Minnesota and Wisconsin have similar raw scores (and family characteristics) but statistically different scores for similar students. Other examples where groups of nearby states show different results are Georgia and Tennessee; Maine, Vermont, and New Hampshire; Montana, North Dakota, Nebraska, Utah, and Idaho; and Rhode Island and Massachusetts. Perhaps the most striking difference is between Texas and California—two states that have similar demographic characteristics. We further analyze these differences below.

TEXAS VERSUS CALIFORNIA

Perhaps the most striking difference among states in these estimates is that between Texas and California.[4] Table 6.2 compares the family characteristics of California and Texas. Both states have fairly

Table 6.2

Comparison of California and Texas Family Characteristics

	California	Texas
Parents college educated (%)	24.8	22.8
Family income ($000)	40.2	32.3
Black (%)	7.5	12.1
Hispanic (%)	37.5	34.5
Teen births (%)	11.0	15.0
Single mother (%)	19.0	19.0
Residential stability	54.0	55.0
SES predicted score	–0.06	–0.14
SES-FE predicted score	–0.04	–0.10

---

[4]The Bonferroni multiple comparison test provides an alternative test for determining the statistical significance of differences in scores for students from similar families. In any single analysis, one would expect some states to have statistically different results at random. However, in repeated tests, the same states would not be expected to show such significance if it is randomly caused. The Bonferroni test takes into account the distribution of estimates across all repeated tests. We ran the models separately for each test and generated seven estimates of score differences for similar students, then used these results in the Bonferroni multiple comparison tests. Even with the more-stringent criteria of the Bonferroni test, the difference between Texas and California scores remained highly statistically significant.

similar family characteristics, and our predicted scores based on these family characteristics show that both states have predicted scores below the national average. Overall, one would expect, based on our SES and SES-FE measures for California, to have higher test scores by about 0.06 to 0.08 standard deviation based on higher family income, more-educated parents, low minority percentage, and lower teen births.

Figures 6.1 to 6.3 compare California and Texas raw NAEP scores for the non-Hispanic white, black, and Hispanic populations across the seven tests. The data show that Texas students of each racial and/or ethnic group scored higher than similar California students on all 21 test comparisons. The differences range from about 0.1 standard deviation to almost 0.7 standard deviation. The average difference is much larger for minority students. Non-Hispanic white students in Texas have scored, on average, 0.24 standard deviation higher, while

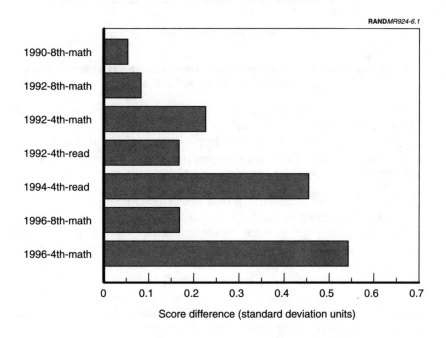

Figure 6.1—Raw Score Differences Between Texas and California Non-Hispanic White Students on Seven NAEP Tests

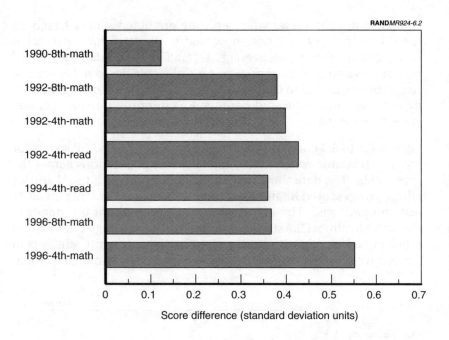

RAND*MR924-6.2*

Figure 6.2—Raw Score Differences Between Texas and California Black
Students on Seven NAEP Tests

black students have scored 0.38 standard deviation higher, and
Hispanic students have scored 0.43 standard deviation higher than
California students.   Thus, the large difference in our estimates
between Texas and California represents large differences in scores
among students with the same race and/or ethnicity.

Texas students are performing well not only with respect to California but with respect to most states—especially on later tests. On the
4th-grade math tests in 1996, Texas non-Hispanic white and black
students were ranked first compared to white and black students in
other states, while Hispanic students were ranked fifth, although
each of the top four states had very small percentages of Hispanic
students. On the same test, California non-Hispanic white students
were ranked third from the bottom, black students last, and Hispanic
students fourth from the bottom among states.

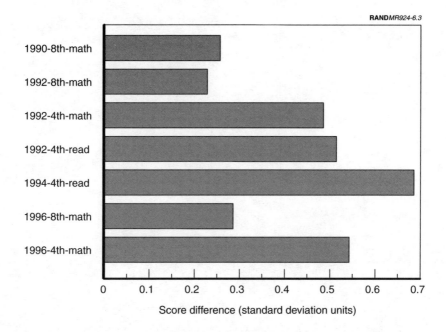

RAND*MR924-6.3*

Score difference (standard deviation units)

**Figure 6.3—Raw Score Differences Between Texas and California Hispanic
Students on Seven NAEP Tests**

Chapter Seven

EFFECTS OF STATE EDUCATIONAL POLICIES AND CHARACTERISTICS

We report the results using three different sets of resource variables. The first results include the most aggregate measure of educational resources only: per-pupil expenditure. The second set of results breaks per-pupil expenditure into four component parts: pupil-teacher ratio, teacher salary, teacher-reported resources, and public prekindergarten participation. These four categories of expenditures (together with a per-pupil transportation, special education, and LEP measure) account for 95 percent of the variance in per-pupil expenditures across states (see Chapter Eight). The third model replaces teacher salary with two categories that explain most of the variance in teacher salaries: teacher experience and teacher education. Teacher salary scales are nearly uniformly structured to provide more pay for experience and education.[1]

RESULTS FOR EDUCATIONAL POLICY AND CHARACTERISTICS VARIABLES[2]

Per-Pupil Expenditure Model

Table 7.1 shows the estimates for per-pupil expenditure. The results show positive, statistically significant effects from increased per-

---

[1]A third variable that would measure relative salary at a given level of education and experience (adjusted for COL) would also be desirable. However, this varies across educational and experience levels because districts have different salary increments and categories for pay scales.

[2]Appendix I contains the full regression results, including family variables and state policy and characteristics variables.

pupil spending for all models. The fixed-effect models show much larger effects than the random-effect models. The results would indicate that an additional $1,000 per student in 1993–1994 dollars over the school career would raise average state scores by 0.04 to 0.10 standard deviation or between 1 and 3 percentile points.

Resource-Utilization Model

Table 7.2 shows the results when resources are disaggregated into pupil-teacher ratio, teacher salary, reported adequacy of teacher resources, and prekindergarten participation. The random-effect models show results indicating increased achievement for additional resources at the 10-percent significance level or better for pupil-teacher ratio in grades 1 through 4, public prekindergarten participation, and resources for teaching (low). Teaching resources (medium) has consistent coefficients with similar signs but is insignificant. Teacher salary is insignificant with different signs, while pupil-teacher ratio (5–8) is insignificant with a perverse sign.

The fixed-effect models show coefficients with generally similar signs, but with similar or smaller magnitude and less statistical significance. An exception is pupil-teacher ratio, which shows a stronger and statistically significant effect for grades 1 through 4 but with opposite signs for 5 through 8. We interpret these results as being partly due to a high correlation between these two variables. Table 7.2 also shows the results when average pupil-teacher ratio (1–8) is entered instead of two variables for pupil-teacher (1–4) and pupil-teacher (5–8). This variable shows consistent coefficients across models, but the fixed-effect coefficients are insignificant.

Our interpretation of the differences between fixed- and random-effect models is that the absence of cross-sectional variation and reduction in degrees of freedom in the fixed-effect models makes the estimates fragile because of the limited sample and the time-series variation in the panel. In all models, the Breusch-Pagan test for random effects is highly significant. The Hausman test shows no systematic difference in fixed- and random-effect coefficients for any of the resource models that use the SES and SES-FE models. However, the Hausman test for all models using the Census-NAEP family variables shows systematic differences in random- and fixed-effect coefficients. The Census-NAEP family variables further reduce the

Table 7.1

Estimated Effects for Per-Pupil Expenditure

	Random Effect			Fixed Effect	
Resource	SES	SES-FE	Census-NAEP	SES	SES-FE
Per-pupil expenditure	0.047^a	0.047^a	0.042^a	0.098^a	0.096^a

[a]Statistically significant at the 1-percent level. Equation (4.3) was used for estimation. The full regression results are given in Appendix I (Tables I.1, I.2, and I.3).

Table 7.2

Results for the Model Disaggregating Educational Resources

	Random Effect			Fixed Effect	
Resource	SES	SES-FE	Census-NAEP	SES	SES-FE
Public prekindergarten	0.004^c	0.004^c	0.005^b	0.003	0.004
Pupil-teacher ratio (1–4)	-0.021^a	-0.020^a	-0.019^b	-0.026^a	-0.026^a
Pupil-teacher ratio (5–8)	0.006	0.006	0.006	0.007^c	0.007^c
Teacher salary	0.001	0.000	-0.003	0.005	0.004
Resources for teaching—low	-0.003^c	-0.003^c	0.003^c	-0.002	-0.002
Resources for teaching—medium	-0.003	-0.003	-0.002	-0.002	-0.002

[a]Statistically significant at the 1-percent level.
[b]Statistically significant at the 5-percent level.
[c]Statistically significant at the 10-percent level.
NOTE: Equation (4.3) was used for estimation. The full regression results are given in Appendix I (Tables I.1, I.2, and I.3).

degrees of freedom, since they include several family variables (fully interacted) rather than a single SES-type family variable. Thus, they will have the least degrees of freedom. A common interpretation of this pattern of results for the Hausman and Breusch-Pagan tests is a preference for the random-effect models.

The public prekindergarten results suggest a gain of 0.03 to 0.05 standard deviation (1–2 percentile points) for a 10-percentage-point increase in public prekindergarten participation. The pupil-teacher ratio (1–4) results suggest that a reduction of one pupil per teacher would raise average achievement scores by approximately 0.020 to 0.025 standard deviation, or about three-quarters of a percentile point. Pupil-teacher (1–8) shows gains of 0.014 to 0.016 standard deviation gain (one-half percentile point) for reduction of one student per teacher.

Teacher Characteristics Model

Table 7.3 provides a model further breaking out teacher salary into teacher education and teacher experience. The results for the prekindergarten, pupil-teacher ratio, and teacher resource variables remain similar to those in Table 7.2. Teacher educational level always has a perverse sign and is generally insignificant. The experience variables generally show that having a high proportion of teachers with more than two years of experience has a positive effect on achievement, but there is no evidence of a learning curve with more than two years of experience. We interpret this as a turnover effect. High levels of teacher turnover usually result in higher levels of teachers with little or no experience.

EFFECTS OF INTERACTION TERMS

We first tested the effects of family interaction terms and a squared term in the case of pupil-teacher ratio using the random-effect model with the SES-FE family variable and the 4th-grade sample only (regression results are in Appendix I).[3] Results are similar using the SES variable. The results show that lower SES families have much larger effects from pupil-teacher reductions than higher SES families, and that marginal effects are larger at higher pupil-teacher ratios than at lower levels.

Table 7.4 contrasts the predictions from a linear model, a model including a squared term (threshold effects), a model with a family interaction term, and finally one with both interaction and squared terms. The predicted result for changes of pupil-teacher reductions of three students per teacher from levels of 26 to 17—the recent

---

[3]We generally believe that the random-effect models provide the "best" results and that the SES-FE variable provides a better estimate of family effects than the SES variable—although the differences are very small using either variable.

Table 7.3

Results for Model Disaggregating Teacher Characteristics

Resource	Random Effect			Fixed Effect	
	SES	SES-FE	Census-NAEP	SES	SES-FE
Public prekindergarten	0.003^c	0.003^c	0.005^b	0.003	0.003
Pupil-teacher ratio (1–4)	-0.020^a	-0.020^a	-0.019^b	-0.028^a	-0.028^a
Pupil-teacher ratio (5–8)	0.007	0.006	0.007	0.007^c	0.007^c
Teaching resources—low	-0.003^c	-0.003^b	-0.003^b	-0.002	-0.002
Teaching resources—medium	-0.002	-0.002	-0.002	-0.002	-0.002
No advanced degrees	0.001	0.001	0.001^c	0.000	0.000
Experience (3–9)	0.008^b	0.008^a	0.007^c	0.005	0.005
Experience (10–19)	0.003	0.003	0.003	0.003	0.003
Experience (20+)	0.005^c	0.005^c	0.004	0.006^c	0.006^c

[a]Statistically significant at the 1-percent level.
[b]Statistically significant at the 5-percent level.
[c]Statistically significant at the 10-percent level.
NOTE: Equation (4.3) was used for estimation. The full regression results are given in Appendix I (Tables I.1, I.2, and I.3).

range of pupil-teacher ratios across states for regular students—is shown. Three family SES levels are shown: *Low* corresponds to Louisiana; *medium* corresponds to such states as Arkansas, North Carolina, and Tennessee; and *high* corresponds to Iowa, Maine, and Massachusetts.

Table 7.4 shows that estimated effects become much larger for lower-SES families and higher beginning class sizes. The predicted gains from reductions of three pupils per teacher can be as large as 0.17 standard deviation (5–6 percentile points) for the lowest SES states with very high pupil-teacher ratios to no effects for states with higher SES.

The results would indicate that targeting reductions in pupil-teacher ratio would increase the effectiveness significantly. Reductions below the current nationwide average in states with the higher level of family resources would have no predicted effect on achievement, while reductions to the nationwide average in states with average levels of family resources and reductions to below the nationwide average in states with low levels of family resources would have significant effects.

We also tested for interaction effects with family variables for prekindergarten and teacher resources. Teacher resource variables showed no significant interaction effects, so this may be an avenue for raising scores at all SES levels. Prekindergarten showed a strong interaction effect—with much stronger effects in states with lower SES at 4th grade. Table 7.5 shows the prediction of effects across SES levels for increased public prekindergarten participation.

TESTING CORRESPONDENCE WITH TENNESSEE

Two problems arose in using our equations to predict a 4th-grade class-size effect for the Tennessee experiment. First, 33 percent of the students in the Tennessee experiment were minority, and over 50 percent were eligible for a free lunch—much higher percentages than for Tennessee students generally (Krueger, 1999a). Our equations could predict a pupil-teacher effect for typical Tennessee students but cannot do so directly for the experimental sample. Second, the class-size reductions of approximately eight students per teacher have to be translated into pupil-teacher reductions, and the pupil-teacher ratios in the experimental schools would have to be known (see Appendix D for more details on these calculations).

Table 7.4

Predicted Achievement Gains for 4th Graders from Reduction of Pupil-Teacher Ratios in Grades 1 Through 4 (standard deviation)

Model	State-SES	Beginning Pupil-Teacher Ratio for Regular Students			
		17	20	23	26
Linear model	All SES	0.02	0.02	0.02	0.02
Squared pupil-teacher term	All SES	−0.06	−0.01	0.03	0.08
Family interaction term	Low family SES	0.12	0.12	0.12	0.12
	Middle family SES	0.04	0.04	0.04	0.04
	High family SES	0.00	0.00	0.00	0.00
Squared and family interaction term	Low family SES	0.04	0.09	0.13	0.17
	Middle family SES	−0.03	0.01	0.06	0.10
	High family SES	−0.06	−0.02	0.03	0.07

NOTE: Full regression results are given in Appendix I (Table I.4).

Table 7.5

Effects of Increasing Prekindergarten Participation by 10 Percentage Points on 4th-Grade Achievement for States with Different Family SES Levels

Model	Prekindergarten Effect (standard deviation)
Linear model	0.04
Model with family interaction term	
Low family SES	0.11
Medium family SES	0.05
High family SES	0.00

NOTE: Full regression results are given in Appendix I (Table I.5).

We estimated an upper limit for the SES-FE variable for the experimental sample using separate Tennessee estimates for the SES-FE variable for black and non-black students and weighting by the proportions in the experimental sample. This is likely to be the upper limit because it still assumes that black and white children in the experimental sample were similar to black and white Tennessee students. White children in disproportionately black schools in Tennessee probably have lower SES than typical white students.

The second method was to find states that had student characteristics similar to those of the experimental sample. Louisiana comes closest to the minority and free-lunch percentages. Our estimated SES-FE variable for the experimental sample from these two methods came very close to the "low family SES" value used in Table 7.4.

If we assume that a class-size reduction of eight students per teacher (the size of the Tennessee class-size reduction) is the same as a pupil-teacher reduction of eight students per teacher, the model with family interactions in Table 7.4 provides an estimate of 0.32 standard deviation.[4] This estimate is in the middle of recent empirical estimates from Tennessee for 4th-grade gains for children in small classes for four years (Krueger, 1999a; Nye et al., 1999a).

---

[4]The more-complex model, with both family interaction and squared terms, needs the beginning pupil-teacher ratio, which cannot be known with any precision. But reasonable assumptions placing beginning pupil-teacher ratios for regular students in 1986 for the experimental schools at 23 to 24 provide similar estimates.

SENSITIVITY TO OUTLIERS

We made estimates using robust estimation with OLS that assign smaller weights to outliers. The regression coefficients for the SES-FE model are given in Appendix J.[5] The two sets of coefficients from the robust and nonrobust regressions show very similar results. We also undertook a number of additional diagnostic analyses on the effects that are due to outliers or particular states and generally found little sensitivity.

EXPLAINING TEXAS-CALIFORNIA DIFFERENCES

The educational variables included in our earlier analysis can explain about two-thirds of the difference between Texas and California scores. Table 7.6 shows the differences in these educational variables and the expected predicted difference in score using the random-effect SES-FE model. California had almost the largest pupil-teacher ratio in the nation in the 1980s and 1990s. Funding for California schools was affected by the property tax relief measures passed in the late 1970s and by a poor economy throughout the late 1980s and 1990s. School funding did not keep pace with the rest of the nation. With a highly paid teaching force, the restricted funding meant larger classes. Recently, California has begun to reverse these trends with significant increases in funding to reduce class sizes in the lower grades.

Texas had the highest proportion of children in any state in public prekindergarten programs—partly because of subsidized prekindergarten for lower-income students started in the early 1980s.[6] Texas teachers also report higher levels of resources available to support

---

[5]The results presented used the default options in STATA. Nine data points were assigned weights less than 0.5, while 34 data points were assigned weights less than 0.75.

[6]The involvement of the business community in Texas schools began in the early 1980s with a commission headed by Ross Perot. Subsidized prekindergarten programs were one outcome of the initial commission. The Texas business community has exercised a strong influence on school policies at the legislative- and executive-branch levels through the Texas—Business Education Coalition from the early 1980s to the present. The coalition's influence has consistently been for assessment and accountability, building strong data systems to support decisionmaking, and using research-based reforms whenever possible.

teaching. This evidence indicates that differences in pupil-teacher ratio alone account for about one-third or more of the difference between Texas and California.

The models including interaction terms and nonlinearity for pupil-teacher effects account for about two-thirds of the Texas-California differences in scores for similar students. They also help explain the wider gap between minority students in Texas and California than for white students in Texas and California. The earlier analysis of differential effects of resources showed that minority students would have disproportionate effects from a higher pupil-teacher ratio and prekindergarten participation.

Table 7.6

Comparing and Estimating the Effects of Educational
Characteristics in Texas and California

Variable	Value of Variable		Estimated Effects		
	California	Texas	Linear Model	Family Interaction Model	Family Interaction and P-T^2
Pupil-teacher ratio	25	18	0.06	0.13	0.16
Public prekindergarten (%)	7	24	0.08	0.08	0.08
Teachers—lowest resource category (%)	46	28	0.07	0.06	0.07
Teachers—middle resource category (%)	49	56	–0.03	–0.03	–0.03
Total			0.18	0.24	0.28
Estimated score difference for similar students— SES-FE			0.41	0.41	0.41

Chapter Eight

ASSESSING THE COST-EFFECTIVENESS OF DIFFERENT RESOURCE UTILIZATIONS

PREVIOUS COST-EFFECTIVENESS MEASUREMENTS

Little research on the cost-effectiveness of educational programs, as opposed to their effectiveness, has been done. Levin (1983) stated the rationale and need for such analysis. Other studies emphasized the importance of focusing on productivity in education that analyzes both outcomes and costs (Hanushek, 1986; Monk, 1990, 1992; Hanushek, 1994; Consortium on Productivity in the Schools, 1995; Grissmer, 1997).

One previous study made estimates of the cost-effectiveness of several major educational policy variables on student achievement: per-pupil expenditure, pupil-teacher ratio, teacher education, teacher experience, and teacher salary (Greenwald et al., 1996). The authors took their estimates of effect sizes on achievement from their meta-analytic analysis of the previous literature, in which they estimated median regression coefficients. Their estimates of the costs of changing each variable came from a classroom model that assumed a class size of 25 students; a teacher salary of $35,000; incremental salaries of $3,500 associated with a master's degree and $1,500 with 3.5 years of additional experience; and that teacher salary costs were 50 percent of total expenditures.[1]

---

[1]Assumptions were also needed concerning the standard deviation of the variables. In particular, the standard deviation of teacher education was assumed to be the movement of the percentage of teachers having masters degrees from 50 to 60 percent, the standard deviation of experience was 3.5 years, and the standard deviation of class size was three students per teacher.

Their estimates showed that the cost of gains of 0.10 standard deviation would be between $230 and $300 per pupil for use as general
per-pupil expenditures, raising teacher salaries, or increasing teacher
education or experience but significantly higher costs of $1,250 per
pupil for decreasing pupil-teacher ratio.[2] However, the estimates
have little reliability because the median regression coefficients
changed dramatically depending on the screening criteria for
included studies.[3] Their cost model also does not estimate marginal
costs accurately.[4]

Cost-effectiveness estimates can be made for class-size reductions
and teacher aides using the Tennessee experimental data (see
Appendix K). The results showed that targeting additional per-pupil
expenditures of about $200 per pupil to class-size reductions would
produce achievement gains of 0.10 standard deviation for the
Tennessee sample students. It would require an additional per-pupil
expenditure of over $1,000 targeted to teacher aides to produce the
same achievement gains. If student achievement gain is the sole
objective, reducing class size looks to be significantly more efficient
than adding teacher aides.

Many researchers consider achievement gains to be important
because of their role in obtaining additional years of education, their
role in greater labor-market success, and their possible link to delinquency behavior (Burtless, 1996; Jencks and Phillips, 1998; Murnane
et al., 1995; Murnane and Levy, 1996). Recently, achievement scores
have taken on even more importance for minority children in the
college admission process—the gateway to more years of education.
While achievement gains can be used as a yardstick to compare the

---

[2]Using the assumptions in their model, we obtained a much larger value for the effect
of teacher education: $65 per-pupil increase for a 0.10 standard deviation gain.

[3]Eliminating earlier studies can change coefficients by factors of 3 to over 100. Using
longitudinal studies often results in sign changes in median coefficients.

[4]Their cost model allows only one-half of marginal increases in per-pupil expenditures to be targeted to the classroom, and their costs are not estimated marginal costs
that take account of the full set of costs incurred with each change. For instance, the
costs of additional classrooms are not included in pupil-teacher ratio reductions, and
teacher salary increases are likely to induce salary increases for other employees
(administrators, aides, janitors) in the long run. Thus, the cost estimates do not reflect
full marginal costs or the possibility of targeting additional resources disproportionately to classrooms.

cost-effectiveness of K–12 expenditures, a much broader set of measures will ultimately be required. For instance, research has shown that achievement gains are often not the primary or most important outcomes of early childhood interventions (Barnett, 1995; Karoly et al., 1998). Positive outcomes can occur in terms of reduced special-education placement and delinquency without large gains in achievement. So, achievement gains may not always be a reliable proxy for significant long-term effects that result in reduced societal outlays. In the long term, the cost-effectiveness of schooling investments must be measured against future labor-force performance and the reduction in future governmental "social" expenditures. Estimates of the present value of programs' costs and savings in government program expenditures show that significant net savings can occur from early intervention efforts (Karoly et al., 1998). However, targeting one program to a more disadvantaged population was necessary to achieve net savings.[5] Preliminary estimates are now also available relating the present values of the costs of class-size reductions to future wage gains linked to higher achievement (Krueger, 1999b).

ESTIMATING COST-EFFECTIVENESS FROM OUR EQUATIONS

Estimates of the per-pupil cost of changing various policy characteristics were obtained by regressing per-pupil expenditures across states against the various resource categories (see Appendix L). We included in the regression the same policy variables as in the resource equations: average teacher salary, pupil-teacher ratio, the two levels of teacher resources, and prekindergarten participation. We also included in the cost regression a per-pupil transportation cost per state and an incidence of IEP and LEP variable to account for differences in special education and transportation costs.

---

[5]The efficiency of this program depended on targeting to a more disadvantaged population. However, a differently designed program might have shown net saving for the higher-functioning population. Generally, the program design has to be appropriate to the needs of the target population regardless of the extent of disadvantage.

The results are shown in Table 8.1. The regression accounts for 95 percent of the variance across states in per-pupil expenditures.[6] The coefficients can be interpreted as the marginal cost per pupil of changing the policy and educational characteristics based on the experience across states of providing these different policies and characteristics. These marginal estimates theoretically include all the long-term costs associated with each action. For instance, raising teacher salaries by $1,000 per teacher probably implies salary increases for nonteaching professional staff and perhaps even support staff. The pupil-teacher ratio coefficient should reflect the full costs of providing classroom capacity and increased salary costs due to higher demand for teachers.[7]

The coefficients all show the expected sign, and nearly all the resource variables are significant at the 10-percent level or better. The results would indicate that raising teacher salaries by $1,000 per teacher would raise per-pupil expenditures by $148 per pupil. Lowering the pupil-teacher ratio by one student would cost an additional $196 per pupil. Increasing the teacher-reported adequacy of resources from each category into the highest category by 1 percentage point would cost an additional $5 to 6 per pupil.[8] Increasing by 1 percentage point the percentage of children in public prekindergarten would cost an additional $12 per pupil.

---

[6]This equation means that these variables include almost all of the variance in per-pupil expenditures. Moreover, including a measure of family (SES-FE) in the regression shows that the additional unaccounted-for expenditure between the highest and lowest SES states is about $300 per pupil—about 5 percent of average per-pupil costs. So, the equation captures most of the differences in resources spent in high- and low-income states.

[7]Alternative cost estimates for each of the categories except teacher resources can be done through simulations. However, it is not clear which would be the more accurate. We have done simulations to verify that the present cost estimates are reasonable. The teacher salary and pupil-teacher ratio cost estimates seem accurate under reasonable assumptions. However, the prekindergarten cost of $12 per pupil seems somewhat high. This may be due to the disproportionate share of special education students attending prekindergarten classes. Thus, the costs of expanding prekindergarten for regular students may be less than $12 per pupil.

[8]This result would imply that it takes about the same investment to move the least adequately resourced teachers by a percentage point than the more adequately resourced teachers. This may indicate that teachers who currently have low levels of resources may be satisfied with less than their better-resourced colleagues.

Table 8.1

Regression Results of Per-Pupil Expenditures (000) Versus
Educational Policy and Characteristics

Variables	Coefficients	T-Statistic
Teacher salary	0.1480	12.7
Pupil-teacher ratio	–0.1960	–7.1
Teacher resources—some	0.0056	1.8
Teacher resources—most	0.0051	1.5
Prekindergarten	0.0120	2.7
Per-pupil transportation	0.0040	4.2
LEP (%)	0.0040	0.3
Individualized learning (%)	0.0160	1.2

NOTES: Equation (4.4) was used for estimation. The full regression results are given in Appendix L (Table L.1).

Using both the expenditure equation and the achievement equation allows estimation of the per-pupil costs of raising achievement scores by 0.10 standard deviation. The results of the estimations are summarized in Table 8.2 for the marginal costs and the range of effects measured across our five specifications.

A cost-effectiveness measure—the per-pupil expenditure necessary to raise average state scores by 0.10 standard deviation—can be derived by dividing the marginal cost per pupil (column 2 of Table 8.2) by the marginal effect (column 4 of Table 8.2). The pupil-teacher estimate assumes that the achievement gains occur only if pupil-teacher ratio is changed for all grades, K–12. Both our results and the Tennessee results indicate that targeted reductions in early grades produce sustained gains. Thus, we have added an estimate for the targeted reduction.[9] Table 8.3 summarizes the results.

Table 8.3 shows that the cost of an increase of 0.10 standard deviation in average student achievement scores can vary between approximately $200 per pupil to over $3,000 per pupil, depending on how increased resources are allocated. The results show generally that allocation to targeted pupil-teacher ratio reduction in grades 1

---

[9]We simply assumed that per-pupil costs are equal across grades and that pupil-teacher ratio reductions in the four early grades would cost 4/13 of reductions across all grades.

Table 8.2

Marginal Cost and Achievement Gains for Each Resource

Cost Equation	Cost per Pupil ($)	Score Equation	Effect Size Range (SD)
Cost per pupil to raise per-pupil expenditures by $1,000	1,000.00	Score gain from general increase of $1,000 per pupil	0.042–0.098
Cost per pupil to lower pupil-teacher ratio by one student (K–12)	196.00	Score gain from lowering pupil-teacher ratio by one student	0.019–0.026
Cost per pupil to raise average teacher salary by $1,000	148.00	Score gain from raising teacher salary by $1,000	0.000–0.005
Cost per pupil to shift teacher responses by 1 percentage point from lowest to highest adequacy level of resources	5.10	Score gain from shifting teacher responses 1 percentage point from lowest to highest category	0.002–0.003
Cost per pupil to shift teacher responses by 1 percentage point from middle to highest adequacy level of resources	5.60	Score gain from shifting teacher responses 1 percentage point from middle to highest category	0.002–0.003
Cost per pupil to increase public prekindergarten participation by 1 percentage point	12.00	Score gain from increasing public prekindergarten by 1 percentage point	0.003–0.005

Table 8.3

Estimates of Additional Per-Pupil Expenditures in Each Resource Category to Raise Average Scores by 0.10 Standard Deviation

Resource	Cost per Pupil ($)
Per-pupil expenditure	1,020–2,380
Pupil-teacher (K–12)	750–1,030
Pupil-teacher targeted (1–4)	230–320
Teacher salary	>>2,900
Teacher resources—low to adequate	170–260
Teacher resources—medium to adequate	190–280
Public prekindergarten	240–400

through 4, expanding prekindergarten programs, and providing teachers more resources for teaching are the most efficient, while allocation to teacher salaries or to general per-pupil expenditures without targeting is least efficient. These results would hold given current allocations of resources. However, each of these resource investments would be expected to have marginally decreasing returns, so the mix of best investments would be expected to change as resources are increased and allocated to specific programs.

Perhaps more importantly, the cost-effectiveness results will change depending on the average SES level of families in a state and the current pupil-teacher ratios. We used the SES-FE random-effect model with interaction terms to estimate the cost-effectiveness of additional expenditures in a low-, a medium-, and a high-SES state (see Table 7.4). The results are shown in Table 8.4. These results imply that expanding prekindergarten, providing teachers more resources, and effecting targeted pupil-teacher ratio reductions would be most efficient for low-SES states, while providing teacher resources appears efficient for all SES states.[10] However, this model cannot take account of the marginally decreasing return to pupil-teacher ratio or determine at what pupil-teacher ratio other resources may become more efficient.

Table 8.5 shows results using the model including family interactions and marginally declining effects from pupil-teacher reductions (see

Table 8.4

Estimate of Additional Per-Pupil Expenditures to Achieve 0.10 Gain in Achievement for States with Different SES ($)

	State SES		
Type of Expenditure	Low	Medium	High
Pupil-teacher (1–4)	150	450	>1,000
Prekindergarten	120	320	>1,000
Teacher resources—low	110	110	110
Teacher resources—medium	140	140	140

---

[10]Both pupil-teacher ratio and prekindergarten have significant interaction terms with the family variable (SES-FE), whereas teacher resources shows no significant interaction term with the family variable.

Table 8.5

**Estimate of Additional Per-Pupil Expenditures to Achieve
0.10 Gain in Achievement for States with Different SES
and Different Initial Pupil-Teacher Ratios ($)**

| | State SES | | |
Type of Expenditure	Low	Medium	High
Pupil-teacher (1–4) from 26	110	180	260
Pupil-teacher (1–4) from 23	140	300	600
Pupil-teacher (1–4) from 20	200	>1,000	>1,000
Pupil-teacher (1–4) from 17	450	>1,000	>1,000
Prekindergarten	120	320	>1,000
Teacher resources—low	90	90	90
Teacher resources—medium	110	110	110

Table 7.4). Efficient strategies for particular states will depend on their current pupil-teacher ratios and SES characteristics. For instance, among states in our sample, only two states (Utah and California) had estimated pupil-teacher ratios for regular students above 23 in 1996. So, the results in the first row of Table 8.5 would apply only to Utah and California.[11] In this row, statewide reductions in pupil-teacher ratio by three appear most efficient for low-SES states, and second in efficiency for medium- and high-SES states.

Only four additional states (Arizona, Idaho, Michigan, and Washington) fall in the second row, having pupil-teacher ratios between 20 and 23 in 1996. These states fall into medium- to high-SES states, in which statewide reductions in pupil-teacher ratio reductions in lower grades are second in efficiency to increasing teacher resources.

All these results point to the importance of targeting in achieving efficiency. While these results cannot automatically be applied to within-state allocations, if the patterns are similar, every state could make achievement gains most efficiently by allocating resources to lower-SES schools. It should be pointed out that the most extreme state in our sample had SES characteristics that were substantially above those in many school districts and schools within states—particularly in urban areas. For instance, the general SES characteristics

---

[11]California has subsequently reduced class sizes significantly in lower grades and so moved below this category.

in Mississippi—the lowest of all states—are still far above the SES characteristics in many schools and school districts in the nation. If the pattern of increasing efficiency evident in these findings continues to lower SES levels, significant gains may be efficiently possible through targeted allocations within states to these districts.

The results also imply—even using an extremely conservative interpretation—that very significant score gains could be obtained for minority and lower-SES students with additional expenditures of less than $1,000 per student if the resources are appropriately targeted. The results would also imply that resources spent in many high-SES states might be quite inefficient.

CAVEATS AND CAUTION

One purpose of these estimates is to display a methodology that has not been previously used to develop cost-effectiveness estimates for educational policies and programs. Further developments and refinements will certainly be made. The full extent of the uncertainty in the estimates has not been included—and uncertainties that approach 50 to 100 percent (factor of two) are possible when including both standard errors and range of estimates. However, even with these uncertainties, the estimates can distinguish more efficient programs, since the efficiency commonly differs by factors of 3 to well over 20.

These levels of efficiency may be difficult to obtain with a political process that, to ensure passage, inevitably widens the targeted groups for any program. Thus, programs to reduce class size for the lowest SES states tend either to be matched with other benefits flowing to other states or to widen the SES category to include medium- or even high-SES states. Targeting appears to be perhaps the most important variable for achieving efficiency, but the most efficient targeting is often impossible in the political process.

We have not included some use of resources in these equations. Perhaps the main omission is teacher professional development. So, estimates of effectiveness and cost-effectiveness cannot be made. We also note that testing students each year costs approximately $5 to $25 a student. These costs may not fully capture the full costs of the systemic reform effort statewide to develop standards, align tests, and provide feedback and accountability. However, if any significant portion of the gains seen in Texas and North Carolina (approximately 0.30 standard deviation) is due to their systemic reform efforts and if the major costs are even $25 per student, this use of resources would be more efficient than the options evaluated here. But more research is required before such estimates can be credibly done.

Chapter Nine

CONCLUSIONS

METHODOLOGICAL CONSIDERATIONS AND INTERPRETATION OF THE RESULTS OF DIFFERENT MODELS

The state NAEP scores are the first achievement scores with representative sampling across states that allow comparison of performance across states. Since states are the leading initiators of educational reform, these scores may be the principle source for evaluating the effectiveness and cost-effectiveness of reform initiatives. These scores are also important because across-state variation accounts for two-thirds of the total variance in per-pupil expenditures among school districts. Because the reasons for variations in expenditures across states may differ from the reasons for variations in expenditures within a state, measurements of resource effects across states are of interest.

However, a number of analytical issues must be addressed in using these data, and some caution is needed in interpreting the results for policy evaluation. One issue is whether to use the individual-level or the aggregate state-level data for evaluation. Both methods should eventually be used, and their results should be compared. Here, we present the aggregate results and suggest several reasons that aggregate-level results may eventually prove less biased than individual-level analysis with NAEP data. The reasons are as follows:

- Higher-quality family variables are available at the state level.
- Higher-quality schooling variables related to major resource expenditures are available at the state level, since they can include estimates from entry into school.

- Evidence from previous measurements of the effects of educational resources shows more-consistent and robust results at the state level of aggregation, and these results are in closer agreement with experimental data than are individual-level results.

- There are no a priori reasons to prefer analysis at the state or individual level, since results should agree if models are linear and well specified.

- There are no a priori reasons to suggest that the net bias introduced by various types of misspecification will be higher for state-level analysis than for individual-level analysis.

- For some forms of misspecification that we know are present (selection, measurement errors, and missing variables at the individual level), there are plausible reasons to suggest that individual-level results will be more biased than state-level results.

Three potential problems with aggregate data are a small sample size, a limited range of variation in variables, and heightened sensitivity to outliers compared to individual-level data. Aggregate models—provided a sufficient range of variation is present in variables—can screen and detect any variables that have large effects but often cannot discriminate variables with weaker effects. Aggregate analysis is less likely to produce statistically significant results and less able to detect low-level effects for resource variables. So, these models should be used to measure effects for major resource variables only.

Insignificant effects may also need a different interpretation for aggregate models. Statistical insignificance may be due to limited sample size and range of variation rather than absence of an actual effect. However, statistically significant results for individual and aggregate results can be interpreted in a similar way.

We specifically addressed whether our results are sensitive to certain specification issues by estimating random- and fixed-effect models that each depend on different, but plausible, sets of statistical assumptions. Since family variables explain much of the variance across state scores, we developed three different sets of family variables using different sources of family data to test the sensitivity of the results to different family variables. Finally, we tested for the influence of outliers on the results.

We generally found consistency in estimates across different model specifications and family variables and little sensitivity to outliers. The fixed-effect models provide coefficients that generally show similar or somewhat smaller effects compared to the random-effects models. Not unexpectedly, the fixed-effect results are also less robust, given our limited time series and the reduced degrees of freedom in these models. The random-effect models provide the most consistent effects and show the closest agreement with the Tennessee results.

Among the six models estimated (random and fixed effect for the three sets of family variables), we found very similar results for the state trends. One set of estimates began to show somewhat different results from the other five estimates for the value-added and policy models. In this model, the family coefficients began to show perverse signs. This model—the fixed-effect estimates with Census-NAEP family variables—also has the fewest degrees of freedom. We have reported these results in the appendixes but have not included them in the main results.

As a test of model validity, we made predictions of the pattern of results from the Tennessee class-size experiment using the 4th-grade scores in our sample. We used only random-effect models because of the reduced sample size of the 4th-grade sample. The three random-effect models predicted results that are very consistent with the size of the Tennessee effects and also the pattern of increasing effects for minority and lower-SES students.

RESULTS

The pattern of achievement across states from 1990 to 1996 suggests that family variables explain most of the variance across scores in states. So, raw scores are of little value as indicators of the effectiveness of the K–12 educational system in states. Our results also show the presence of significant state-specific effects on achievement that make scores differ across states for students with similar family background. Some of these differences in scores can be explained by specific characteristics of the educational systems in the states. These results suggest that the level of per-pupil expenditures and how they are allocated and targeted can make significant differences in student achievement. The results also suggest that there is a wide variation in the cost-effectiveness of expenditures, depending on the grade level, the programs targeted, and the SES level of students.

Finally, the results suggest that significant gains in math scores occurred from 1990 to 1996, but there is wide variation in gains across states. Our resource variables cannot explain much of the overall gains or the pattern of gains by state.

More specifically, the results show the following:

- Public elementary students across participating states had statistically significant gains in mathematics of about 1 percentile point a year between 1990 and 1996.

- The rate of math improvement varied significantly across states with a few states making gains of about 2 percentile points a year, while other states had little or no gain.

- These gains cannot be explained by changes in levels or allocation of the major resource variables (per-pupil expenditure, teacher salaries, pupil-teacher ratio, teacher resources, and levels of public prekindergarten participation). Differences in systemic reform initiatives across states are the leading candidates for explaining these gains in scores.

- Students from similar family backgrounds had statistically significant score differences across states that can be as large as 11 to 12 percentile points. States with both higher and lower scores for students from similar families are in all regions of the country.

- The characteristics of state educational systems can account for some of the score differences for students from similar families. Other things being equal, higher per-pupil expenditures, lower pupil-teacher ratio in lower grades, higher reported adequacy of teacher-reported resources, higher levels of participation in public prekindergarten, and lower teacher turnover all show positive, statistically significant effects on achievement. Other things being equal, higher teacher salaries, higher teacher educational levels, and increased experience over the past three years do not show significant effects on achievement. However, these variables explain one-half or less of the nonfamily differences in achievement across states.

- The cost-effectiveness of expenditures varied widely, depending on how the expenditures are directed, the SES level of the state, the current allocation of expenditures, and the grades targeted. The most efficient uses of educational expenditures among those evaluated here were providing all K–8 teachers more-adequate resources for teaching, expanding public prekindergarten in lower-SES states, and targeting reductions in pupil-teacher ratios in lower grades in lower-SES states to well below the national average and in medium-SES states to the national average. Estimates of the cost-effectiveness of teacher aides from Tennessee experimental data show that they are far less cost-effective than class-size reductions.

Evidence for the Effects of Reform

The effects of the wave of reform initiatives that began in the later 1980s would be expected to begin showing up in achievement scores in the 1990 to 1996 period. But it will take much longer for the full effects to be reflected. These reform initiatives are of two types: Some are related to changes in the level and allocation of resources, while others are more structural or pedagogical. Since the pace and structure of reform vary considerably by state, such efforts would be expected to show uneven results across states. However, only gains that are unrelated to traditional resource variables would provide evidence for the effect of structural reform.

The analysis provides strong evidence that math scores from 1990 to 1996—controlling for student demographic changes and NAEP participation rates—increased in most states for public students by statistically significant amounts. Eighth-grade math scores increased much more than 4th-grade scores. The average annual gain across states is about 1 percentile point a year. A few states gained about 2 percentile points a year, while some states had little or no gain.

Three sources of evidence point to structural reform as the cause of these gains, but much more research is needed into the pattern of specific reforms across all states before a compelling linkage can be made. First, these gains cannot be explained by major changes in resources. Second, the rate of gains varied widely by state, as did the structure and intensity of reform efforts. Third, a case study of two states with the largest gains—Texas and North Carolina—suggested that a series of similar reforms in both states linked to aligned standards, assessments, and accountability was the most plausible cause of the gains.

Scores for Students from Similar Family Backgrounds

Since achievement is strongly linked to family characteristics, only score differences for students with similar family backgrounds indicate the presence of state-specific effects that might be linked to the quality of educational systems and other factors. Our results indicate the strong presence of differences in scores across states for students from similar families. The analysis was able to distinguish three groups of states: those whose students with similar family backgrounds are significantly above and below the median state, and a broad middle group. Texas and California—two states with fairly similar family characteristics—are ranked the highest and lowest, respectively, and have score differences for students with similar family backgrounds of about 12 percentile points. The variables in our model explain about two-thirds of the difference in these scores. The major contributions to the higher Texas scores are lower pupil-teacher ratio, a much larger percentage of children in public prekindergarten, and teachers who report having more of the resources necessary to teach.

The Effects and Cost-Effectiveness of Resources

States have widely different levels of per-pupil expenditures, which are spent in significantly different ways across states. The result is wide variance in pupil-teacher ratios, teacher characteristics, and salaries; different levels of teacher-reported adequacy of resources; and different support for public prekindergarten programs. Such large differences would be expected to show up in achievement scores across states if these variables actually affect achievement in significant ways. States also have wide variation in the SES characteristics of their students, so it is possible to measure whether these resource variables have different effects across SES levels.

The results imply that resources in public education must be allocated to specific programs and grade levels and toward specific students to be most effective and cost-effective. The cost-effectiveness of resource expenditures can change by more than a factor of 25, depending on which programs and grade levels are funded and which types of students are targeted. The analysis suggests that providing all K–8 teachers additional resources, expanding prekindergarten in low-SES states, reducing pupil-teacher ratios in lower grades in lower-SES states to well below the national average, and reducing pupil-teacher ratio in medium-SES states to the national average are most efficient. This analysis suggests that significant gains in achievement for students in lower-SES states can be achieved through modest increases in resources, if allocated to specific programs. Conservative estimates show predicted score gains of 12 to 15 percentile points from additional targeted expenditures of less than $1,000 dollars a pupil in the states with the lowest SES.

INTERPRETATIONS

Improving American Education

The most widely accepted explanation of the pattern of previous measurements on the effects of educational resources has been that public education shows great inconsistency in the effectiveness with which it uses additional resources. This explanation does not rule out the occasional effective use of resources but generally proposes that public schools have used additional resources ineffectively and inefficiently. One explanation for this ineffectiveness is that sufficient incentives do not exist in the public school systems to drive effective use of resources.

The major evidence that supports this explanation comes from previous empirical measurements of the effect of a wide variety of resources made at the individual, classroom, school, and district levels that show highly inconsistent results. While the overall results suggest a net positive effect for resources, the wide inconsistency is interpreted as indicating that public schools do not reliably and effectively convert resources into better outcomes.

This explanation implies that providing more resources for public education is not the answer to school improvement without fundamental reforms that can change the organizational climate and incentives in education. An underlying thesis is that the public school system is too bureaucratic to reform itself and that it is necessary to create alternatives outside the current system or increased choice within the system to produce an environment of greater competition. Policies advocated with this approach include vouchers, school choice, charter schools, and contracting out of schools.

Recent research has suggested three major problems with this explanation. First, there were significant score gains nationwide for minority and disadvantaged public school students in the 1970s and 1980s. This period was characterized by social and educational policies focused on these groups and by disproportionate allocation of relatively modest levels of additional educational resources to programs that primarily benefited these groups. Second, the results of the Tennessee class-size experiment showed large and significant effects from class-size reductions in public schools, and these results appear robust to the inevitable flaws in experimental design and execution. Third, previous measurements at the state level of aggregation, unlike lower levels of aggregation, showed consistent statistically significant positive effects from additional resources. The usual explanation given is that state-level effects are biased upward with respect to the more-accurate measurements made at lower levels of aggregation, but no credible source of bias has been suggested.

We suggest a competing explanation for the pattern of results in the previous literature that is consistent with the results from the Tennessee experiment, the pattern of national score gains and expenditures from 1970 through 1996, and the new results in this report. This explanation suggests that measurements at the state level may provide the most-accurate results among previous measurements and that less-aggregate measurements may be biased downward. The newly available state NAEP scores provided a test of whether using much-higher-quality achievement data at the state level could also provide effects consistent with past state measurements. We found positive and statistically significant effects from higher levels of resources across states and found that certain resource uses can be highly effective and efficient in raising achievement.

These results also suggest that additional resources are most effective and efficient when spent in states with higher proportions of minority and disadvantaged students. Thus, these results suggest that the modest additional resources spent in the 1970s and 1980s might account for significant national minority and disadvantaged score gains in this period. In particular, national pupil-teacher ratios declined significantly, and evidence from our model and from the

Tennessee experiment would suggest that such reductions are consistent with explaining part or most of the gains in the 1970s and 1980s. Our state NAEP model also provides pupil-teacher effects consistent with the size and pattern of larger effects for minority and lower-SES students found in the Tennessee experiment.

We also suggest that specific forms of bias are known to exist in educational data that could plausibly bias previous measurements made at the individual, classroom, school, and district levels downward but that these introduce much less bias at the state level of aggregation. One form of such bias is clearly indicated by the Tennessee experimental data: missing variables on schooling conditions from school entry. These variables are missing in almost all previous measurements and would probably create a larger bias in a less-aggregate analysis, likely in a downward direction.

The Tennessee data also suggest that production-function models that contain a pretest measure—generally thought to be the highest-quality specifications and often used at less-aggregate levels of analysis—are untenable and can lead to significant bias, likely in a downward direction. Selection effects—widely acknowledged to exist in education—also have the potential to produce more bias at less-aggregate levels.

This explanation does suggest a different approach to improving public education. The public-education system can and has used some additional resources effectively, particularly when directed to minority and disadvantaged students. Our results suggest that such resources need to be effectively targeted to specific programs, matched to particular types of students, and toward early grades. Targeting resources toward states with lower-SES students appears to be the most efficient. The current disparity in per-pupil spending across states represents a source of major inefficiency in educational spending.

Our results also show that significant gains are occurring in math scores across most states, with sizable gains in some states. The source of these gains cannot be traced to resource changes, and the most likely explanation would suggest that ongoing structural reform **within** public education might be responsible. This reform suggests that well-designed standards linked to assessments and some forms of accountability may change the incentives and productivity within public schools and even introduce competition among public schools. Thus, these results certainly challenge the traditional view of public education as "unreformable." Public education may be a unique type of public institution in which competition and accountability work because of the large number of separate units whose output can be measured.

There are reasons to believe that improvements in achievement could be expected to continue. The full effect of structural reform initiatives is not reflected in current achievement, and the identification of successful initiatives will likely result in diffusion across states. Better allocation of future resources can also raise achievement. Finally, new data, improving methods of nonexperimental analysis, and new experimentation could also be expected to contribute to future gains.

Interpreting the Effects of Teacher Salary and Teacher Working Conditions

The variables in our analysis that are most efficient seem to involve improving the classroom teaching environment or "working conditions" for teachers. Smaller pupil-teacher ratios and higher levels of satisfaction with resources for teaching appear to make teachers more productive. Prekindergarten participation may improve the classroom environment by providing better-prepared students for teachers. However, our equations imply that, other things being equal, states having higher average salaries do not have higher achievement.

This analysis would suggest that salary increases might come at the expense of providing teachers the working conditions that make them more productive. The analysis suggests that, if investments were made to improve teacher working conditions in the ways recommended, the **current** teachers in our schools would produce significant gains in achievement scores. The Tennessee experiment also supports the conclusion that changes in the conditions facing teachers in the classroom result in higher achievement. The efforts to increase the quality of teachers in the long run are important, but this analysis would suggest that significant productivity gains can be obtained with the current teaching force if their working conditions are improved. It further suggests that teachers by and large respond to better conditions and know what to do to raise achievement.

The low cost-effectiveness of direct investment in salaries can have at least four interpretations. The first explanation assumes the measurements are accurate and attempts to explain the ineffectiveness of increases in teacher salary. The second explanation is that the teacher salary coefficient is biased downward because of its correlation with family variables. The third explanation posits that measurements of interstate salary differences may show different effects from measurements of intrastate salary differences. The fourth interpretation attributes the weak salary effect to the excess supply of teachers in the 1980s and early 1990s.

The ineffectiveness of teacher compensation could result from the inefficient structure of the current teacher compensation system and the inability to target salary increases to higher-quality teachers effectively (Grissmer and Kirby, 1997; Hanushek, 1994; Ballou and Podgursky, 1995, 1997). Unlike class size, which can be targeted to early grades and lower-SES students, salaries are, by and large, raised for all teachers. If the system could distinguish and provide higher compensation for higher-quality teachers and those who are more effective with lower-scoring students, for whom there is more leverage for raising scores, one would expect a dollar of compensation to be more effective. However, the differential pay by school districts in the current salary system is insufficient to prevent higher-quality teachers from teaching in districts with higher-SES students.

A second problem is that salary increases are usually given for more education and experience. Teacher educational level is a weak and inconsistent predictor of achievement. For universities and colleges, providing teachers with master's degrees produces significant income but seems to have little effect on improving teachers' abilities to raise achievement. Teachers themselves are motivated to spend significant time and money on pursuing such degrees largely because of the structure of the current compensation system. It is arguably one of the least-efficient expenditures in education.[1]

---

[1]More master's degrees in education are awarded annually than in any other subject, constituting one in four master's degrees awarded in the nation, with more than 100,000 awarded annually. Assuming the cost of tuition, transportation costs, and the

Teacher experience shows somewhat stronger and more consistent results, but other teacher characteristics generally show more-consistent relationships with achievement. Verbal ability, test scores of teachers, and degrees in subjects taught are three such characteristics, and others may exist. So, part of the ineffectiveness of the current compensation structure is that pay is not directed toward rewarding characteristics that are related to producing higher achievement.

The second explanation is that the coefficient of teacher salary is biased downward because of its correlation with social capital. An overlooked source of social capital can be teachers, who are usually seen as part of the schooling effect. If teachers disproportionately choose to teach in or are more often hired to teach in schools whose students have family characteristics similar to their own, the teachers must be considered as part of social capital. It is almost certainly the case that teachers from backgrounds with more family resources are more likely to teach students with more family resources and vice versa. This is partly due to the fact that teachers usually teach in the same state in which their own schooling occurred, often returning to the same city and county of their own schooling. Hiring practices that often attempt to match the characteristics of students and teachers probably reinforce this trend.

Thus, correlation probably exists between teacher characteristics and student characteristics. The highest correlation between family and school characteristics is between teacher salary and family characteristics (approximately 0.60). If the characteristic of teachers that determines their effectiveness partially has its origin in family capital (i.e., verbal ability), part of the effects of higher-quality teachers may appear in the social-capital effect.

However, two effects are possible when teachers and students are matched. If effective teaching has a component linked to intrinsic characteristics correlated with the teacher's family background (i.e., verbal ability), matching teacher and student characteristics will have net positive effects on achievement of students in families with more resources. However, a second effect can arise if teachers can

---

opportunity costs of time, a master's degree conservatively costs $20,000. Annual national expenditures by teachers or subsidized by school districts would be approximately $2 billion.

more effectively teach students from backgrounds similar to their own: the mentoring effect.

Given the current situation, in which teachers are more likely to be matched to student backgrounds, both of these effects would be positive for students with high family resource backgrounds. For students from lower family resource backgrounds, one effect would be positive and one negative, and whether the net effect is positive or negative would depend on the relative strength of the two. Regardless of which effect dominates, the net effects are likely to be captured in the social-capital effect unless specific variables are introduced measuring the intrinsic abilities of teachers (teacher test scores) and the characteristics of the match between student and teacher.

A third explanation is that the effects of interstate salary differentials may be different from intrastate differentials. Teachers tend to teach in their home states and may be sensitive to salary differentials across districts within a state but are less sensitive to salary differentials across states. Part of the reason may be that women constitute over two-thirds of the teaching workforce and do not have the same job mobility as men in seeking higher-paying jobs. Thus, intrastate differences in salary may affect the distribution of quality teachers much more than the interstate salary differentials. In this case, an intrastate analysis may show salary to be more effective in increasing achievement.

Last, more sensitivity to salary would be expected when teacher labor markets are tight. The period of this analysis was characterized by a teacher surplus across most teacher categories. However, the teacher labor market will become much tighter from 2000 to 2010 for several highly predictable reasons. An aging teacher force will have increasing retirement rates, and attrition rates will also stay high if outside job opportunities remain plentiful. Reductions in class size will also likely increase demand for new teachers.

The supply of new teachers depends partially on the labor market for college graduates, which has been strong in recent years. Beginning teacher salaries are not competitive with most alternative job opportunities. Thus, it may be difficult to expand supply without significant salary growth.

A teacher shortage disproportionately affects schools in lower-SES districts, where the leverage is greatest for boosting scores but also where the risk is greatest for achievement declines. So, the tightening teacher labor market might be expected to heighten the sensitivity of achievement to salary levels—especially for lower-SES states and localities.

RESEARCH IMPLICATIONS

It would not be surprising if some educational resources had not been used effectively in education because policymakers and educators have had little help from the research and development (R&D) community in identifying what is effective and efficient. Successful R&D is the engine that drives productivity improvement in every sector of our economy. Until educational R&D can play the role that R&D does in virtually every other sector of our economy, continual educational improvement cannot be taken for granted.

Experimentation

More experimentation in education seems critical. However, in the long run, confidence in nonexperimental results is needed for policy guidance, since only a limited number of experiments are possible, and contextual effects will likely be important influences in education. Thus, the generalizability of experimental data may always be limited, and we will have to depend on improved nonexperimental analysis. Therefore, experimentation should be directed not only toward variables that have major resource implications but also toward hypotheses that can significantly improve our specifications with nonexperimental models.

Obtaining accurate estimates of resource and policy effects is only the first step needed for policy guidance. The second is to estimate the costs accurately and to compare the cost-effectiveness across resource uses and policies. Cost analysis needs to be built into experimentation, and nonexperimental analysis needs to be more focused on cost-effectiveness analysis.

Improving Nonexperimental Analysis

Besides experimentation focused on testing assumptions in nonexperimental analysis, there are several research directions to improve the reliability of nonexperimental analysis. Use of individual-level longitudinal data that begin at school entry can sort out many of the specification problems that may exist in previous analyses. There are two new sources of such longitudinal data that will have school, teacher, and family characteristics and achievement data. First, there are newly emerging longitudinal state databases that link student achievement across years. Such data have very large samples, and linkages are possible with teacher data and school characteristics. These data should help sort out many of the potential specification issues involving dependence of later achievement on previous years' class sizes and thresholds and on interactions with teacher characteristics. However, certain forms of bias may still be a problem with individual-level data, even if it is longitudinal from kindergarten.

It will also likely be possible to determine class-size effects for various combinations of large and small classes in early and later grades and the importance of small classes in later grades. The subject of differential bias across levels of aggregation can also be partially addressed with these data through direct testing.

The second source will be the Early Childhood Longitudinal Study funded by the U.S. Department of Education, which will collect very detailed data on children, their families, and their schools. The data will be much richer in variables but will have much smaller sample sizes.

A second approach to improving the reliability of nonexperimental analysis is to use empirical analysis to test and better understand the assumptions upon which such analysis depends. Why do students in large and small classes have different characteristics? How important are parent and teacher selection processes in determining class size? Do more-senior teachers choose smaller classes? Are assumptions more valid in some kinds of schools? Are class sizes in rural areas mainly randomly determined, with more selection occurring in cities? There are many empirical approaches to addressing these kinds of questions that would give us a better idea whether assumptions made in specifications are reasonable.

Finally, it now appears that specifying models will require more knowledge about classroom behavior and children's cognitive development. Neither the classroom nor the child can be treated as a black box. There is a great deal of research on patterns of physical, emotional, and social development in children from birth, covering such areas as differences across children, delays in development, and dependence on previous mastery. Studies involving long-term developmental outcomes—especially for children at risk—identify resiliency factors that enable development to occur even in highly risky situations. Much can be learned from this literature to help prevent the use of poor modeling assumptions.

Building Theories

Experimentation and improved nonexperimental analysis alone will not build scientific consensus. Theories need to be developed that link classroom behavior and its effect on student development with resource variables. Theories that can successfully predict more-aggregate phenomena and that can continually be tested with new empirical analysis are what ultimately generate scientific consensus. More theory building is needed in educational research.

Time on task still appears to be a central organizing concept in learning. A secondary concept involves the productivity and optimal division of that time among the different alternatives: presentation of new material through lectures, supervised and unsupervised practice, periodic repetition and review, and testing. Students have a wide variance in the ways they spend time in school. Part of the variance appears to depend on teacher characteristics, characteristics of other students in the class, and the amounts of time parents spend at home instructing children. Theories of learning need to be developed that incorporate school and home time and the various trade-offs and differences that exist across teachers, classrooms, and SES levels. Such a theory would generate a number of testable hypotheses for research that would then allow better and probably more-complex theories to be developed. Such theories can then provide guidance about which research is important to undertake.

The differences in effects between low- and high-SES students are particularly important to understand. One reason for this is that resource substitutions can occur between families and schools that can affect achievement. High family resources may often substitute for and supplement school resources in indirect and unmeasured ways that affect the accurate measurement of policy variables. Parental time spent on homework may substitute for individual teacher time in the classroom, allowing the teacher of higher SES students to spend more time lecturing and thus avoiding the opportunity costs of individualized instruction inside the classroom.

Families may also shift more resources of time and money when school resources are lowered, and less when schools are devoting more resources to students. Thus, students with higher levels of family resources will be more immune to changing school resources than students with lower levels of family resources. This could help explain the weaker schooling effects for students in higher-resource families. Students from families with few resources show the most sensitivity to levels of school resources because the substitution potential is weak or nonexistent. However, the results of this analysis would imply that more school resources could substitute for lower family resources. These substitutions need to be the focus of much more research.

Improving NAEP Data

If NAEP would collect a **school district** sample rather than a **school** sample, historical data from school districts (not available at the school level of aggregation) and Census data could be used to obtain decidedly superior family and schooling variables for models. Census data can provide good family characteristics for school districts but not generally for schools. The necessity of including variables since school entry in specifications makes district-level samples necessary for developing analytical models below the state level of aggregation.

One additional advantage of moving to a district sample is that comparison of scores could be made for major urban and suburban school districts. Urban school systems pose the greatest challenge to improving student achievement, and being able to develop models of NAEP scores across the major urban school districts could provide critical information in evaluating effective policies across urban districts. The samples would be much larger than at the state level and could be expected to provide more-reliable results than for states.

If NAEP does not move toward a district-level sample, collecting a very limited set of data from parents should be considered. The critical parental information could be obtained with no more than 10 questions.

LIMITATIONS AND CAUTION

No single analysis of achievement scores is definitive. Rather, the coherent pattern that emerges across experimental and nonexperimental measurements and the associated theories that explain the mechanisms causing achievement gains in classrooms ultimately build scientific consensus and confidence in informing policymaking. We are still far from achieving this kind of consensus for the effects of educational policy variables. Until this happens, there will always be legitimate differences of opinion about the importance and interpretations of any empirical results.

We believe that providing a new explanation that more successfully encompasses the pattern of previous nonexperimental results, the Tennessee experimental data, the pattern of score gains in the 1970s and 1980s, and the new results in this report may be the most important part of this report for policy. While the results of the analysis of state scores can be important, developing an explanation that accounts for a much wider set of results—in the absence of competing explanations—is more important for policy purposes. However, competing explanations need to be proposed, and more research is needed that can test this explanation.

Finally, achievement scores are not the only, and arguably may not be the most important, output of schools. It may be possible to have good schools that are responsive to students and parents that do not place strong emphasis on achievement scores. It is certainly necessary to collect wider measures than achievement when assessing schools.

Although NAEP strives to reflect a broad range of items, so that some items reflect skills learned at earlier grades and some at later grades, the scores can reflect the timing of when students learn skills. Students in different states do not learn particular skills in the same sequence or at the same grade level. The types of state assessments done and whether these assessments are more or less similar to NAEP tests may also influence scores. States that have assessment systems that are similar to NAEP might be expected to score higher because of the alignment of curriculum with NAEP items.

The effects measured should be seen primarily as long-term effects of differences in characteristics. States should not necessarily expect to see the full effects measured here in the first few years. The state differences measured here have, for the most part, existed over long periods, allowing students, teachers, parents, and curriculum to make longer-term adjustments.

"Teaching to the test" is often cited as a concern in assessments. Such a term carries three connotations. One connotation is a temporary inflation of achievement. Teachers are doing something that can result in a short-term achievement gain only, but the student's achievement will not benefit in the long term. In this case, achievement scores can be misleading indicators, and testing can provide perverse incentives. A second connotation of "teaching to the test" is more positive and suggests that tests reflect accepted standards for what children should know and that review and repetition are necessary to achieve both short- and long-term gains in achievement. This possibility should be of less, if any, concern. A third connotation is that an imbalance occurs in the time spent on and the priority of tested versus untested subjects, or between educational goals related to achievement and those not related directly to achievement. If achievement gains occur at the expense of untested subjects or other socially desired objectives, some concern is warranted. In this case, broader measures are needed, and priorities should be set across objectives.

These concerns are more prevalent for "high stakes" tests, those for which there are consequences for students, teachers, or administrators. These concerns are minor for the NAEP, since no feedback or consequences are provided to students or teachers for NAEP tests. However, high-stakes state assessments could certainly be reflected in NAEP assessments to the extent that the tests are similar.

STATE NAEP TEST SCORES AND STATE FAMILY AND EDUCATIONAL SYSTEM CHARACTERISTICS

STATE NAEP SCORES

Figures A.1 through A.7 show the ranked results of the seven state NAEP tests given from 1990 to 1996 for public school students. The results for each test are normalized to a mean of zero, and score differences are divided by the standard deviation of the nationally representative NAEP test. The scores incorporate the latest corrections to the test results that are published in the 1994 and 1998 documentation (Shaughnessy et al., 1998; Miller et al., 1995) and subsequent corrections from the NCES Web site. Table A.1 provides the correlation coefficients among the tests for states taking all tests. The test results are highly correlated at 0.77 or above. The correlation is higher when types of tests are similar (reading or math) or grade levels are similar. Table A.2 ranks each state for each test. The overall ranking is computed by normalizing the mean score for each test to zero and computing the average score across the tests in which each state participated.

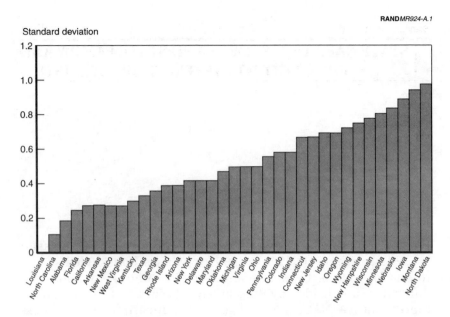

Figure A.1—Results of the 1990 8th-Grade Math Test

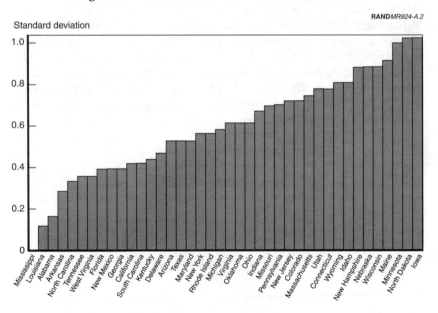

Figure A.2—Results of the 1992 8th-Grade Math Test

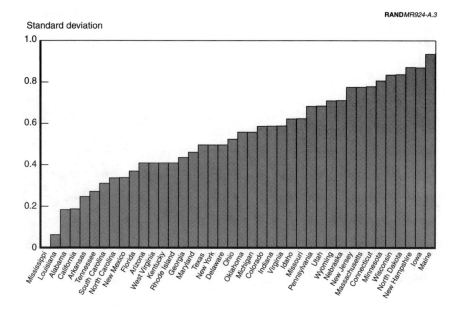

Figure A.3—Results of the 1992 4th-Grade Math Test

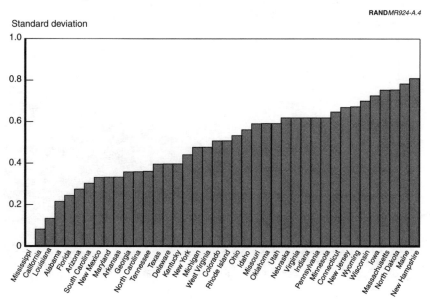

Figure A.4—Results of the 1992 4th-Grade Reading Test

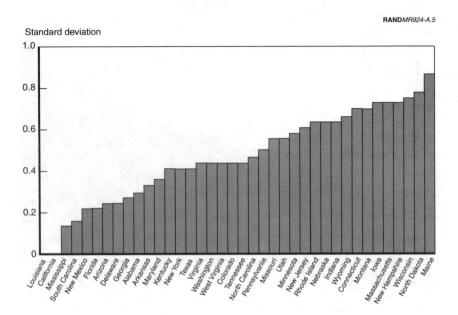

Figure A.5—Results of the 1994 4th-Grade Reading Test

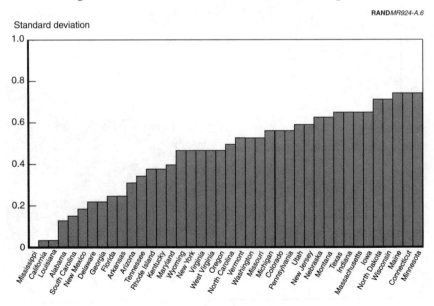

Figure A.6—Results of the 1996 4th-Grade Math Test

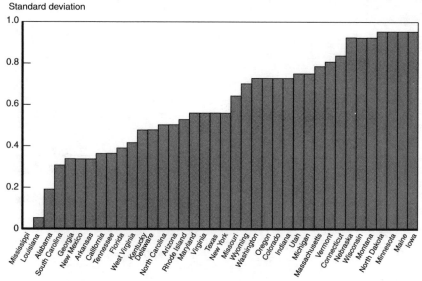

Figure A.7—Results of the 1996 8th-Grade Math Test

Table A.1

**Correlation Among States' Reading and Math Tests Given
Between 1990 and 1996 for States Taking All Tests**

	1990 Math 8th	1992 Math 8th	1992 Math 4th	1992 Read 4th	1996 Math 8th	1994 Read 4th	1996 Math 4th
1990 Math 8th	1.00						
1992 Math 8th	0.97	1.00					
1992 Math 4th	0.95	0.96	1.00				
1992 Reading 4th	0.88	0.87	0.93	1.00			
1996 Math 8th	0.94	0.97	0.96	0.88	1.000		
1994 Reading 4th	0.81	0.81	0.86	0.94	0.861	1.00	
1996 Math 4th	0.77	0.83	0.88	0.87	0.910	0.88	1.00

Table A.2

Summary of State Rankings Across Seven NAEP Tests

	1990 8th Math	1992 8th Math	1992 4th Math	1992 4th Read	1996 8th Math	1994 4th Read	1996 4th Math	Overall Rank
Maine	NA	4	1	2	1–4	1	1–3	1–2
North Dakota	1	1–2	4–5	3–4	1–4	2	4–5	1–2
Iowa	3	1–2	2–3	5	1–4	4–6	6–9	3
New Hampshire	7	5–7	2–3	1	NA	4–6	NA	4
Montana	2	NA	NA	NA	5–7	7–8	10–11	5
Wisconsin	6	5–7	4–5	6	5–7	3	4–5	6
Minnesota	5	3	6	10–14	1–4	14	1–3	7
Nebraska	4	5–7	10–11	10–14	5–7	10–12	10–11	8
Massachusetts	NA	12	7–9	3–4	10	4–6	6–9	9
Connecticut	11–12	10–11	7–9	9	8	7–8	1–3	10
New Jersey	11–12	13–14	7–9	7–8	NA	13	12–13	11
Wyoming	8	8–9	10–11	7–8	17	9	21–25	12
Vermont	NA	NA	NA	NA	9	NA	17–19	13
Idaho	9–10	8–9	14–15	18	NA	NA	NA	14
Utah	NA	10–11	12–13	15–17	11–12	15–16	12–13	15
Indiana	13–14	17	16–18	10–14	13–16	10–12	6–9	16
Oregon	9–10	NA	NA	NA	13–16	NA	21–25	17
Pennsylvania	15	15–16	12–13	10–14	NA	17	14–16	18
Missouri	NA	15–16	14–15	15–17	18	15–16	17–19	19

Table A.2—Continued

	1990 8th Math	1992 8th Math	1992 4th Math	1992 4th Read	1996 8th Math	1994 4th Read	1996 4th Math	Overall Rank
Colorado	13–14	13–14	16–18	20–21	13–16	19–23	14–16	20
Washington	NA	NA	NA	NA	13–16	19–23	17–19	21
Michigan	16–18	21	19–20	22–23	11–12	NA	14–16	22
Oklahoma	19	18–20	19–20	15–17	NA	NA	NA	23
Virginia	16–18	18–20	16–18	10–14	19–22	19–23	21–25	24
Ohio	16–18	18–20	21	19	NA	NA	NA	25
Rhode Island	23–24	22–23	27–30	20–21	23	10–12	27–28	26
Texas	26	24–26	22–24	25–27	19–22	24–26	6–9	27
New York	20–22	22–23	22–24	24	19–22	24–26	21–25	28
Maryland	20–22	24–26	25	31–33	19–22	27	26	29
West Virginia	28–31	34–35	27–30	22–23	28	19–23	21–25	30
Kentucky	27	28	27–30	25–27	26–27	24–26	27–28	31
Delaware	20–22	27	22–24	25–27	26–27	31–32	33–34	32
Arizona	23–24	24–26	27–30	35	24–25	31–32	30	33
North Carolina	34	36	32–33	28–30	24–25	18	20	34
Tennessee	NA	34–35	35	28–30	30–31	19–23	29	35
Georgia	25	31	26	28–30	32–34	30	33–34	36
Florida	32	32–33	31	36	29	33–34	31–32	37
New Mexico	28–31	32–33	32–33	31–33	32–34	33–34	35	38
Arkansas	28–31	37	36	31–33	32–34	28	31–32	39

Table A.2—Continued

	1990 8th Math	1992 8th Math	1992 4th Math	1992 4th Read	1996 8th Math	1994 4th Read	1996 4th Math	Overall Rank
South Carolina	NA	29–30	34	34	35	35	36	40
Alabama	33	38	37–38	37	36	29	37	41
California	28–31	29–30	37–38	39	30–31	37–38	38–39	42
Louisiana	35	39	39	38	37	37–38	38–39	43
Mississippi	NA	40	40	40	38	36	40	44

STATE FAMILY CHARACTERISTICS

The states have much variability in the average characteristics of their families, and since family characteristics explain most of the variance in cross-sectional models of achievement at the individual level, it would be expected that differing family characteristics would account for an important part of state test-score variance. Figures A.8 through A.15 show measures of selected family characteristics by state: percentages of minorities, family income levels, parental education, teen births, single parents, mothers working, and residential stability of home environment.

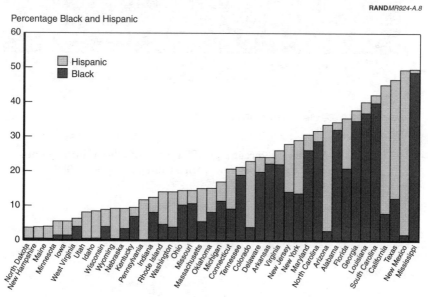

SOURCE: 1990 Census for families with children 8–10.

Figure A.8—Estimated Percentage of 4th-Grade Student Population That Is Black or Hispanic—1990

RAND*MR924-A.9*

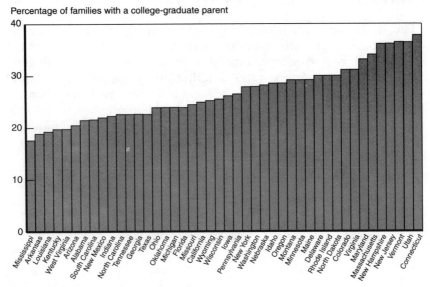

Percentage of families with a college-graduate parent

SOURCE: 1990 Census for families with children 8–10.

**Figure A.9—Estimated Percentage of Families of 4th-Grade Students
Having at Least One Parent with a College Degree—1990**

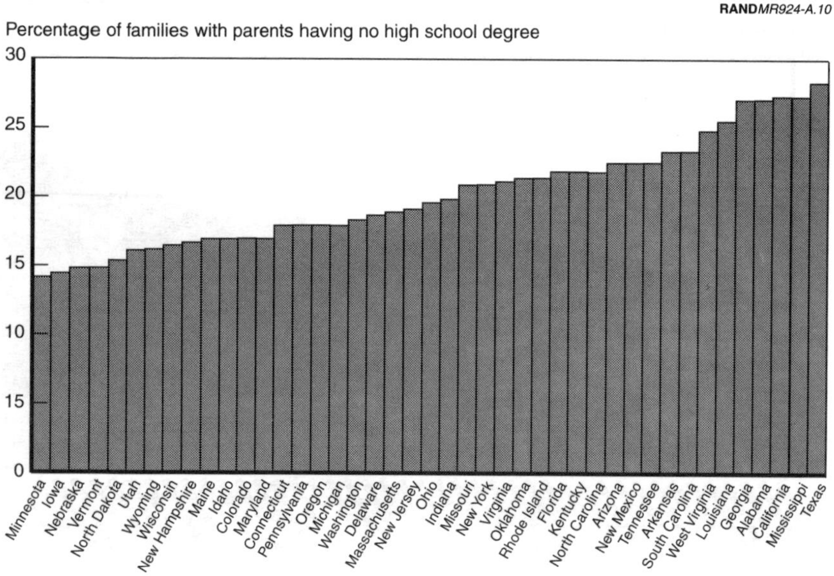

RAND*MR924-A.10*

Percentage of families with parents having no high school degree

SOURCE: 1990 Census for families with children 8–10.

Figure A.10—Estimated Percentage of Families of 4th-Grade Students Having the Highest Parental Education as Non–High School Graduate—1990

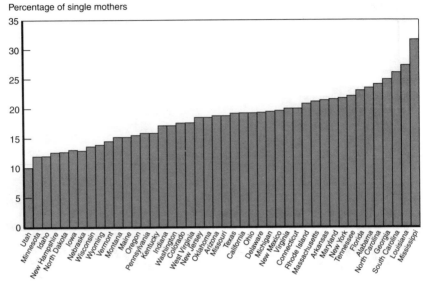

SOURCE: 1990 Census for families with children 8–10.

Figure A.13—Estimated Percentage of Single-Parent Families of 4th-Grade Students

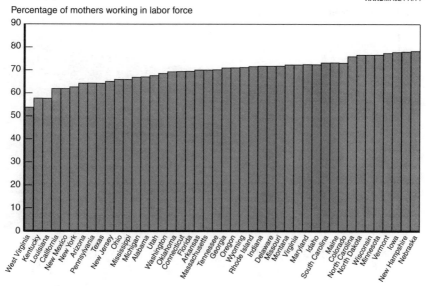

SOURCE: 1990 Census for families with children 8–10.

Figure A.14—Estimated Percentage of Mothers Working Full or Part Time of 4th-Grade Students

No change in residence in last two years (percent)

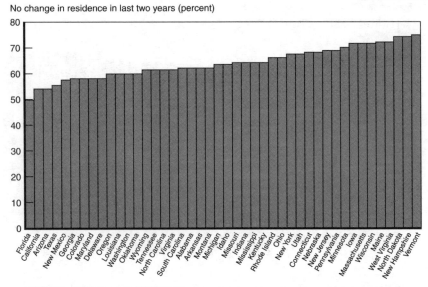

SOURCE: 1992 4th grade NAEP tests.

Figure A.15—Estimated Percentage of 4th-Grade Students Reporting No Residential Relocation Over Last Two Years

STATE EDUCATION CHARACTERISTICS

The states have a remarkable variance in key characteristics of their educational systems and teachers. These differences are partly the result of correlation with family characteristics and partly due to nonfamily factors. The correlation coefficients with family characteristics are shown in Table A.3. The correlation between specific educational characteristics and specific family characteristics is generally around 0.5 or less. The schooling variables most correlated are teacher salary and per-pupil expenditure. The highest correlation (0.63) is between teacher salary and family income. The correlation of pupil-teacher ratio and family characteristics is below 0.3, with even less correlation between family and public prekindergarten.

Figures A.16 through A.22 show seven measures of the educational policies and teacher characteristics among states that might be hypothesized to lead to score differences: pupil-teacher ratio, per-pupil spending, average teacher salary, percentage of teachers with no degree beyond the bachelor's, percentage of teachers with more than 20 years of experience, proportion of children in public prekindergarten, and percentage of teachers responding in the lowest (least adequate) category of the adequacy of their resources for teaching. These variables have generally been constructed using data from the *Digest of Educational Statistics* (NCES, 1996, 1990, 1986), but several refinements, such as COL adjustments, have been made. The teacher resource variables are taken from the NAEP teacher surveys administered with the test. See Appendix F for detailed definitions of these variables.

Table A.3

Correlation Coefficients Among Family and Educational Policy Variables

	SES	SES-FE	Family Income	Parents' Education (College)	Single Parent	Black (%)	Hisp (%)
Per-pupil expenditure	0.48	0.44	0.51	0.50	–0.24	–0.26	–0.11
Pupil-teacher ratio	–0.27	–0.25	–0.15	–0.20	0.16	0.08	0.29
Teacher salary	0.44	0.40	0.63	0.54	–0.17	–0.28	0.04
Teacher degree (BA)	0.17	0.20	–0.26	0.08	–0.36	–0.19	0.04
Prekindergarten	0.02	0.01	0.22	0.10	–0.09	0.01	0.14
Teacher experience							
4–9 years	–0.21	–0.17	–0.39	–0.20	–0.04	–0.04	0.34
10–20 years	–0.17	–0.17	–0.16	–0.24	0.16	0.12	–0.19
20+ years	0.26	0.23	0.45	0.29	–0.04	–0.03	–0.17

RAND*MR924-A.16*

Estimated pupil/teacher ratio (regular students)

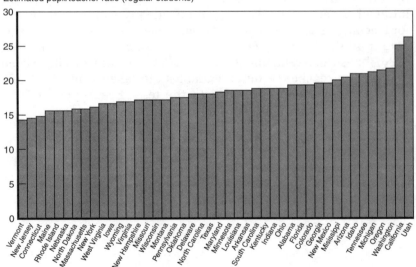

Figure A.16—Estimated Pupil-Teacher Ratio for 4th-Grade NAEP Test
States in 1992 Averaged Over Years in School

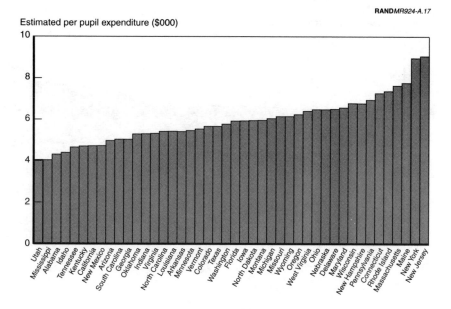

Figure A.17—Estimated Per-Pupil Expenditures for NAEP 4th-
Grade Test States in 1992 Averaged Over Years in School
(Adjusted for COL, 1993–1994 Dollars)

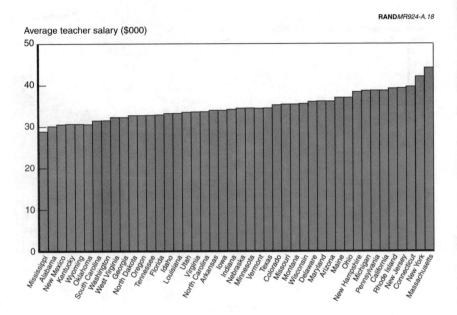

RAND*MR924-A.18*

Figure A.18—Average Teacher Salary
(Adjusted for COL Differences)

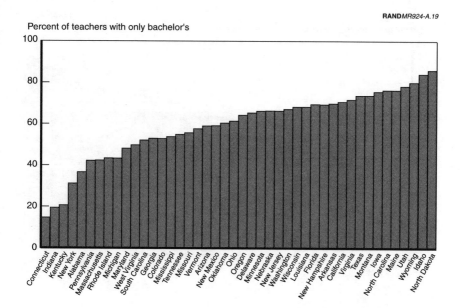

Figure A.19—Estimated Percentage of Teachers Having No Degree Beyond Bachelor's for 1992 4th-Grade NAEP Test States Averaged Over Years in School

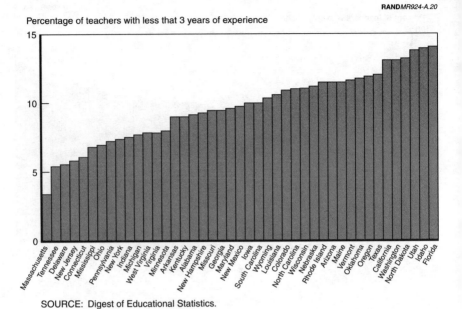

SOURCE: Digest of Educational Statistics.

**Figure A.20—Estimated Percentage of Teachers with Less Than
Three Years of Experience for 4th-Grade NAEP Test States in
1992 Averaged Over Years in School**

RAND*MR924-A.21*

Percentage of teachers with over 20 years of experience

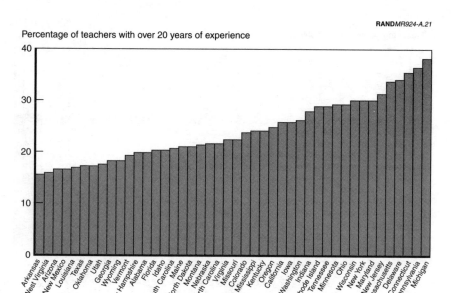

Figure A.21—Estimated Percentage of Teachers with Over 20 Years of Experience for 4th-Grade NAEP Test States in 1992 Averaged Over Years in School

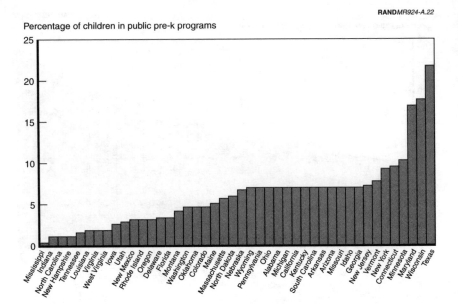

Figure A.22—Estimated Percentage of 4th-Graders in Test
States Who Attended a Public Prekindergarten Program

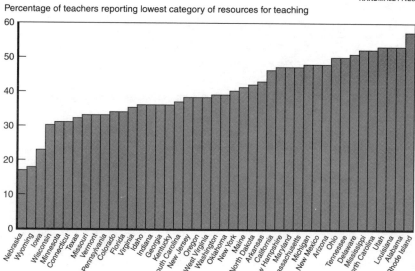

SOURCE: 1992 4th grade math NAEP test-teacher survey.

Figure A.23

Figure A.23—Percentage of 4th-Grade Teachers in 1992 Responding in
Lowest (Most Inadequate) Category for Adequacy of Resources to Teach

NAEP EXCLUSION AND PARTICIPATION RATES

The actual sample of students completing NAEP tests varies from the public school population because of the exclusion of certain categories of students and because of nonparticipation. We will review these data to help assess the extent of possible bias due to exclusion and nonparticipation

STUDENT EXCLUSIONS

Exclusion criteria have been established for two categories of students from the tests: LEP and IEP/DS. These students include those who have IEPs or who are receiving special services as a result of section 504 of the Rehabilitation Act. The criteria used in NAEP's assessments state that IEP/DS students could be excluded only if they were mainstreamed in academic subjects less than 50 percent of the time and/or judged to be incapable of participating meaningfully in the assessment. Furthermore, LEP students could be excluded if they were native speakers of a language other than English, had been enrolled in an English speaking school for less than two years, and were judged to be incapable of taking part in the assessment. The criteria for exclusion are applied across states resulting in approximately 2 to 3 percent of public school students excluded for LEP and 5 percent for IEP/DS.

IEP/DS Exclusions

Table B.1 presents the weighted percentages of IEP/DS students excluded from the seven NAEP assessments. The range of variation

141

Table B.1

Weighted Percentages of IEP Students Excluded by State

	Mathematics					Reading		
	1990 8th	1992 4th	1992 8th	1996 8th	1996 4th	1992 4th	1994 4th	Avg.
Florida	5	7	5	7	7	7	9	6.71
Oklahoma	5	7	6	NA	NA	8	NA	6.50
West Virginia	6	4	6	8	8	5	7	6.29
Arkansas	8	5	6	7	6	5	6	6.14
Maine	NA	6	4	4	8	5	9	6.00
Ohio	6	6	6	NA	NA	6	NA	6.00
Texas	5	5	5	6	8	5	7	5.86
Wisconsin	4	5	4	7	8	6	7	5.86
Massachusetts	NA	6	6	6	7	5	5	5.83
Mississippi	NA	5	7	7	5	5	6	5.83
South Carolina	NA	5	6	5	6	6	7	5.83
New Mexico	6	6	4	4	8	6	6	5.71
Alabama	6	4	5	8	6	5	5	5.57
Virginia	5	5	5	6	6	6	6	5.57
Connecticut	6	4	5	7	6	4	6	5.43
Delaware	4	5	4	8	5	5	6	5.29
Maryland	4	3	4	5	7	6	7	5.14
Michigan	4	5	6	4	6	4	6	5.00
New York	5	3	6	6	6	4	5	5.00
Oregon	NA	NA	NA	4	6	NA	NA	5.00
Tennessee	NA	4	5	4	6	5	6	5.00
Vermont	NA	NA	NA	4	6	NA	NA	5.00
Colorado	4	4	4	4	7	5	6	4.86
Georgia	4	5	4	5	6	5	5	4.86
Louisiana	4	4	4	5	7	4	6	4.86
Missouri	NA	4	4	7	5	4	5	4.83
Arizona	4	3	4	5	7	5	5	4.71
New Hampshire	5	4	5	4	NA	4	6	4.67
Washington	NA	NA	NA	5	5	NA	4	4.67
Kentucky	5	3	5	5	6	4	4	4.57
New Jersey	6	3	6	5	5	3	4	4.57
Utah	NA	4	4	5	5	4	5	4.50
Indiana	5	3	4	5	5	4	5	4.43

Table B.1—Continued

	Mathematics				Reading		
	1990 8th	1992 4th	1992 8th	1996 8th	1996 4th	1992 4th	1994 4th	Avg.
Rhode Island	5	4	4	5	5	4	4	4.43
California	4	3	4	4	6	4	5	4.29
North Carolina	3	3	3	4	7	4	5	4.14
Nebraska	3	4	4	4	5	4	4	4.00
Pennsylvania	5	3	4	NA	4	3	5	4.00
Iowa	4	3	4	4	4	4	4	3.86
Montana	NA	NA	NA	3	5	NA	3	3.67
Minnesota	3	3	3	3	4	4	4	3.43
Wyoming	4	3	4	1	4	4	4	3.43
Idaho	2	3	3	NA	NA	3	4	3.00
North Dakota	3	2	2	4	3	2	2	2.57
Average	4.61	4.20	4.60	5.15	5.9	4.65	5.38	4.96

across states is fairly small—approximately ±2 percentage points around the average. There is a high correlation across tests, indicating a fairly consistent identification of IEP/DS students over time in the states. There is a slight trend upward, with the 1994 and 1996 tests having exclusion rates about 0.75 to 1.5 percentage points higher than the 1990-1992 tests.

The pattern of IEP/DS exclusions across states cannot be easily characterized. The incidence of learning and emotional disabilities tends to be spread throughout all types of family and demographic groups. Mild mental retardation appears to be more prevalent for blacks, but other learning and emotional disabilities are not (Reschly, 1996). In addition, the identification and screening of children for learning and emotional disabilities is done with different intensities in different states (Reschly, 1996). Decisions to classify children have fiscal implications and implications for providing a special learning environment, so the decisions of parents and school systems to pursue such classifications can vary by state. Some higher-educated, higher-income parents may be more aggressive in pursuing certain classifications, and certain states with higher levels of spending may be more likely to classify children as IEP/DS.

It cannot be determined whether the differences among states reflect a uniform application of criteria that have detected actual differences in the incidence of IEP/DS or whether part of the state variation reflects different criteria or different intensities of screening applied in states. A regression of exclusion rate on SES-FE shows higher exclusion with lower SES with a $t = 3.3$ for SES-FE, but only 20 percent of the variance is explained. The maximum residuals for a state in this regression show ±1.5 percent in unexplained exclusion rate. Also, a regression of our value-added measure against the exclusion rate shows that the exclusion rate is highly insignificant ($t = 1.08$) and the wrong sign (higher exclusion leads to lower value added). It is possible that different criteria and screening intensity could change exclusion rates among states by 1 or 2 percentage points. At the extreme, two states may differ by 3 percentage points because of different criteria and exclusion rates, but this would occur for very few states. These differences would introduce some bias in the average state scores. The amount of bias would depend on the proportion of children in a state "misclassified" and on the average scores of the children. While the average scores of such children would be expected to be low, the percentage misclassified also appears to be fairly low.

Assuming scores for these misclassified students of two standard deviations below the mean would indicate a potential maximum state average score bias of 0.06 standard deviation between two states with the most differences in classification and screening. For most states, the amount of potential bias would be expected to be significantly less. The estimates of policy coefficients are insensitive to these small biases. The value-added estimates are more sensitive, but the range of value-added estimates is around 0.35 standard deviation. So, the maximum potential bias would move states several positions in the value-added rankings but would never result in dramatic shifts of state value added.

However, our methodology accounts for at least part of the effects of differences in exclusion rates. We account for the part of exclusion rate differences that would affect the percentage of each race and/or ethnic group taking the test. We do this by developing our family variables based on the percentage of children actually taking each test by race by state. However, the methodology does not account for within-race differences from different exclusion rates.

The story is similar for our trend estimates. IEP exclusion has increased between 1990 and 1996 for math scores at an approximate rate of 0.3 percentage point per year. Assuming that students 2 standard deviations below the mean are the marginal exclusions, this would introduce an upward trend in scores of 0.006 standard deviation per year. Our average trend in overall math scores is 0.032 per year, so, under these conservative assumptions, the exclusion rates could potentially account for only a small part of the trend. But our methodology accounts for part of the changes in exclusion rates that affect racial and/or ethnic proportions taking each test. So, actual bias would be less.

LEP Exclusions

Table B.2 presents the weighted percentages of LEP students excluded from the NAEP assessments. Most states exclude less than 2 percent of students because of LEP, but states with a high proportion of Hispanics, such as California, Texas, Arizona, New Mexico, and New York, have excluded a much larger percentage of LEP students. California excludes the largest percentage by a wide margin. If all exclusions were Hispanics, approximately one in five Hispanic students in California would be excluded from the tests, while in Texas, Arizona, and New Mexico, only approximately one in ten Hispanics would be excluded. However, the higher California exclusion probably represents a combination of exclusions due to immigrants from Asia and a higher incidence of recent Hispanic immigrants.

The correlation between average LEP exclusion and the percentage of Hispanic students in a state is 0.66. Most of the state differences appear traceable to the Hispanic population, but this relationship leaves little room for any significant bias from this exclusion for almost all states. But the Texas-California difference bears further scrutiny. For instance, even if we assume that the entire California-Texas difference represents misclassifications due to different criteria, it would separate the two average state scores by 0.10 standard deviation, assuming students would score two standard deviations below mean scores. The direction of the bias would be upward for California average scores. Scores in California would be lifted to the extent that differences exist in classification criteria in Texas and California. That is, if the two states had similar classification criteria,

Table B.2

Weighted Percentages of LEP Students Excluded by State

| | NAEP Mathematics | | | | | NAEP Reading | | |
	1990 8th	1992 4th	1992 8th	1996 8th	1996 4th	1992 4th	1994 4th	Avg.
California	5	10	5	6	13	11	9	8.43
Texas	2	4	2	3	5	3	5	3.43
Arizona	2	2	2	4	7	3	3	3.29
New York	2	2	3	2	4	2	3	2.57
New Mexico	1	1	1	4	5	2	2	2.29
Rhode Island	2	3	2	2	2	4	1	2.29
Connecticut	1	3	1	2	2	3	3	2.14
Florida	2	2	2	2	3	2	2	2.14
Massachusetts		2	2	1	2	2	3	2.00
Oregon	NA	NA	NA	1	3	NA	NA	2.00
New Jersey	2	2	1	2	1	2	2	1.71
Colorado	1	1	1	1	2	2	2	1.43
Maryland	1	1	1	1	1	1	1	1.00
Utah		1	0	2	1	1	1	1.00
Virginia	1	1	1	1	1	1	1	1.00
Washington	NA	NA	NA	1	1	NA	1	1.00
Delaware	1	1	0	0	2	0	1	0.71
Georgia	0	1	0	1	1	1	1	0.71
Wisconsin	0	1	0	1	1	1	1	0.71
Pennsylvania	0	1	0	NA	1	1	1	0.67
Idaho	0	1	0	NA	NA	1	1	0.60
Nebraska	0	0	0	1	1	1	1	0.57
North Carolina	0	0	0	1	1	1	1	0.57
Michigan	0	1	0	0	1	1	0	0.43
Minnesota	0	0	0	0	1	1	1	0.43
Ohio	0	0	0	NA	NA	1	NA	0.25
Oklahoma	0	0	0	NA	NA	1	NA	0.25
Maine	NA	0	0	0	0	0	1	0.17
Missouri	NA	0	0	1	0	0	0	0.17
Tennessee	NA	0	0	0	1	0	0	0.17
Arkansas	0	0	0	1	0	0	0	0.14
Iowa	0	0	0	0	1	0	0	0.14
Alabama	0	0	0	0	0	0	0	0.00

Table B.2—Continued

	NAEP Mathematics					NAEP Reading		
	1990 8th	1992 4th	1992 8th	1996 8th	1996 4th	1992 4th	1994 4th	Avg.
Indiana	0	0	0	0	0	0	0	0.00
Kentucky	0	0	0	0	0	0	0	0.00
Louisiana	0	0	0	0	0	0	0	0.00
Mississippi	NA	0	0	0	0	0	0	0.00
Montana	NA	NA	NA	0	0	NA	0	0.00
New Hampshire	0	0	0	0	NA	0	0	0.00
North Dakota	0	0	0	0	0	0	0	0.00
South Carolina	NA	0	0	0	0	0	0	0.00
Vermont	NA	NA	NA	0	0	NA	NA	0.00
West Virginia	0	0	0	0	0	0	0	0.00
Wyoming	0	0	0	0	0	0	0	0.00
Average	0.70	1.03	0.60	1.05	1.56	1.23	1.20	1.01

the large value-added differences between Texas and California would become even larger. However, our methodology probably accounts for much of this bias, since LEP directly affects the percentage of Hispanic students taking the test.

There is a slight upward trend in LEP exclusion of approximately 0.2 percentage points a year. Using the conservative assumption of marginal excluded students scoring 2 standard deviations below the mean would mean an upward trend of 0.004 per year. However, our methodology probably accounts for much of this bias.

NONPARTICIPATION RATES

The NAEP tests are voluntary for states, schools, and students. At the school and student levels, substitution is attempted when schools and students refuse to participate. In 1990, the NCES established the following guidelines to ensure the absence of significant nonresponse biases in school and student participation rates for reported scores:

1. Both the state's weighted participation rate for the initial sample of schools below 85 percent *and* a weighted school participation

rate after substitution below 90 percent; *or* a weighted school participation rate of the initial sample of schools below 70 percent

2. The nonparticipating schools include a class of schools with similar characteristics, which together account for more than 5 percent of the state's total 4th- or 8th-grade weighted sample of public schools

3. A weighted student response rate within participating schools below 85 percent

4. The nonresponding students within participating schools include a class of students with similar characteristics, who together constituted more than 5 percent of the state's weighted assessable student sample (Mullis, 1993).

Each state or jurisdiction is required to meet the NCES standards. States and jurisdictions receive a notation in published NAEP reports if any of the guidelines presented above are not met. If a jurisdiction fails to meet all of the requirements, its results are not reported. The results for several states have been excluded over time because of low participation, and the results for several states in each test contain a notation for low participation.

The NCES guidelines presented above governed the 1992 state mathematics assessment. There have been a few modifications and consolidations to the guidelines. In 1996, the weighted student response rate within participating schools could not be below 80 percent, compared to below 85 percent in pervious assessments.

Table B.3 presents the rank of each state's participation rate after substitution by test and an average participation rate across tests. Participation rates after substitution for each test range from 100 to 63 percent. Table B.4 presents a correlation matrix of weighted overall participation rate. There is a moderately positive correlation, showing that if state participation is low in a given year, it is more likely to be low across all years. Thus, participation rates are not random across tests, but states have persistent patterns in participation rates.

These differences are not important if nonparticipants are similar to participants. We tested for bias by regressing the participation rate

Table B.3

Weighted School Participation Rate After Substitution

	Mathematics					Reading		
	1990 8th	1992 4th	1992 8th	1996 8th	1996 4th	1992 4th	1994 4th	Avg.
Nation	88	86	88	81	83	86	86	85.5
Alabama	86	75	66	84	79	76	87	79.0
Arizona	97	100	99	87	87	99	99	95.5
Arkansas	100	90	89	70	76	87	86	85.4
California	94	91	93	83	80	92	80	87.6
Colorado	100	100	100	100	99	100	100	99.9
Connecticut	100	99	99	100	100	99	96	99.0
Delaware	100	92	100	100	100	92	100	97.7
Florida	98	100	100	100	100	100	100	99.7
Georgia	100	100	99	99	98	100	99	99.3
Idaho	97	84	85	NA	NA	82	69	83.4
Indiana	89	76	79	88	87	77	83	82.7
Iowa	91	100	99	74	79	100	85	89.7
Kentucky	100	93	96	88	88	94	88	92.4
Louisiana	100	100	100	100	100	100	100	100.0
Maine	NA	57	92	90	87	58	94	79.7
Maryland	100	99	89	86	93	99	94	94.3
Massachusetts	NA	87	83	92	97	87	97	90.5
Michigan	90	83	78	70	76	83	63	77.6
Minnesota	90	82	81	86	91	81	86	85.3
Mississippi	NA	98	99	89	92	98	95	95.2
Missouri	NA	89	92	93	96	90	96	92.7
Montana	NA	NA	NA	72	70	NA	85	75.7
Nebraska	87	80	75	99	100	76	71	84.0
New Hampshire	91	69	80	66	NA	68	71	74.2
New Jersey	97	76	69	64	73	76	85	77.1
New Mexico	100	75	77	100	100	76	100	89.7
New York	86	78	81	71	73	78	75	77.4
North Carolina	100	95	94	100	97	95	99	97.1
North Dakota	96	73	78	83	75	70	80	79.3
Ohio	96	79	77	NA	NA	78	NA	82.5
Oklahoma	78	86	82	NA	NA	86	NA	83.0
Oregon	NA	NA	NA	86	86	NA	NA	86.0

Table B.3—Continued

	Mathematics				Reading		
	1990 8th	1992 4th	1992 8th	1996 8th	1996 4th	1992 4th	1994 4th	Avg.
Pennsylvania	90	84	81	NA	73	85	80	82.2
Rhode Island	94	83	85	90	89	83	80	86.3
South Carolina	NA	98	94	86	87	98	95	93.0
Tennessee	NA	92	87	92	94	93	72	88.3
Texas	88	93	95	90	95	92	91	92.0
Utah	NA	99	100	100	100	99	100	99.7
Vermont	NA	NA	NA	74	78	NA	NA	76.0
Virginia	99	99	97	100	100	99	98	98.9
Washington	NA	NA	NA	94	99	NA	100	97.7
West Virginia	100	100	100	100	100	100	99	99.9
Wisconsin	99	100	100	78	92	99	79	92.4
Wyoming	100	97	99	100	100	97	98	98.7

Table B.4

Correlation Matrix of Weighted School Participation Rate After Substitution

	Mathematics					Reading	
	1990 8th	1992 4th	1992 8th	1996 8th	1996 4th	1992 4th	1994 4th
1990 8th math	1.00						
1992 4th math	0.38	1.00					
1992 8th math	0.41	0.77	1.00				
1996 8th math	0.30	0.39	0.49	1.00			
1996 4th math	0.38	0.40	0.55	0.78	1.00		
1992 4th reading	0.37	0.99	0.77	0.43	0.44	1.00	
1994 4th reading	0.37	0.41	0.42	0.43	0.28	0.41	1.00

by test against SES-FE. The SES-FE was positive and statistically significant, suggesting that participation is higher in states with higher SES. Thus, schools and students not participating in the NAEP analysis are probably lower-scoring schools or students. Almost all of the nonparticipation is by school rather than by student, so schools choosing not to take the tests are probably more often schools with lower-scoring students. We take differences in participation rates into account in two ways. First, we included the participation rate variable in all our regressions. The variable is always negative, but never statistically significant. The t-statistic is in the range of –0.75 to –1.35. The coefficient is approximately 0.001, indicating that states that differ in participation rates by 15 percentage points would be expected to have differences of 0.015 standard deviation in scores because of differences in participation. Thus, the variable does correct for some bias due to low participation. Second, our methodology accounts for differences in participation to the extent that it results in differences in race and/or ethnic participation by test.

SOURCES OF BIAS

INTRODUCTION

Reviews of the literature show that educational resource variables are likely to have positive, statistically significant results only when measurements are at the state level of aggregation (Hanushek et al., 1996). Measurements at lower levels of aggregation show no consistent effects. The state-level measurements are thus more consistent with the experimental Tennessee class-size effects than measurements at lower levels of aggregation.

Aggregation in and of itself does not introduce bias into correctly specified linear models, although the standard errors can change with the level of aggregation. Thus, there is no a priori reason results from one level of aggregation should be different or be preferred over another level. Despite this neutrality, the presumption in the literature has been that the less-aggregated measurements are more accurate, while the more-aggregated measurements are biased upward (Hanushek et al., 1996).

This presumption partly arises because well-designed and collected individual-level data used in well-specified models can potentially provide superior estimates because the sample sizes are inherently larger and because there are generally more of and a greater range of variables. Other things being equal, researchers prefer individual-level data. However, the amount of bias can change across levels of aggregation, and larger samples and greater variation cannot generally compensate for bias. The level of bias will partly depend on the characteristics of specific data sets and the specifications used. Given the characteristics of the data sets actually used in current and previous educational research, it is possible that aggregate measurements are less biased than measurements at lower levels of aggregation.

If it could be shown that individual-level measurements carry differential bias in the downward direction, a more-consistent explanation of the previous nonexperimental measurements and experimental measurements would be possible. That explanation would be that aggregate-level measurements that show the most consistent and robust results in the nonexperimental literature and that are in closer agreement with the experimental data are the most accurate and that previous measurements at lower levels of aggregation are biased downward.

To pursue this hypothesis, we would need to identify factors causing more-pronounced bias at lower levels of aggregation. For models that are nonlinear or not correctly specified, more bias can be introduced at one level of aggregation than another, making results differ across levels of aggregation. Determining which set of results is more accurate entails knowing which forms of misspecification or nonlinearity are present and how each affects the results at each level of aggregation. There are usually several possible misspecification problems present, making it difficult to determine whether measurements at one level of aggregation are to be preferred over another.

In this appendix, our discussion is meant to suggest the factors that need to be explored further. We suggest one candidate implicated by the Tennessee experiment: missing variables describing previous years of schooling characteristics. We provide arguments that these missing variables would likely cause downward bias. We have tested this hypothesis empirically with our data set on one variable—pupil-teacher ratio—and found that the results are consistent with this hypothesis. We also argue below that the bias from these missing variables will be greater at lower levels of aggregation.

We also suggest other factors that might bias measurements at lower levels of aggregation downward. These effects need to be explored mathematically, through simulation, and empirically with existing and emerging data sets. If solid evidence emerges of downward bias at lower levels of aggregation in previous measurements, one of the more vexing issues in education research would be solved—the cause of differences in results between experimental and nonexperimental results and among nonexperimental measurements at different levels of aggregation.

After reviewing two recent articles that address aggregation issues in education production functions, we describe some forms of misspecification that might support this conjecture. The discussion assumes that model specifications do not include a test score from a previous year as a control. We address this issue in the final section.

CURRENT ANALYSIS OF THE EFFECTS OF MISSPECIFICATION IN EDUCATIONAL PRODUCTION FUNCTIONS

One form of misspecification in education production functions that would bias more-aggregate measurements upward has been analyzed (Hanushek et al., 1996). The analysis suggested that measurements done at the state level would be biased upward if there were missing state-level policy variables correlated with observed variables, while such a bias would not be present for less-aggregate measurements. The authors suggest that this may be the reason that state-level measurements of resource variables are "biased" upward, while the less-aggregate measurements showing little effect of resources are unbiased.

One possible problem with this analysis is that it assumes an unspecified set of state regulatory policies that have significant influence on educational outcomes, while concluding that resource variables (per-pupil expenditures, class size, and teacher education and experience) have little effect on outcomes. It is hard to see how the political decisionmaking process that underlies both state resource allocations and regulatory decisions could result in one set of policies having significant effects, while the other set has little effect. There is also little empirical evidence that state regulatory policies existing at the time of previous measurements affected educational outcomes.

Goldhaber and Brewer (1997) provided empirical evidence suggesting that unobservables do not bias the measured effects of teacher characteristics at the individual and school levels. Using NELS, they estimated achievement models using random and fixed effects at the teacher and school levels to account for unobservables. They concluded that unobserved teacher and school effects influence achievement but introduce no bias in the measured effect, implying that there is no correlation between the unobservables and included teacher characteristics.

The result cannot be generalized beyond the current data set because an observed variable in one data set may be unobserved in another. The equations estimated included a quite diverse set of teacher and school characteristics compared to previous measurements, so it is difficult to assess whether results would apply to historical measurements. The results also apply to teacher characteristics of 10th-grade teachers but would not apply to longer-term effects from teachers or characteristics of previous years. This study also addressed a single type of potential bias at the individual level.

FACTORS THAT CAN PRODUCE DOWNWARD BIAS AT LOWER LEVELS OF AGGREGATION

Some types of misspecification may introduce more bias at less aggregate levels of measurement. One example frequently cited is measurement error in the explanatory variables at lower levels of aggregation. Other conditions that might produce more bias at lower levels of aggregation include the following:

- Variables are missing at the lower level.
- Factors causing bias are more prevalent at lower levels of aggregation.
- Factors causing bias at lower levels tend to cancel out when aggregated to higher levels, such as measurement error.

The argument here is that differential bias can occur because differential quality of data can exist at different levels of aggregation, the presence of factors causing bias can be differentially present, and certain forms of bias may cancel at higher levels of aggregation.

Unobserved Variables at Lower Levels of Aggregation

The results of the Tennessee experiment suggest that class-size effects can depend in complex ways on class size in all previous grades (see Appendix D). The total class-size effect appears to depend on each previous grade, as well as on the current grade. Thus, models should ideally include class size from all previous grades in specifications. It is not known whether this phenomenon extends to other resource variables, but it is plausible. It would not be surprising, for instance, to find that good teachers have long-lasting influence.

If so, a major set of variables has been missing from almost all previous analysis regardless of level of aggregation. The likely effect of these missing variables is to bias measurements **downward** at any level of aggregation. Only including the current grade inevitably misses part of the cumulative effect, and so the bias is toward zero. However, the absence of variables for previous years can bias individual-level estimates more than aggregate estimates because of higher student migration at the individual level.

The amount of bias will depend partly on the correlation between the current year's class size and class sizes in previous years. A perfect correlation, meaning that all students maintain the same relative class size across grades, would result in no bias in the cumulative effect of class size, but the interpretation that the effect is due to the class size in the current grade would be in error.

An imperfect correlation among current and previous class sizes would generally bias the cumulative effect toward zero. The degree of bias can be greater at the individual level because higher correlation of class size across grades may exist at higher levels of aggregation because of differential migration effects.

Class size for a cohort can change from year to year within a school due to changing enrollment and policies. However, a significant source of variation may be migration between schools. Migration across districts and states is much less than between schools, so average class size across districts and states between grades can be more highly correlated than at the individual or school level. Thus, aggregate measurements would be less biased to the extent that migration is a major source of changes in class size across grades.

Migration can bias results in two other ways. Since migration is higher in lower-income schools and districts, the correlation between grades might be lower in disadvantaged school districts. If class-size effects are larger for minority and disadvantaged students, this higher migration could produce an additional downward bias. This bias would also be greater for measurements done at higher grades, since correlation between current grades and early grades would decline as the gap between grades grows. If class-size effects mainly arise in early grades, measurements at higher grades are likely to be even more biased toward zero.

Although variables from previous years can be introduced into analysis at any level of aggregation, they have been much more available in previous aggregate data sets than individual-level data sets. Only individual-level data collected from kindergarten would have previous years' class sizes, and virtually no such longitudinal data sets have existed until recently. However, such information is more readily available at the district or state level because resource variables have been commonly collected as part of the administrative system. Thus, average class size and per-pupil expenditures for students in a district or state are available for their previous grades. However, this information has probably rarely been included in the models.

We tested whether results for pupil-teacher ratio differed in our data set when the variables were defined using averages during time in school versus the value in the year of the test only. We used the state average pupil-teacher ratio during all years in school, the average during grades 1 through 4, and the value in the year of the test. The estimates for these variables are shown in Table C.1 for the policy model using SES. The results are very similar for SES-FE and Census-NAEP. The results show that including current-year pupil-teacher ratio instead of information from previous years causes the coefficients generally to weaken in both random- and fixed-effect models and to change signs in one model. This effect can be peculiar to our data set, and more widespread testing with other data sets is needed.

The Quality of Family Variables

The effects of family variables in estimates of education production functions, including cross-sectional data, dwarf any schooling effects. Family variables are also moderately correlated with most schooling variables, so missing, inaccurate, and misspecified family variables have great potential to bias schooling effects.

Table C.1

Comparing Three Pupil-Teacher Coefficients That Incorporate Differing Information About Previous Grades

Variable	Random Effect		Fixed Effect	
	Coef	T–Value	Coef	T–Value
Average pupil-teacher ratio during school years	–0.015	–2.41	–0.014	–1.16
Average pupil-teacher ratio in grades 1–4	–0.020	–2.69	–0.026	–2.60
Pupil-teacher ratio in year of the test	–0.008	–1.32	0.014	1.57

The completeness and accuracy of family variables are highly dependent on the source of the family data in particular analysis. It is possible that the quality of family data systematically varies across levels of aggregation. Census data can be used to generate family variables at the state and district level, but not at the school or individual level. At the school and individual levels, family variables must come from surveys of parents or from student reports. Student reporting can be problematical. While it is possible that well-designed and well-collected survey data from parents might approach, if not improve on, Census data, the level of response rates and missing values is likely higher on such data used in previous data sets—particularly for lower-income families.

Missing family variables alone cannot explain a downward bias at lower levels of aggregation, since this generally results in upward bias on schooling effects. However, inaccurate reporting and missing values could cause bias in either direction. Again, since the quality of data is probably poorer for students that have larger class-size effects, there may be greater sensitivity to the poor quality of data among lower-income families.

Nonlinearities in Family Variables

Significant nonlinearities appear to be present in family variables. One study showed significant squared terms for many family variables, as well as several interaction terms (Grissmer et al., 1996). In the previous literature, these have rarely, if ever, been fully included.

The bias caused by the absence of nonlinear terms in models might bias individual-level data more due to the usually wider range of variation of both independent and dependent variables at the individual level, where nonlinear terms can be important in estimating accurate relationships at more-extreme values.

Bias from Selection Effects

In the case of class size, parents may select districts, schools, or classes based partly on class size, and teachers may also select districts, schools, or classes based partly on class size. To the extent that this causes students and teachers with different characteristics and abilities to be in small or large classes, a potential for bias is present in measuring class-size effects. There is agreement that significant selection effects are present in education and that these effects are complex because they can vary considerably in strength and even direction across schools and districts.

These effects can vary in strength and direction partly because of the strong countervailing forces that help produce actual class size. Most parents prefer smaller classes, but more highly educated parents with higher incomes generally have an advantage in this pursuit. However, equity concerns expressed through court decisions, federal and state legislative resource allocations, or district- and school-level decisions can also have a decided countereffect. These two forces are unlikely to exert the same influence across schools, districts, and states, possibly resulting in a complex set of different and changing selection effects.

Selection effects can also occur for teachers, resulting in differential quality of teachers in classrooms with possible interactive effects on other resource variables. Again, contrasting forces can be present. Teachers generally seek schools and districts with higher-scoring students, higher salaries, and good working conditions (including class size). Teachers with more seniority may be more successful at this pursuit. However, administrators may try to place teachers where they are most effective. For instance, new teachers may be placed in less-challenging environments in smaller classes. Again, the strength of the relative forces probably differs across schools, school districts, and states.

The strongest selection effects arguably occur within and between school districts, with much weaker effects at the state level.[1] For instance, parents often select neighborhoods among choices within a district or between neighboring districts, usually in the same state. It seems possible that selection effects would cause more bias at lower levels of aggregation if the selection primarily results in changes within the unit of aggregation, rather than between units. For instance, if selection effects are limited to within school districts, aggregate analysis across school districts might be less biased.

This lower bias at higher levels of aggregation might occur because selection effects may partially cancel out as we move to higher levels of aggregation. If selection is a zero-sum game in which one student obtaining a smaller class size results in another being in a larger class size, the effect would tend to cancel for higher levels of aggregation.

Endogeneity Effects

We include here resource allocations to education at the family, school, district, or state level that occur in reaction to, rather than cause, achievement. Parents may vary their resources (time and monetary inputs) devoted to education depending on the achievement of specific children and/or may vary their inputs over time in response to changes in their children's educational circumstance. When students encounter higher class sizes or less-able teachers, parents may devote more time or resources (tutoring). Schools, districts, and states may also vary resources based on achievement. If the general direction were to devote more resources in response to poorer conditions or achievement, the direction of bias would generally be downward on resource variables. For instance, if higher-income parents are more likely to adjust resources, effects for higher-income children may be biased downward—a possible explanation for the lower class-size effects for higher-income students.[2]

---

[1]Selection effects at the state level can arise mainly from the location decisions of businesses that will affect the type of families relocating to new business locations. State selection can also occur where two or more states intersect and families can choose locally in which state to reside.

[2]This phenomenon may also explain why higher-income parents pursue smaller classes—not because of higher achievement, but less of their time and resources would be needed to produce a given level of achievement.

This source of bias might be different across levels of aggregation because these effects generally are much more prevalent at lower levels of aggregation. The major reallocation of resources that might be based on achievement is the district allocation made at the state level. About 50 percent of public educational resources come from the state level, and these resources are usually allocated to address equity concerns. While the federal government allocates some resources across states, in response mainly to family income, to equalize spending across states, this is a fairly small proportion of total educational resources. Such differences appear to have the potential to produce a different bias at each level of aggregation below the state.

Effects from Adding Previous Years' Test Scores to Models (Production-Function Approaches)

The current analysis of Tennessee data shows that two children can have the same score at the end of 6th grade, the same inputs in 7th grade, and emerge with different scores based on previous educational resources. Even though educational resources were similar in grades 4–8, scores changed during this period based on the number of years in smaller classes in K–3. Scores declined for those with 1–2 years in small classes, while scores appeared steady for those with 3–4 years in small classes. Production functions with a pretest cannot reflect this effect.

The Tennessee data warn us not to try to isolate schooling effects within specific grades or time periods but rather assume that achievement can depend in complex ways on all earlier characteristics. Achievement in a given grade appears to depend on interaction terms between present schooling characteristics and previous schooling characteristics. But more-complex scenarios seem possible. If the same two children were placed in a smaller class in 7th grade, it is not unreasonable to think that their score gains in 7th grade would depend on how many previous years they were in small classes. Those with two years might benefit more from the third year than those with four years would benefit from the fifth year. The concepts of risk and resiliency may apply here. Children with similar scores at a given grade may have different vulnerability to next year's schooling conditions that can best be reflected in interaction terms between present and previous conditions. For instance, students who have had three to four years in small classes may be more resilient to future conditions than those with less.

The Tennessee data tell us that the class-size effect cannot be isolated to a particular grade, but its size will depend on future schooling conditions. For instance, the effect of a smaller class size at 2nd grade cannot be known until the 8th grade or longer because its size will depend on what the conditions of schooling were between 2nd and 8th grade.

These issues call into question the entire production-function approach to modeling achievement using a pretest as control. These production function models assume that changes in achievement in a period can be traced to changes in inputs during the period. When inputs in a period can affect scores in several future periods, the conceptual framework has to shift to modeling capital flows. Basically, the achievement at a given time is a function of capital inputs in all previous periods, and the productivity of capital investments in a given period also depends on the level of previous investments. Among the current model specifications used, aggregate models that include information about previous years' class sizes but without previous years' scores come closest to reflecting the issues discussed here.

It is possible that the use of pretest approaches has biased measurements downward, since coefficients from such models usually reflect only part of the effect. Upward bias is also possible. However, production-function estimation with pretest scores has been more prevalent at lower levels of aggregation—particularly at the individual level. So, differential bias across levels of aggregation is possible.

THE TENNESSEE EXPERIMENT

We used the results of the Tennessee class-size experiment for two purposes in this study. First, we used it to guide the specification of the model. Second, we used our equations to predict a "class-size" effect for a group of students with characteristics similar to those of the Tennessee experimental sample. Being able to predict an effect for similar students that are similar to the experimental effects measured in Tennessee provides a "validity" check on the models. Since most estimations with nonexperimental data do not provide results consistent with Tennessee, it is important to do this type of validity check with experimental data to try to understand why certain model specifications may be better than others (Grissmer, 1999).

THE DESIGN OF THE TENNESSEE EXPERIMENT

The multidistrict Tennessee STAR experiment randomly assigned a single cohort of kindergarten students in 79 participating schools to three treatment groups: large classes (approximate mean of 22–24 students) with or without an aide and small classes (approximate mean of 15–16 students). The students entering at kindergarten were scheduled to maintain their treatment through 1st, 2nd, and 3rd grades. However, the treatment groups changed in significant ways after kindergarten because of attrition and late-entering students.

Students newly entering a participating school in 1st, 2nd, or 3rd grade were also randomly assigned to treatment groups, but these late-entering students came from schools outside the sample and had likely been in large classes in earlier grades. Many students entering the experiment between kindergarten and 3rd grade moved away from a participating school after one or more years of participation, so students could have spent from one to four years in small classes in different combinations of grades. For instance, the combination of late entries and attrition left the 3rd-grade small-class sample with only one-half the students who had been in small classes all four years. The remaining part of the sample had spent one to three years in small classes.

The experimental sample changed in another important way after kindergarten, since late-entering students had lower average scores than beginning students had and since those leaving the original sample had lower scores than those who remained all four years. The 3rd-grade small-class sample then contained a higher-scoring group who remained all four years, and a lower-scoring group with fewer and later years in small classes.

The sample of participating students in any grade was over 6,000, but late entries and exits meant that about 12,000 students were included over the four years. The characteristics of the students were different from those of average Tennessee students. The experimental sample contained approximately 33-percent minority students, and over 50 to 60 percent of all students were eligible for free or reduced-price lunches, compared to 23-percent minority students and about 43 percent free or reduced-price lunch students for Tennessee in 1986. The sample was also quite different from students nationwide in the United States, where approximately 30 percent were minority students and 37 percent were eligible for free and reduced-price lunches in 1990.

THE RESULTS FROM THE EXPERIMENT

Finn and Achilles (1999) restated the measured achievement differences for the Tennessee experiment between those in large and small classes at each K–3 grade in each subject tested. The results showed that these class-size reductions had statistically significant effects in each K–3 grade and all subjects tested, showing that achievement rose by 0.15 to 0.25 standard deviation. The size of the reported effects increased markedly from kindergarten to 1st grade, but remained fairly constant or even declined in grades 2 to 3. Effects for math and reading were 0.15 and 0.18 in kindergarten, respectively, and 0.27 and 0.24 in 1st grade.

Krueger (1999a) and Nye et al. (1999a), using models that control for school effects and teacher and classroom covariates, also estimated these basic results. The results of these analyses show substantial agreement both in the magnitude of the effect by grade and its pattern. Thus, the use of more-sophisticated models, including covariates and school and classroom effects, does not seem to substantially alter the reported effects.

All students were in large classes in grades 4 through 7, and Finn and Achilles (1999) reported statistically significant effects, between 0.10 and 0.16 standard deviations, in each subject through 7th grade. Nye et al. (1999a, 1999b) also reported effects for 4th, 6th, and 8th grades using two-level HLM, including student and school characteristics, that show statistically significant effects in three subjects for each grade. Their estimates are between 0.11 and 0.20 standard deviation. Since the effects at 3rd grade tend to be in the range of 0.15 to 0.20, the long-term effects show little sign of declining from the time students left smaller classes.

The reported results using the entire sample are increasingly hard to interpret past kindergarten, since any changes in the reported effects across grades might be due to either a different average duration in small classes or different student characteristics. So, the key question is whether achievement rises with more years in small classes. The three measurements that address this question have some inconsistency among them.

Nye et al. (1999a, 1999b) analyzed the short-term effects through 3rd grade with HLM comparing results for four groups: students in small classes in any grade, two or more grades, three or more grades, and four grades. Each estimate was made using the remaining part of the sample as the contrasting group. Their results show effects for those in small classes in all four years versus the remaining sample to be 0.35 to 0.39 standard deviation. Corresponding estimates for the group with three or more years, two or more years, and at least one year in small classes are 0.26 to 0.27, 0.19 to 0.24 and 0.15 to 0.16, respectively. All these results are statistically significant.

Nye et al. (1999a, 1999b) did similar estimates for long-term effects at 4th, 6th, and 8th grades. Their results show continuing statistically significant effects in three subjects and all grades, with increasing effects for longer time spent in small classes in K–3. The 8th-grade estimates are 0.30 to 0.41 for those in small classes all four years, 0.23 to 0.29 for three or more years in small classes, 0.16 to 0.24 for two or more years in small classes, and 0.06 to 0.20 for one or more years in small classes. There appear to be no differences between subjects or significant trends from 4th through 8th grade. So, the pattern and magnitude of effect size appear to remain fairly stable from 3rd to 8th grade for each duration group.

Krueger (1999a) made separate short-term estimates of the effects by year of entry and grade. These estimates essentially contrast groups having different duration and student characteristics. His results for the group entering in kindergarten and staying all four years show a gain in kindergarten but show no evidence of additional gains with each additional year in small classes. However, for groups entering in 1st and 2nd grade, there is evidence of significant gains from each additional year, with somewhat smaller first-year gains.

Krueger (1999a) also estimated a pooled model that assumes equal first-year gains, regardless of year of entry, and equal incremental gains for each additional year regardless of year of entry or duration. His estimates show statistically significant gains for both first-year and incremental effects but larger first-year gains with only small incremental gains. For instance, estimates made from his equations would predict a cumulative effect from four years in small classes of 0.19 to 0.25 standard deviation with approximately two-thirds of the effect in the first year.

Krueger's (1999a) results and those of Nye et al. (1999a, 1999b) on the short-term effects of more years in smaller classes seem inconsistent. Krueger's predicted results for four years in small classes at 3rd grade (0.19 to 0.25) are significantly smaller than Nye et al.'s (0.35 to 0.39). Nye et al.'s estimates also understate what the effects would be for students in small classes all four years. However, unlike Krueger, the results in Nye et al. do not imply that most of the short-term effect happens in the first two years. In fact, the long-term effects imply that the sustained effects occur only if students are in small classes for three or four years. More years in small classes may be most important for sustaining long-term effects. This explanation would be consistent with previous early intervention research that shows short-duration interventions produce significant short-term effects that usually fade over time, but long duration interventions produce more long-term effects (Barnett, 1995; Ramey and Ramey, 1998).

A common interpretation of the results of the Tennessee experiment is that effect sizes are around 0.2 standard deviation for four years in small classes. *The results on duration would suggest that this common interpretation of the Tennessee results might substantially understate the sustained class-size effect for those in small classes all four years, for whom long-term effects might be as large as 0.4 standard deviations.* From a policy perspective, the differences in both magnitude and duration of effects are critical, since significant funding is associated with class-size reduction for each grade, and the cost-effectiveness of class-size reduction would change significantly.

Finn and Achilles (1999) reported minority effects that are approximately double those for white students in grades K–3. Krueger (1999a) also reported larger effects for minority students. Estimated short-term effects for minority students from four years in small classes would be 0.3 standard deviation or greater, with effects for remaining students closer to 0.2 standard deviation or greater. Current analysis also indicates that free-lunch students have larger short-term effects than their counterparts. Estimates from Krueger for free-lunch and non–free-lunch students are 0.27 and 0.21, respectively. A nonexperimental analysis of large class-size reductions in 17 of the poorest school districts in Tennessee measured effects from 0.4 to 0.6 standard deviation (Achilles et al., 1993; Nye et al., 1999). While nonexperimental, the reductions all started in a single year and continued for four years. Comparisons were made to scores prior to reductions and to the most similar districts available. These data would suggest that effects continue to grow for the most disadvantaged students.

No separate *long-term* estimates have been made for minority or free-lunch students. No separate long- or short-term estimates have been made for more-advantaged white students.

SENSITIVITY TO FLAWS IN EXPERIMENTAL EXECUTION

We now turn to questions concerning whether deviations from ideal experimental design and execution could affect the present results. Well-designed and well-implemented experimental studies yielding data that are accurately analyzed and replicated remain as close as we can come to causal evidence in social science. The basic premise of experimentation—choosing two groups of subjects through randomization or preselection such that the only difference between them is the variable of interest—remains the ideal method of building social science knowledge. While experiments are potentially capable of providing the most compelling evidence, they often fall far short of achieving this objective (Boruch, 1994; Heckman and Smith, 1995; Manski, 1996).

Hanushek (1999) summarized potential issues that need to be taken into account when analyzing and interpreting the Tennessee results. He included differences between random and actual classroom assignment, nonrandom test-taking and attrition, lack of randomization of schools, potential problems in teacher assignments, lack of knowledge of prior class sizes for students entering after kindergarten, and Hawthorne effects. The effects of most of these deviations have been tested.

Not all students initially assigned to large or small classes remained in these classes. Krueger (1999a) and Nye et al. (1999a, 1999b) compared results using the actual and assigned treatments. No significant differences in effects were discovered in these studies. The issue of differential attrition in test and control groups was also addressed in these studies. All found significant differences between students staying in the experiment (continuers) and those that either enter after kindergarten (late entries) or leave (leavers), with continuers having higher scores than leavers and late entries. However, none of the studies found significant differences in the characteristics of leaving and entering students between small and large class groups. Only differences in effects between small and large class groups would bias the net effects.

These studies did not address the issue of non–test-taking for students present in the classes. About 8 to 11 percent of children in classes did not take tests because of absences or other reasons. Hanushek (1999) provided data that show that the percentage excluded is similar in test and control groups for each grade, so the characteristics of the students excluded would have to vary widely in small and large classes to have any effect on the results. This certainly needs to be analyzed further.

Krueger (1999a) analyzed available teacher characteristics (experience and education) and found no evidence of nonrandom teacher assignment. While other teacher characteristics (teacher test scores and verbal ability) may be more closely related to teacher quality, it would be highly unlikely that randomization did not distribute these characteristics nearly equally between small and large classes (Ehrenberg and Brewer, 1994, 1995; Ferguson, 1991, 1998a; Ferguson and Ladd, 1996).

Schools were not randomly selected. Since students were randomized within each school, it seems unlikely that school characteristics could bias the effects. Nye et al. (1999a, 1999b) and Krueger (1999a) allowed school effects in their specifications and found little difference in effect coefficients. However, the selection of schools is important for generalizability. The schools selected were not representative of Tennessee schools and were even less representative of students in the nation as a whole.

A second concern for the generalizability of the results may be the variance of the results across schools. Hanushek (1999) presented evidence of a distribution of class-size effects across schools in kindergarten that suggested that small-class achievement exceeded *both* large treatment groups in less than one-half of the schools. This may indicate the presence of interactive effects below the school level that are important. However, Nye et al. (1999a, 1999b) used a three-level HLM that suggested the effects were fairly uniform across schools.

For students entering the experiment after kindergarten, no data were collected on the class size in their previous schools. Since most migrating students would be from Tennessee, presumably most would have been in large classes in previous grades. The randomization process would in all likelihood account for any differences in previous class sizes for late-entering students.

It is possible for further analysis to find a flaw in the experiment that significantly affects the results, but extensive analysis to date has eliminated most of the potential problems.

SPECIFICATION LESSONS FROM TENNESSEE

Hanushek (1999) reviewed the nonexperimental evidence from over 250 measurements in studies of effects of class size and/or pupil-teacher ratio. The results show many studies with statistically significant positive and negative effects but with approximately equal numbers of positive and negative results. It is not clear whether a meta-analysis taking the sample sizes into account would shift the results significantly. Hanushek further provided separate results by elementary and secondary school and for value-added models within and across states. Use of value-added models with previous year's test scores as a proxy for all earlier experience and missing family variables has been considered to be among the best specifications. Hanushek separated production-function studies using previous test score as a control and showed that these produce no consistent positive effects.

The current evidence from nonexperimental data seems in conflict with the results from experimental data. Several explanations have been proposed for these differences (Grissmer, 1999). One reason may be that the different studies have students with different characteristics. The experimental sample contained mostly disadvantaged students, whereas most nonexperimental measurements contain much broader samples. If large class-size effects are confined to more-disadvantaged students, differences in effects between Tennessee and nonexperimental measurements might be expected. However, the differences can also arise from specification problems inherent in the model specifications used in most nonexperimental analysis.

One problem with the production-function specification may be that a previous year's test score may be a poor control because student achievement changes significantly over the summer, with differential effects for students from different family backgrounds (Alexander and Enthisle, 1998). Thus, a test score used for control at the beginning of the school year may produce a result different from that at the end of the last school year for different students.

Production-function techniques assume that changes in achievement during a period can be accounted for by changes in input variables during the period. The Tennessee data seem to contradict this assumption. A substantial effect remained at 8th grade in Tennessee that was traceable to small classes years earlier. Moreover, the achievement of students from 4th to 8th grade changed based on the number of years in small classes in K–3. The K–3 small-class experience set in motion a series of long-term changes in achievement that cannot be accounted for by inputs during the 4th- to 8th-grade period. Grissmer and Flanagan (2000) have suggested that these multiple-year effects imply that a single year of previous scores is insufficient for control of previous schooling experience. Rather, models that account for the characteristics of schools since entry —without using previous years' scores as controls could reproduce the Tennessee results. Krueger (1999a) also suggested that the pattern of results in Tennessee cannot be obtained with production-function techniques using a previous year's score as control except in the first year of the intervention.

ESTIMATING THE TENNESSEE EFFECT

We used the results from Table 7.3 for 4th-grade students to compute a Tennessee class-size effect. The actual class sizes in Tennessee were reduced from approximately 24–25 to 16–17 students per class. In comparison with the other students in the state, the Tennessee experimental sample was disproportionately black (33 percent versus 21 percent) and eligible for free lunches (55 percent versus 40 percent) (Krueger, 1999a). These characteristics make the experimental sample more similar to Alabama and Louisiana students than to Tennessee students.

To estimate the effects of the Tennessee experiment, we needed to determine the SES-FE value for the Tennessee sample and the pupil-teacher reduction. We estimated an upper limit for the Tennessee sample by simply using the race specific value of SES-FE for Tennessee. These values are –0.46 and –0.53 for black Tennessee students for reading and math, respectively, with corresponding values for white students of 0.045 and 0.040. Weighting these values by the proportion of minority to nonminority students in the experiment gave values of –0.12 and –0.15 for reading and math, respectively. These are upper-level limits, since the experimental white sample drawn from high-minority schools likely had lower income and education than typical white Tennessee students.[1]

_____

[1]This can also be seen from comparing the free-lunch percentages. Overall, 26 percent of Tennessee students were eligible for free lunches in 1987. Younger students always have higher eligibility. In Tennessee, the difference between eligibility at 4th and 8th grade is typically 12 percentage points. So, approximately 40 percent of Ten-

Another approximate estimate can be made by finding a state with characteristics similar to those of the experimental sample. Only Mississippi has a free lunch percentage as high as 55 percent, and the value of SES-FE is approximately –0.25. Louisiana has 40 percent minority and 46 percent free lunch, with an SES-FE value of –0.19. The SES-FE for the experimental sample is certainly in the range of –0.15 to –0.25.

The random-effect model, which is linear in pupil-teacher ratio, would predict gains of approximately 0.10 standard deviation for pupil-teacher reductions of eight students per teacher—the amount of the Tennessee class-size reduction. However, the random-effect model with a family-interaction term would predict gains of 0.28 standard deviation using an SES-FE of –0.20 and a reduction of eight students per teacher. Our estimates using the model with squared and family-interaction terms are sensitive to the value of beginning pupil-teacher ratio, but values from 0.20 to 0.30 occur when using reasonable assumptions.[2] The estimated values for the difference in scores at the end of the 3rd grade in the Tennessee class-size experiment from Krueger (1999a) are approximately 0.19 to 0.24, while Nye et al. (1999a, 1999b) estimates are as high as 0.40 standard deviation for four years in small classes. The estimates from our model are certainly in the current range of experimental estimates.

Our current model would also predict larger effects for minority and disadvantaged students. We cannot make estimates for minority students alone, since no state has more than 50 percent minority students, making these estimates far outside the current range of family values in our model.

---

nessee students in K–3 were eligible for free lunches, compared to about 55 percent in the experimental sample. This difference cannot all be accounted for by higher minority percentages.

[2]We made two estimates translating class-size reduction into pupil-teacher ratio reduction. We first assumed that a reduction of eight in class size translates into a pupil-teacher reduction of eight. Second, we used 1990 to 1991 data from the Schools and Staffing Survey (SASS), in which K–6 teachers reported actual classroom size, and regressed pupil-teacher ratio against actual size. The coefficient of class size is 0.84, indicating that reducing class size reduces pupil-teacher ratio by only 0.84. Thus, a reduction of eight in class size would produce only a reduction of 6.7 in pupil-teacher ratio.

FAMILY VARIABLE DEVELOPMENT

THE CENSUS-NAEP FAMILY CONTROL VARIABLES

The major problem with NAEP data for analyzing the effect of policies is the lack of accurate and detailed family variables. Since family variables account for most of the variance in state NAEP scores and are correlated with policy variables, their accuracy is important for estimating unbiased policy effects.

Accuracy of NAEP Family Variables

We used the 1990 Census data to check the accuracy of the student-reported NAEP family variables. We have derived a set of family variables (parent educational level, family income, race and/or ethnicity, and family type) for each state from the 1990 Census for families with students at the NAEP ages. For 4th-grade students, we chose 8- to 10-year-old students, while for 8th grade, we chose 12- to 14-year-old students. We chose a somewhat wider age range to increase the sample size of minority populations in small states.

Not surprisingly, Census and student-reported NAEP data on race and/or ethnicity and family type (one versus two parents) show strong agreement (correlation of 0.95 and above). However, we find major differences between student-reported parental education and parent-reported education from the Census—particularly for 4th-grade students. About one-third or more of 4th-grade students do not report parental education, and the nonreporting is higher for disadvantaged and minority students. Table E.1 compares, for those responding, the 4th-grade NAEP estimates for highest parental

Table E.1
NAEP and Census Estimates: Highest Parental Education for 4th-Grade Students

	No High School			High School			Some College			College		
	NAEP	CEN	Diff	NAEP	CEN	Diff	NAEP	CEN	Diff	NAEP	CEN	Diff
Alabama	11.3	14.4	-3.1	26.8	34.5	-7.8	12.7	29.5	-16.9	49.3	21.5	27.8
Arizona	7.1	17.3	-10.2	19.6	26.2	-6.5	14.3	35.9	-21.7	58.9	20.5	38.4
Arkansas	10.6	13.5	-2.8	27.3	39.7	-12.4	13.6	28.0	-14.4	48.5	18.9	29.6
California	9.1	20.1	-11.1	14.5	22.4	-7.8	12.7	32.7	-19.9	63.6	24.8	38.8
Colorado	6.3	8.0	-1.6	15.9	24.1	-8.2	14.3	36.8	-22.5	63.5	31.1	32.4
Connecticut	6.2	10.1	-4.0	15.4	25.5	-10.2	10.8	26.7	-15.9	67.7	37.7	30.0
Delaware	7.7	9.2	-1.5	21.5	31.6	-10.1	10.8	29.5	-18.7	60.0	29.7	30.3
Florida	6.5	13.5	-7.0	21.0	29.8	-8.8	12.9	32.6	-19.7	59.7	24.1	35.5
Georgia	7.5	15.3	-7.8	26.9	35.0	-8.1	10.4	27.0	-16.6	55.2	22.7	32.5
Idaho	5.0	7.2	-2.2	20.0	23.8	-3.8	15.0	40.7	-25.7	60.0	28.4	31.6
Indiana	9.1	9.5	-0.4	27.3	36.0	-8.8	12.1	32.1	-20.0	51.5	22.3	29.2
Iowa	4.6	4.4	0.2	20.0	31.7	-11.7	13.8	37.6	-23.7	61.5	26.3	35.2
Kentucky	15.2	14.6	0.6	30.3	38.6	-8.3	13.6	27.2	-13.5	40.9	19.6	21.3
Louisiana	9.1	17.4	-8.4	24.2	37.1	-12.9	12.1	26.1	-14.0	54.5	19.3	35.2
Maine	6.2	5.9	0.3	24.6	34.7	-10.1	13.8	30.3	-16.4	55.4	29.2	26.2
Maryland	6.2	8.8	-2.6	18.5	29.1	-10.6	12.3	29.1	-16.8	63.1	33.1	30.0
Massachusetts	3.0	10.2	-7.1	16.7	25.7	-9.0	10.6	30.2	-19.6	69.7	33.9	35.8

Table E.1—Continued

	No High School			High School			Some College			College		
	NAEP	CEN	Diff	NAEP	CEN	Diff	NAEP	CEN	Diff	NAEP	CEN	Diff
Michigan	4.7	8.4	-3.7	21.9	29.7	-7.8	14.1	37.9	-23.8	59.4	24.0	35.4
Minnesota	3.4	4.4	-0.9	20.7	27.5	-6.8	10.3	39.0	-28.6	65.5	29.1	36.4
Mississippi	11.9	21.4	-9.5	26.9	33.3	-6.4	9.0	27.5	-18.5	52.2	17.8	34.4
Missouri	7.7	9.3	-1.6	23.1	34.1	-11.0	13.8	32.0	-18.2	55.4	24.6	30.7
Nebraska	4.5	4.9	-0.3	19.7	26.0	-6.3	16.7	41.2	-24.5	59.1	28.0	31.1
New Hampshire	4.5	5.2	-0.7	19.4	26.9	-7.5	13.4	31.8	-18.4	62.7	36.1	26.6
New Jersey	4.3	9.9	-5.5	15.9	28.2	-12.3	11.6	25.7	-14.1	68.1	36.2	31.9
New Mexico	11.3	14.9	-3.7	24.2	31.2	-7.0	14.5	32.1	-17.5	50.0	21.8	28.2
New York	6.3	13.9	-7.6	17.5	29.2	-11.7	11.1	29.2	-18.1	65.1	27.7	37.4
North Carolina	8.7	13.8	-5.1	23.2	32.3	-9.1	13.0	31.3	-18.3	55.1	22.6	32.5
North Dakota	4.6	3.6	1.0	18.5	20.7	-2.2	10.8	45.4	-34.7	66.2	30.3	35.9
Ohio	7.6	9.2	-1.6	25.8	35.4	-9.6	12.1	31.7	-19.5	54.5	23.8	30.8
Oklahoma	7.6	10.8	-3.3	24.2	31.0	-6.7	15.2	34.4	-19.2	53.0	23.8	29.2
Pennsylvania	6.1	8.7	-2.6	24.2	38.0	-13.7	13.6	26.7	-13.0	56.1	26.7	29.4
Rhode Island	8.3	13.4	-5.1	18.3	27.7	-9.4	13.3	28.6	-15.3	60.0	30.3	29.7
South Carolina	7.7	14.7	-7.0	26.2	34.4	-8.3	10.8	29.4	-18.6	55.4	21.5	33.8
Tennessee	11.6	13.3	-1.8	26.1	36.1	-10.1	13.0	27.9	-14.8	49.3	22.6	26.6
Texas	11.5	19.9	-8.5	21.3	27.2	-5.9	13.1	30.1	-17.0	54.1	22.8	31.3
Utah	4.9	4.7	0.2	16.4	19.1	-2.7	13.1	39.8	-26.7	65.6	36.4	29.2

Table E.1—Continued

	No High School			High School			Some College			College		
	NAEP	CEN	Diff	NAEP	CEN	Diff	NAEP	CEN	Diff	NAEP	CEN	Diff
Virginia	8.5	10.5	-2.0	19.7	27.3	-7.6	11.3	31.0	-19.7	60.6	31.2	29.3
West Virginia	11.8	12.8	-1.1	30.9	42.2	-11.3	13.2	25.3	-12.0	44.1	19.7	24.4
Wisconsin	4.8	7.1	-2.3	23.8	33.7	-9.9	15.9	33.7	-17.8	55.6	25.5	30.0
Wyoming	6.3	5.7	0.5	18.8	27.5	-8.7	17.2	41.5	-24.3	57.8	25.4	32.5
Average	7.5	11.0	-3.5	21.9	30.6	-8.7	12.9	32.1	-19.2	57.7	26.3	31.4
Standard Dev.	2.8	4.7	3.3	4.2	5.3	2.6	1.8	5.0	4.6	6.6	5.3	3.8

educational level with the Census estimates for families with 8- to 10-year olds. Fifty-eight percent of 4th-grade NAEP students reported a parent with a college degree, compared to 26 percent in the Census. The difference between NAEP and Census varies considerably by state, from 20 percentage points to almost 40 percentage points, so the amount of inflation appears to depend on student characteristics.

There are corresponding underestimates for parents with no high school education, high school only, and some post–high school education. Generally, the estimates are closer for the first two categories than for the last. Parental education is the strongest family variable correlated with achievement. Given the nonrandomness of both missing data and bias in reporting, the NAEP-reported data on parental education are problematical in any analysis of NAEP data.

Accuracy of Census Variables

Census data derived for families with children of similar ages similar to those of NAEP test-takers do not reflect with complete accuracy the family characteristics of actual NAEP test-takers. NAEP excludes private-school students, disabled students, LEP students, and non-participants—all of whom are sampled on Census files (see Appendix D for data on the NAEP exclusions). The 1990 Census data also do not reflect the demographic changes in the NAEP test-taking population from 1990 to 1996. In addition, the NAEP sample reflects normal sampling variation from test to test.

Census data would be a representative sample of NAEP test-takers only if exclusions, nonparticipants, private-school students, and demographic changes were random—which is certainly not the case. Our analysis of these differences (Grissmer et al., 1998e) shows that the small differences between NAEP and Census in race and/or ethnicity and family type primarily arise from nonrandom exclusions in the NAEP sample, while the large differences in parental education are primarily due to inaccuracy in student reporting and bias in missing data.

Family Variables Used in the Census-NAEP Regressions

The NAEP variables **where they are accurately reported** tend to be better variables than the Census variables, since they better reflect the actual sample of public school students taking the test. The NAEP and Census estimates by state for race and/or ethnicity and family type are very similar, but the differences seem to be accounted for by NAEP exclusions. The NAEP estimates, then, actually reflect these family characteristics of the test-taking samples by state better than the Census estimates do. So, we used the NAEP estimates for race and/or ethnicity and family type by state and test. We also used a family mobility variable from NAEP—whether the family has changed houses in the last two years—that is probably the type of information that can be accurately reported and is not on Census files.

The Census variables tend to be much better in the case of parental education because of the nonuniformly inflated values given by students. The Census-reported family income is probably a better measure of income than free lunches or Title I participation because it contains more information about income distribution and because changes in eligibility requirements occur in these programs over time that are not related to real income changes. However, the Census estimates of education and income can be adjusted to better reflect the NAEP test-taking population in each state by adjusting the state estimates using the racial and/or ethnic makeup of each test-taking population.

We first derived from Census the family income and parental education by race and/or ethnicity and state. We then developed a composite statewide estimate of family income and parental education for each NAEP test by using the NAEP race and/or ethnicity percentages taking each test in the state as weights with the Census-derived income and parental education estimates by race and/or ethnicity. For instance, the Census data may show that 35 percent of non-Hispanic white Indiana parents with children 8 to 10 are college graduates, 15 percent for similar black parents, and 10 percent for similar Hispanic parents. If 80 percent of NAEP test-takers in Indiana for the 1990 test were white, 12 percent black, and 8 percent Hispanic, the SES composite would be (0.35) x (0.80) + (0.15) x (0.12) + (0.10) x (0.08) = 0.306. The estimated percentage of NAEP test-takers in Indiana who have college graduate parents is 30.6.

This method allowed us to account partially for differential state exclusions, nonparticipation, and private-school students, but it also partially took into account changing state demographics from 1990 to 1996 as well as simple random differences in the racial and/or ethnic test-takers for each test. So, if states experienced an influx of Hispanic students from 1990 to 1996, this would affect the percentage taking the NAEP, and our family characteristics would be adjusted to take this into account. Likewise, if a state suddenly excluded a larger proportion of Hispanics because of LEP, this would be reflected in our family variables. This method captures the between-race part of the differences in sample between Census and NAEP test-takers but does not reflect the within-race differences. This method also introduces some limited time-series variation into the Census family variables, since the demographic mix of the test-taking population in each state changes for each test.

Thus, we used NAEP variables in our analysis that seem to be reported accurately (race and/or ethnicity, family type, family mobility). For parental education and income, we used Census estimates by state, but adjusted these estimates using the race and/or ethnicity percentages of NAEP test-takers. These variables include family income and four classifications of the highest-educated parent: college graduate, some postsecondary education, high school graduate only, and less than high school graduate. These variables were entered directly into the regressions, allowing their influence to be determined by the variation of the 271 state scores themselves.

THE TWO COMPOSITE SES FAMILY CONTROL VARIABLES

SES Variable

An alternative method of controlling for the effects of family characteristics in our equations is to develop a composite SES variable using individual-level data. Since individual-level NAEP data do not include accurate data for key family variables and are also missing some important family variables, we used NELS data that contain **parent-reported** family characteristics and student achievement scores. These data were collected for a nationally representative sample of about 25,000 8th-grade students in 1988. The method used here parallels that used in an earlier study, in which more detail is provided about estimation (Grissmer et al., 1994).

First, we regressed reading and math achievement scores on eight parent-reported family characteristics using the NELS sample. The family characteristics are mother's education, father's education, family income, family size, age of mother at child's birth, family type, race and/or ethnicity, and mother's labor-force status. The definitions of the variables are given in Table E.2. We include missing-value dummy variables for each variable.

The results of these estimations are given in Table E.3 for math and reading. The coefficients all have the expected sign. Other things being equal, achievement scores are lower for students with parents who are minority, have less education, less income, more children, a lower age at birth of the child, and single parents. Mother's work-force status is insignificant. The race and/or ethnicity, parental education, and family income are the most significant of the variables, but mother's age at birth, family size, and single-parent status are also highly significant.

Table E.2

Family Variable Definitions for NELS Estimation

Variable	Type	Definition
MOM-NHS	Dummy	Mother's education—non–high school graduate = 1
MOM_HS+	Dummy	Mother's education—high school + post high school = 1
MOM-COLL	Dummy	Mother's education—college graduate=1
FATH-NHS	Dummy	Father's education—non–high school graduate = 1
FATH-HS+	Dummy	Father's education—High School + post high school = 1
FATH-COLL	Dummy	Father's education—college graduate = 1
FEMALE	Dummy	Gender—female = 1
INCOME		Family income
MOM_AGEB		Mother's age at child's birth
MOM_WORK	Dummy	Mother's labor force status—working = 1
SIBS_T		Number of siblings
Single Ma	Dummy	Single mother = 1
Hispanic	Dummy	Hispanic = 1
Black	Dummy	Black = 1
MV_AGE	Dummy	Missing value—age
MV_FAED	Dummy	Missing value—father education
MV_INC	Dummy	Missing value—income
MV_MAED	Dummy	Missing value—mother education
MV_SIBS	Dummy	Missing value—number of siblings
MV_SING	Dummy	Missing value—single mother
MV_WORK	Dummy	Missing value—mother working

Table E.3

NELS Regression Results for Reading and Math —SES Variable

Variable	Math			Reading		
	Coef	SE	T-Stat.	Coef	SE	T-Stat.
INTERCEP	−0.213	0.031	−6.9	−0.285	0.031	−9.100
MOTH–NHS	−0.155	0.019	−8.3	−0.180	0.019	−9.400
MOTH–HS+	0.132	0.016	8.2	0.140	0.016	8.500
MOTH–COLL	0.395	0.020	20.1	0.347	0.020	17.400
FATH–NHS	−0.149	0.019	−7.9	−0.146	0.019	−7.600
FATH–HS+	0.150	0.017	8.8	0.150	0.017	8.600
FATH–COLL	0.409	0.019	21.9	0.345	0.019	18.200
FEMALE	−0.026	0.012	−2.3	0.216	0.012	18.400
INCOME	0.002	0.000	14.7	0.002	0.000	9.300
MOM_AGE	0.007	0.001	6.8	0.008	0.001	7.600
MOM_WORK	−0.008	0.012	−0.7	0.000	0.013	−0.000
SIBS_T	−0.018	0.004	−4.4	−0.038	0.004	−9.100
SINGLEMA	−0.034	0.018	−1.9	−0.034	0.018	−1.900
BLACK	−0.606	0.019	−32.7	−0.508	0.019	−27.000
HISPANIC	−0.351	0.018	−19.3	−0.297	0.019	−16.000
MV_AGE	−0.099	0.037	−2.7	−0.116	0.037	−3.460
MV_FAED	−0.108	0.026	−4.2	−0.127	0.026	−7.158
MV_INC	−0.002	0.029	−0.1	−0.018	0.029	−0.761
MV_MAED	−0.119	0.048	−2.5	−0.162	0.048	−3.658
MV_SIBS	−0.132	0.053	−2.5	−0.114	0.053	−3.197
MV_SING	−0.201	0.032	−6.3	−0.134	0.033	−6.303
MV_WORK	−0.066	0.047	−1.4	−0.065	0.047	−1.303
Adjusted R^2	0.28			0.23		

We then extracted a Census sample of families from each state with children 12 to 14 or 8 to 10 years old and obtained the same eight family characteristics for each family. We next used the NELS equation to project a score for each child given his or her eight family characteristics. We implicitly assumed here that the family equations are similar for 4th- and 8th-grade students. The mean value of these scores by state provided an overall SES measure for the Census sample of families in the state.

However, the NAEP test-taking sample differs from the Census sample in each state because NAEP excludes private-school students, LEP and IEP students, and nonparticipants. In addition, the NAEP sample differed because of demographic shifts from 1990 to 1996 and because of normal sampling variation. If we could identify the Census students excluded from the NAEP (LEP, disabled, nonparticipants, and private-school students), we could simply develop the average predicted scores for the Census students taking the NAEP. However, we do not know who in the Census sample would not have taken the NAEP. We do know that those in private schools are more often white, those excluded for IEP (disabled) are more often minority, and those excluded by LEP are most often Hispanic.

So, each of these will change the racial and/or ethnic percentage in each state taking the NAEP. We also know that perhaps the most significant demographic shift in population occurring in states from 1990 to 1996 involves increases in the Hispanic population as this population continues to move northward.

We used a procedure similar to that described above in the Census-NAEP family variables to correct partially for these differences between Census and NAEP test-taking samples. We took the racial and/or ethnic percentage taking each of the seven tests in each state and used it to weight the predicted SES score in each state. We did this by developing the average predicted score by racial or demographic group in each state and developing a composite state SES using the percentage of each racial and/or ethnic group taking the NAEP in each state. For instance, the average predicted NELS score by racial and/or ethnic group in Indiana might be –0.7 for blacks, –0.2 for Hispanics, and 0.10 for white students. If 80 percent of NAEP test-takers in Indiana for the 1990 test were white, 12 percent black, and 8 percent Hispanic, the SES composite would be (0.80) x (0.10) + (0.12) x (–0.7) + (0.08) x (–0.20) = –0.02.

This method allowed us to account partially for differential state exclusions, nonparticipation, and private-school students, and it also partially took into account changing state demographics from 1990 to 1996, as well as simple random differences in the racial and/or ethnic test-takers for each test. This method adjusts for the between-race and/or -ethnicity component of different exclusions, nonparticipation, and private schools. It still left a within-race component not taken into account. It also introduced a time-series variation into the SES variables.

SES-FE Variable

SES-FE followed the same procedure as SES, except that it started with different NELS equations. In this variable, we tried to further isolate the family influence by running a school fixed-effect model with the NELS data. NELS has more than 1,000 schools. We ran the same model with eight family characteristics, as used in SES, but added the school fixed effects. This procedure decreased the family influence somewhat because it removed some of the joint variance due to family and schools. This variable reflects relatively more of the within-family influence because it eliminates some of the family social-capital influence.

The results in Table E.4 show that the family variables are somewhat weaker in statistical significance, with coefficients that reflect less influence on achievement than the model without fixed effects. However, the statistical significance and influence are still strong.

In estimating a test score for each child in the Census sample from these equations, we used only the equation constant and family coefficients, ignoring the school fixed effects.

Table E.4

NELS Regression Results for Reading and Math—SES-FE Variable

Variable	Math			Reading		
	Coef	SE	T-Stat.	Coef	SE	T-Stat.
INTERCEP	0.161	0.171	0.9	0.142	0.177	0.8
MOTH–NHS	–0.121	0.019	–6.5	–0.135	0.019	–7.1
MOTH–HS+	0.108	0.016	6.9	0.130	0.016	8.0
MOTH–COLL	0.293	0.020	15.0	0.274	0.020	13.5
FATH–NHS	–0.106	0.018	–5.7	–0.112	0.019	–5.9
FATH–HS+	0.139	0.017	8.3	0.142	0.017	8.2
FATH–COLL	0.319	0.019	17.1	0.285	0.019	14.8
FEMALE	–0.034	0.011	–3.0	0.213	0.012	18.1
INCOME	0.001	0.000	4.8	0.001	0.000	3.2
MOM_AGE	0.004	0.001	3.9	0.006	0.001	5.4
MOM_WORK	–0.003	0.012	–0.2	0.006	0.013	0.5
SIBS_T	–0.011	0.004	–2.7	–0.030	0.004	–7.3
SINGLEMA	–0.036	0.018	–2.1	–0.030	0.018	–1.6
MV_AGE	–0.114	0.036	–3.1	–0.114	0.037	–3.0
MV_FAED	–0.069	0.025	–2.7	–0.085	0.026	–3.3
MV_INC	–0.021	0.028	–0.7	–0.028	0.029	–1.0
MV_MAED	–0.116	0.047	–2.5	–0.163	0.049	–3.4
MV_SIBS	–0.108	0.052	–2.1	–0.090	0.053	–1.7
MV_SING	–0.170	0.032	–5.4	–0.102	0.033	–3.1
MV_WORK	–0.011	0.046	–0.2	–0.027	0.047	–0.6

VARIABLE DEFINITIONS

This appendix provides information on variable construction and the sources of data for each variable used in the analysis. Table F.1 briefly defines the variables; the variable name is enclosed in parentheses. Table F.2 provides means and standard deviations for all variables.

- Definition of Dependent Variable Test Score

  — **NAEP test score (score).** The raw NAEP scores were converted to standard deviation units for the analysis. Each test was normalized using the national mean and standard deviation from the earliest test given by subject and grade. For instance, 8th-grade math scores in 1992 and 1996 are normalized to 8th-grade math scores in 1990. Thus, the standard deviation unit scores reflect increases over time.

- Variables Generated from NAEP and Census Data

  — Variables from NAEP Data Sources Only[1]

    – **Percentage of blacks (black).** The NAEP-reported percentage of students **in a state** who took the NAEP tests who were black. This variable is reported for all seven state tests.

---

[1]The NAEP-generated variables are taken from the following: Mullis et al. (1991), Mullis et al. (1993), Miller et al. (1995), Reese et al. (1997), and Shaughnessy et al. (1998).

Table F.1

Variable Names

	NAEP, NELS, and Education Policy Variables
SCORE	NAEP test scores, by subject, grade, and year
SES	NELS-predicted test scores, by age
SES-FE	NELS-predicted test scores, by age and fixed effects
INC87	Median family income, 1987
BLACK	Percentage of black
HISP	Percentage of Hispanic
HS	Percentage of parents with a high school diploma
HSPLS	Percentage of parents with some college
COLLEG	Percentage of parents with a college degree
MOBILITY	Percentage of students reporting no change in residence in the past two years
PARTIC	School participation rate
PPEXP	Per-pupil expenditure
Pup-Tchr (1-4)	Average pupil-teacher ratio, grades one through four
Pup-Tchr (5-8)	Average pupil-teacher ratio, grades five through eight
SALARY	Average teacher salary
PRE KNDGRTN	Percentage of public prekindergarten
TCH-Res-Low	Percentage of teachers reporting receiving some of the resources needed
TCH RES-Med	Percentage of teachers reporting receiving most of the resources needed
TCHR BA	Percentage of teachers with a bachelor's degree
TCHR Exp (3-9)	Percentage of teachers with 3–9 years of experience
TCHR EXP (10-20)	Percentage of teachers with 10–20 years of experience
TCHR EXP (20+)	Percentage of teachers with 20 plus years of experience
IEP	Percentage of Disadvantaged students
LEP	Percentage of Students with limited English proficiency
BUS	Transportation expenditures per-pupil
TREND	= 0 if score relates to the 1990 8th-grade math test, 1992 4th-grade math test, or the 1992 4th-grade reading test
	= 2 if score relates to the 1992 8th-grade math test or the 1994 4th-grade reading test
	= 4 if the score relates to the 1996 4th-grade math test
	= 6 if the score relates to the 1996 8th-grade math test
READ4	= 1 if score relates to a 4th-grade reading test
	= 0 otherwise

Table F.1—Continued

	NAEP, NELS, and Education Policy Variables
EIGHT	= 1 if score relates to an 8th-grade test
	= 0 otherwise
NORTH	= 1 if state is northern
	= 0 otherwise
SOUTH	= 1 if state is southern
	= 0 otherwise
MDWEST	= 1 if state is midwestern
	= 0 otherwise
WEST	= 1 if state is western
	= 0 otherwise
URBAN	Percentage of population living in urban area
SUBURBAN	Percentage of population living in suburban area
RURAL	Percentage of population living in rural area
Gain 90-92 8mth	= 1 if relates to the 1992 8th-grade math test
	= 0 otherwise
Gain 90-96 8mth	= 1 if relates to the 1996 8th-grade math test
	= 0 otherwise
Gain 92-94 4rd	= 1 if relates to the 1994 4th-grade reading test
	= 0 otherwise
Gain 92-96 4mth	= 1 if relates to the 1996 4th-grade math test
	= 0 otherwise
NOPREK	= 1 if prekindergarten data are available
	= 0 otherwise
SES X 4th R	= SES if score relates to 4th-grade reading test
	= 0 otherwise
SES-FE X 4thR	= SES-FE if score relates to 4th-grade reading test
	= 0 otherwise
INC X 4thR	= INC87 if score relates to a 4th-grade reading test
	= 0 otherwise
Sngl-Par X 4thR	= ONEPAR if score relates to a 4th-grade reading test
	= 0 otherwise
BLACK X 4thR	= BLACK if score relates to a 4th-grade reading test
	= 0 otherwise
HISP X 4thR	= HISP if score relates to a 4th-grade reading test
	= 0 otherwise
HGH X 4thR	= HS if score relates to a 4th-grade reading test
	= 0 otherwise

Table F.1—Continued

NAEP, NELS, and Education Policy Variables	
HGH+ X 4thR	= HSPLS if score relates to a 4th-grade reading test
	= 0 otherwise
COLL X 4thR	= COLLEG if score relates to a 4th-grade reading test
	= 0 otherwise
Mobility X 4thR	= CHANGE if score relates to a 4th-grade reading test
	= 0 otherwise
Income x 8th	= INC87 if score relates to an 8th-grade test
	= 0 otherwise
Sngl-Par X 8th	= ONEPAR if score relates to an 8th-grade test
	= 0 otherwise
BLACk X 8th	= BLACK if score relates to an 8th-grade test
	= 0 otherwise
HISP X 8th	= HISP if score relates to an 8th-grade test
	= 0 otherwise
HGH SCH X 8th	= HS if score relates to an 8th-grade test
	= 0 otherwise
HGH SCH + X 8th	= HSPLS if score relates to an 8th-grade test
	= 0 otherwise
COLL X 8th	= COLLEG if score relates to an 8th-grade test
	= 0 otherwise
MOBILITY X 8th	= CHANGE if score relates to an 8th-grade test
Pup-Tchr X SES-FE	Interaction between PTGR14 and SES-FE
PT2	Pupil-teacher ratio squared
Pre-KNDGRTN X SES_FE	Interaction between PREK and SES-FE

Table F.2

Variable Summary Statistics

Variable	Variable Name	Mean	Stand. Dev.
Score	score	0.082	0.241
Family, SES	SES	−0.004	0.118
Family, SES-FE	SES-FE	−0.003	0.089
Family income, 1987 (000)	inc87	35.896	5.764
Percentage of Black	black	13.466	12.306
Percentage of Hispanic	hisp	12.994	10.928
Percentage of Students with one parent	onepar	19.335	3.041
Percentage of Parents, less than high school education	nohs	11.270	4.906
Percentage of Parents, high school graduates	hs	30.447	5.400
Percentage of Parents, high school plus some college	hspls	32.195	5.201
Percentage of Parents, College degree	colleg	26.089	5.204
Percentage of Students with change in residence	mobilty	70.189	8.453
Participation rate	partic	94.384	6.624
Per-pupil expenditure	ppexp	5.482	1.046
Pupil-teacher ratio, grades 1-4	ptgr14	18.266	2.421
Pupil-teacher ratio, grades 5-8	ptgr58	7.556	9.080
Teacher salary ($000)	salary	33.318	2.987
Percentage of Public prekindergarten	prek	6.290	4.716
Percentage of Teachers responding, some resources	smeres	34.807	9.487
Percentage of Teachers responding, most resources	mstres	52.596	6.415
Teachers with BA	tchba	53.051	14.673
Teacher experience, 3 to 9 years	t9yrs	26.064	4.238
Teacher experience, 10 to 20 years	t20yrs	39.588	4.596
Teacher experience, 20 plus years	t20pls	25.023	6.799
Percentage of Disadvantaged students	iep	4.930	1.379
Percentage of Students with limited English proficiency	lep	1.023	1.737
Transportation expenditures per pupil	bus	226.791	82.881
Trend	trend	2.007	2.133
Dummy Variables			
4th-grade reading	read4	0.288	0.454
South (%)	south	0.391	0.489
Midwest (%)	mdwest	0.214	0.411

Table F.2—Continued

Variable	Variable Name	Mean	Stand. Dev.
West (%)	west	0.203	0.403
Urban (%)	urban	30.116	10.176
Suburban (%)	suburb	34.489	16.421
Rural (%)	rural	35.432	19.654
1992 8th-grade math	d92m8	0.148	0.355
1996 8th-grade math	d96m8	0.140	0.348
1994 4th-grade reading	d94r4	0.140	0.348
1996 4th-grade math	d96m4	0.148	0.355
Dummy variable, no prekindergarten data	noprek	0.262	0.441
Interaction Terms			
SES—4th-grade reading	nos4r	0.000	0.043
SES-FE—4th-grade reading	sch4r	0.000	0.056
Family income (1987)—4th-grade reading	inc4r	10.091	16.183
% Single parent—4th-grade reading	one4r	5.502	8.826
% Black—4th-grade reading	blk4r	3.970	9.164
Hispanic—4th-grade reading	hsp4r	3.947	8.363
Parent education, H.S. —4th-grade reading	hs4r	8.775	14.121
Parent education, H.S.+—4th-grade reading	pls4r	9.249	14.825
Parent education, College—4tDchg4r grade reading	col4r	7595	12.282
Change—4th-grade reading	dchg4r	18.744	29.712
SES—8th grade	nos8	−0.003	0.061
SES-FE—8th grade	sch8	−0.004	0.081
Family income (1987)—8th-grade reading	inc8	15.474	18.721
% Single parent—8th-grade reading	one8	8.363	10.099
% Black—8th-grade reading	blk8	5.420	10.061
* Hispanic—8th-grade reading	hsp8	4.939	9.484
Parent education, H.S. —8th-grade reading	hs8	12.686	15.443
Parent education, H.S.+—8th-grade reading	pls8	13.427	16.276
Parent education, College—8th-grade reading	col8	10.718	13.147
Change—8th-grade	dchg8	32.398	38.518
Pupil-teacher ratio—SES-FE	ptsch	−0.114	1.682
Pupil-teacher ratio squared	pt2	339.477	95.622
% Prekindergarten—SES-FE	pksch	−0.014	0.620

- **Percentage of Hispanics (hisp).** The NAEP-reported percentage of students in a state who took the NAEP tests who were Hispanic. This variable is reported for all seven state tests.
- **Percentage of single parents (onepar).** The student-reported percentage of NAEP families in a state that were headed by a single parent. The wording of the question shifted in 1996, and we imputed the 1996 data for students living with only one parent using both 1992 and 1996 data.
- **Teachers reproting some resources (smres).** The percentage of teachers responding, "I get some or none of the resources I need" to the question, "How well are you provided with instructional materials and the resources you need to teach?"
- **Teachers reproting most resources (mstres).** The percentage of teachers responding, "I get most of the resources I need" to the question "How well are you provided with instructional materials and the resources you need to teach?"
- **Stability of the home environment (mobilty).** The mobility variable entered as the percentage of students reporting no change in schools in the past two years required by a change in residence. Missing 1990 data were imputed by using data on the percentage of students reporting living in the same house for two consecutive years (1990–1991).
- **NAEP school participation rate (scrate).** The percentage of schools chosen in the original sample that participated in the tests.
- **Type of Community (urban, suburb, rural).** Whether the community is urban, suburban or rural, rom the NAEP sampling data.

— Variables Generated from 1990 Census Files and NAEP Data

- **Parental education variables (nhs, hs, hspls).** The highest education for either parent: non–high school (nhs), high school (hs), high school plus (hspls), college (colleg). The Census-derived percentage of NAEP families that have the highest parental-educational level to be non–high school graduate, high school graduate, high school plus additional years, but no college degree and college degree. These variables were derived by using the 1990 Census estimates of highest parental education by state and by race and/or ethnicity, weighted by the racial and/or ethnic percentage taking each NAEP test. It thus takes the 1990 Census estimates and incorporates the specific racial and/or ethnic group taking each NAEP test. It thus partially adjusts for the NAEP exclusions of LEP, IEP/DS, and private school students, as well as picking up the natural sampling variation of each test and the changes in demography over time (see Appendix E for more detail).

–   **Census income variable: Median household income (Income).** The Census income data were adjusted to reflect differences in incomes by racial and/or ethnic groups. The percentages of NAEP students reported, by race, were used to weight the income data. Again, this correction partially accounts for NAEP exclusions and natural sampling variations.

- Variables Generated from Non-NAEP Sources

—   **Pupil-teacher ratio, by grade groups (Pup-Tchr [1–8], Pup-Tchr [1–4], and Pup-Tchr [5–8]).** (National Center for Education Statistics [NCES], 1998.) The pupil-teacher ratio (1–8) for a given year and grade taken as the average pupil-teacher ratio in the state from the first year of schooling to the year of a particular test. Pup-Tchr (1–4) is the average pupil-teacher ratio in the state during the first four years of schooling, while Pup-Tchr (5–8) is the average pupil-teacher ratio in the state for the years spent in grades 5–8. When data for a particular year were not available, the next available data were used. For example, 1982 data were not available; therefore, 1983 data were substituted when calculating the average pupil-teacher ratio experienced by an 8th-grade student taking the 1990 NAEP. An adjustment was made to these estimates to obtain an estimate closer to the pupil-teacher ratio for regular students. The pupil-teacher ratio for special-education students and LEP students is much smaller than for regular students. We used the NAEP-reported data for the percentage of LEP and IEP/DS students to estimate the number of students excluded from the NAEP sample. This percentage was used to adjust the data to estimate a pupil-teacher ratio for NAEP students only. We assumed IEP students had pupil-teacher ratios that were one-half those of regular students and that LEP students had ratios 20 percent larger than those of regular students. Both are conservative estimates. These adjustments resulted in increases in pupil-teacher ratios for regular students of approximately two students per teacher. Thus, states with larger numbers of LEP and IEP students had larger adjustments than states with smaller numbers of such students.

— **Average teacher salary (salary).** (NCES, 1998.) A series of average annual teacher salaries calculated to reflect the average annual salary of teachers experienced by NAEP test-takers. Constant 1993 to 1994 dollar average annual salaries were adjusted for COL differences between states. State COL adjustments were taken from Chambers (1996).

— **Per-pupil expenditure (ppexp).** (NCES, 1998.) A series of average per-pupil expenditures calculated to reflect the average yearly per-pupil expenditure on a student from entry into the educational system to the time of the NAEP tests. Constant 1993 to 1994 per-pupil expenditures were adjusted by a COL adjustment for differences in the COL between states. The state COL adjustments were taken from Chambers (1996).

Adjustments were also made to reflect expenditures for regular students only. Assumptions were made about the relative costs of educating excluded students (LEP and IEP). We assumed that IEP students were twice as expensive to educate and that LEP students required 20 percent more per student. Both are conservative estimates of the added expenditures necessary. The NAEP-reported data for the percentage of LEP and IEP/DS students were used to estimate the number of students excluded.

— **Percentage of teachers with bachelor's degrees (tchba).** (NCES, 1998.) The percentage of teachers reporting a bachelor's degree as the highest degree obtained, by state. For each test, the percentage relates to the median year of schooling for NAEP students. For example, the 1985 values were used for the 1990 8th-grade NAEP mathematics test.

— **Years of teacher experience (t9yrs, t20yrs, t20pls).** (NCES, 1998.) The percentage of teachers, by state, with three to nine years (t9yrs), 10 to 20 years (t20yrs), and more than 20 years (t20pls) of experience. For each test, the percentage relates to the median year of schooling for NAEP students. For example, the 1985 values were used for the 1990 8th-grade NAEP mathematics test.

— **Percentage of prekindergarten (pksch).** (NCES, 1998.) The percentage of students enrolled in public prekindergarten, defined as the ratio of prekindergarten students to students in 1st grade. For example, the percentage of prekindergarten students in 1986 corresponded to students taking the 1992 NAEP tests.

— **Regional variables (south, mdwest, neast, west).** The standard Census definition by state.

STATISTICAL RESULTS FOR ESTIMATING
STATE TRENDS

This appendix provides the regression results for estimating national and state achievement gains described in Chapter Five. Tables G.1, G.2, and G.3 show the results presented in Table 5.1 for estimates of national gain across repeated tests. The tables show both random- and fixed-effect results using the SES (Table G.1), SES-FE (Table G.2), and Census-NAEP (Table G.3) family variables.

These random-effect models are estimated using the Mixed Procedure in SAS using the maximum likelihood estimator and a variety of variance component structures. The results were insensitive to the choice of variance structure (unstructured, compound symmetry, or variance component) or the estimation technique (maximum likelihood estimator, restricted maximum likelihood). SAS was used rather than STATA because it provided a standard error estimate on the random-effect residuals. The standard errors are the standard errors of the predictions. All fixed-effect models were estimated using STATA (xtreg.fe), which is essentially an OLS procedure.

Tables G.4, G.5, and G.6 show the regressions used to estimate the annualized state gains in Table 5.3 that include all seven tests. Table G.7 shows the correlation matrix for the six annualized state gain estimates. For these trends, the correlation among model results is 0.8 or above. If the Census-NAEP fixed-effect model is eliminated, the correlation among results is 0.92 or above. Thus, the state trend results are relatively insensitive to the model used.

Tables G.8, G.9, and G.10 provide the regression results used in Table 5.4. These results include only the five math tests in the analysis. These random-effect models were estimated using the general linear estimator with the exchangeable correlation structure (xt.gee) in STATA. This estimator provides robust standard errors and takes account of unbalanced panels. For fixed-effect models, we used the fixed-effect estimator in STATA—essentially OLS estimation.

Table G.11 provides the correlation matrix for annualized state gain estimates across the six models. For these math trends, the correlation among model results is 0.95 or above. Thus, the state trend results are relatively insensitive to the model used.

We also provide the results of the Hausman test for no differences between random- and fixed-effect coefficients (see Tables G.12, G.13, and G.14). A statistically significant result for this test indicates that random- and fixed-effect coefficients are likely different. The models show statistically significant results in five of the nine estimations, indicating probable different coefficients for random- and fixed-effect models. The cause of the difference in coefficients appears to be the change in the value of the family coefficients rather than trend coefficients. The stability of the trend coefficients across models is illustrated by the high correlation among trend estimates across models. Essentially, the different models provide different estimates of the effects of family variables, and the state trends are relatively insensitive to these differences in family coefficients across models.

Table G.1

Regression Results for Estimated Score Gains
for Repeated Tests Using SES
(t-statistics in parentheses)

	Random Model	Fixed Model
Number of observations	271	271
Dependent variable	Score	Score
Intercept	–0.233	–0.226
	(–1.230)	(–1.110)
Dummy—4th-grade reading	–0.278	–0.275
	(–2.750)	(–2.240)
Dummy—8th grade	0.182	0.213
	(1.010)	(1.320)
Gain 90–92 8th grade math	0.104	0.104
	(10.440)	(6.760)
Gain 92–96 8th grade math	0.229	0.227
	(12.740)	(10.210)
Gain 92–94 4th-grade reading	–0.092	–0.094
	(–6.610)	(–5.490)
Gain 92–96 4th-grade math	0.096	0.095
	(5.770)	(5.850)
Mobility—4th-grade reading	0.004	0.004
	(2.750)	(2.240)
Mobility—8th grade	–0.003	–0.004
	(–1.450)	(–2.020)
SES—4th-grade reading	–0.075	–0.149
	(–0.850)	(–1.260)
SES—8th grade	0.351	0.386
	(3.960)	(5.170)
SES	1.301	0.888
	(11.660)	(3.100)
Mobility	0.006	0.006
	(2.450)	(1.990)
Participation	–0.001	–0.001
	(–1.370)	(–1.260)
R^2	NA	0.944

Table G.2

**Regression Results for Estimated Score Gains
for Repeated Tests Using SES-FE
(t-statistics in parentheses)**

	Random Model	Fixed Model
Number of observations	271	271
Dependent variable	Score	Score
Intercept	−0.263	−0.248
	(−1.370)	(−1.130)
Dummy—4th-grade reading	−0.337	−0.296
	(−3.250)	(−2.420)
Dummy—8th grade	0.173	0.217
	(0.980)	(1.370)
Gain 90–92 8th-grade math	0.104	0.104
	(10.480)	(6.740)
Gain 92–96 8th-grade math	0.230	0.226
	(12.880)	(10.220)
Gain 92–94 4th-grade reading	−0.097	−0.099
	(−6.860)	(−5.810)
Gain 92–96 4th-grade math	0.095	0.092
	(5.670)	(5.680)
Mobility—4th-grade reading	0.005	0.005
	(3.240)	(2.420)
Mobility—8th grade	−0.003	−0.004
	(−1.470)	(−2.170)
SES-FE—4th-grade reading	−0.79	−0.282
	(−1.520)	(−1.930)
SES-FE—8th grade	0.495	0.567
	(4.220)	(5.580)
SES-FE	1.683	0.815
	(10.730)	(2.120)
Mobility	0.006	0.007
	(2.630)	(2.210)
Participation	−0.001	−0.001
	(−1.440)	(−1.390)
R^2	NA	0.943

Table G.3

Regression Results for Estimated Score Gains for Repeated Tests Using Census-NAEP (t-statistics in parentheses)

	Random Model	Fixed Model
Number of observations	271	271
Dependent variable	Score	Score
Intercept	−1.516	1.148
	(−1.540)	(0.890)
Dummy—8th grade	−0.137	−0.110
	(−0.210)	(−0.200)
Dummy—4th-grade reading	0.530	0.502
	(0.990)	(0.890)
Gain 90–92 8th-grade math	0.126	0.125
	(9.380)	(8.580)
Gain 92–96 8th-grade math	0.242	0.238
	(11.360)	(11.560)
Gain 92–94 4th-grade reading	−0.073	−0.061
	(−5.460)	(−3.460)
Gain 92–96 4th-grade math	0.094	0.102
	(6.250)	(6.480)
Mobility—8th grade	−0.002	−0.003
	(−0.800)	(−1.150)
Mobility—4th-grade reading	0.001	0.001
	(0.600)	(0.480)
Income—4th-grade reading	−0.011	−0.011
	(−3.360)	(−2.920)
Income—8th grade	−0.002	−0.001
	(−0.420)	(−0.240)
Single parent—4th-grade reading	0.012	0.012
	(1.310)	(1.310)
Single parent—8th grade	−0.002	−0.002
	(−0.210)	(−0.230)
Black—4th-grade reading	−0.003	−0.003
	(−1.380)	(−1.310)
Hispanic—4th-grade reading	−0.003	−0.003
	(−1.410)	(−1.430)

Table G.3—Continued

	Random Model	Fixed Model
High school—4th-grade reading	−0.006	−0.006
	(−0.940)	(−0.940)
High school+—4th-grade reading	−0.009	−0.008
	(−1.510)	(−1.560)
College—4th-grade reading	0.003	0.003
	(0.740)	(0.500)
Black—8th grade	−0.001	−0.001
	(−0.500)	(−0.840)
Hispanic—8th grade	0.001	0.002
	(1.180)	(1.010)
High school—8th grade	0.002	0.000
	(0.290)	(0.090)
High school +—8th grade	0.005	0.008
	(0.980)	(1.530)
College—8th grade	0.004	0.001
	(0.450)	(0.270)
Income	0.009	0.014
	(1.950)	(0.990)
Single parent	−0.012	−0.012
	(−1.450)	(−1.590)
Black	−0.006	−0.010
	(−2.340)	(−2.500)
Hispanic	−0.002	−0.015
	(−0.990)	(−3.010)
High school	0.019	0.001
	(1.820)	(0.060)
High school+	0.014	−0.029
	(1.570)	(−2.010)
College	0.018	−0.009
	(1.900)	(−0.660)
Mobility	0.003	0.002
	(1.230)	(0.650)
Participation	−0.001	−0.001
	(−1.070)	(−0.750)
R^2	NA	0.958

Table G.4

Regression Results for Estimating the Annualized State Trends by State for Seven Tests—SES Family Variable (t-statistics in parentheses)

	Random Model	Fixed Model
Number of observations	242	242
Dependent variable	Score	Score
Intercept	0.218	0.455
	(0.980)	(1.840)
Dummy—8th grade	0.416	0.491
	(2.010)	(2.320)
Dummy—4th-reading	−0.157	−0.157
	(−0.920)	(−0.920)
Mobility —8th grade	−0.005	−0.005
	(−1.670)	(−1.690)
Mobility —4th-grade reading	0.001	0.001
	(0.560)	(0.570)
SES —8thgrade	0.314	0.293
	(2.580)	(2.270)
SES —4th-grade reading	0.039	0.050
	(0.280)	(0.310)
SES	1.610	1.686
	(9.840)	(3.630)
Mobility	−0.001	−0.005
	(−0.250)	(−1.760)
Participation	−0.001	−0.001
	(−0.970)	(−0.380)
Alabama (annualized gain)	0.021	0.023
	(1.570)	(1.710)
Arizona (annualized gain)	0.022	0.023
	(1.640)	(1.670)
Arkansas (annualized gain)	0.012	0.014
	(0.830)	(0.940)
California (annualized gain)	0.030	0.039
	(2.280)	(2.760)
Colorado (annualized gain)	0.027	0.029
	(2.030)	(2.070)

Table G.4—Continued

	Random Model	Fixed Model
Connecticut (annualized gain)	0.033	0.033
	(2.580)	(2.460)
Delaware (annualized gain)	0.012	0.015
	(0.910)	(1.070)
Florida (annualized gain)	0.034	0.038
	(2.580)	(2.760)
Georgia (annualized gain)	0.008	0.001
	(0.590)	(0.100)
Indiana (annualized gain)	0.041	0.038
	(3.150)	(2.840)
Iowa (annualized gain)	0.023	0.019
	(1.760)	(1.380)
Kentucky (annualized gain)	0.031	0.036
	(2.420)	(2.640)
Louisiana (annualized gain)	0.020	0.021
	(1.540)	(1.540)
Maine (annualized gain)	0.027	0.017
	(1.910)	(1.120)
Maryland (annualized gain)	0.037	0.042
	(2.750)	(2.910)
Massachusetts (annualized gain)	0.012	0.008
	(0.840)	(0.570)
Michigan (annualized gain)	0.050	0.051
	(3.830)	(3.730)
Minnesota (annualized gain)	0.041	0.042
	(3.140)	(3.080)
Mississippi (annualized gain)	0.018	0.014
	(1.300)	(0.890)
Missouri (annualized gain)	0.014	0.008
	(1.010)	(0.550)
Nebraska (annualized gain)	0.036	0.033
	(2.730)	(2.410)
New Jersey (annualized gain)	0.026	0.026
	(1.260)	(1.130)
New Mexico (annualized gain)	0.025	0.021
	(1.860)	(1.510)

Table G.4—Continued

	Random Model	Fixed Model
New York (annualized gain)	0.033	0.034
	(2.510)	(2.530)
North Carolina (annualized gain)	0.056	0.056
	(4.370)	(4.180)
North Dakota (annualized gain)	0.021	0.015
	(1.600)	(1.120)
Pennsylvania (annualized gain)	0.010	0.010
	(0.490)	(0.490)
Rhode Island (annualized gain)	0.022	0.029
	(1.730)	(2.160)
South Carolina (annualized gain)	0.029	0.026
	(1.990)	(1.720)
Tennessee (annualized gain)	0.017	0.018
	(1.260)	(1.250)
Texas (annualized gain)	0.055	0.047
	(4.160)	(3.430)
Utah (annualized gain)	0.006	0.008
	(0.390)	(0.550)
Virginia (annualized gain)	0.014	0.013
	(1.090)	(0.930)
West Virginia (annualized gain)	0.029	0.029
	(2.230)	(2.150)
Wisconsin (annualized gain)	0.033	0.027
	(2.440)	(1.910)
Wyoming (annualized gain)	0.012	0.011
	(0.920)	(0.830)
R^2	NA	0.665

Table G.5

Regression Results for Estimating the Annualized State Trends Including Seven Tests—SES-FE Family Variable (t-statistics in parentheses)

	Random Model	Fixed Model
Number of observations	242	242
Dependent variable	Score	Score
Intercept	0.213	0.471
	(0.940)	(1.880)
Dummy—8th grade	0.435	0.541
	(2.060)	(2.530)
Dummy—4th-grade reading	−0.249	−0.230
	(−1.450)	(−1.330)
Mobility—8th grade	−0.005	−0.006
	(−1.750)	(−1.940)
Mobility—4th-grade reading	0.003	0.003
	(1.080)	(0.970)
SES-FE—8th grade	0.461	0.498
	(2.790)	(2.860)
SES-FE—4th-grade reading	−0.080	−0.159
	(−0.430)	(−0.800)
SES-FE	2.073	1.482
	(9.560)	(2.360)
Mobility	0.000	−0.005
	(−0.070)	(−1.550)
Participation	−0.002	−0.001
	(−1.140)	(−0.730)
Alabama (annualized gain)	0.019	0.020
	(1.450)	(1.470)
Arizona (annualized gain)	0.021	0.023
	(1.510)	(1.590)
Arkansas (annualized gain)	0.009	0.013
	(0.640)	(0.810)
California (annualized gain)	0.029	0.034
	(2.170)	(2.420)
Colorado (annualized gain)	0.026	0.027
	(1.910)	(1.900)

Table G.5—Continued

	Random Model	Fixed Model
Connecticut (annualized gain)	0.036	0.034
	(2.750)	(2.520)
Delaware (annualized gain)	0.012	0.013
	(0.910)	(0.940)
Florida (annualized gain)	0.033	0.034
	(2.450)	(2.460)
Georgia (annualized gain)	0.008	0.001
	(0.610)	(0.060)
Indiana (annualized gain)	0.040	0.036
	(3.040)	(2.670)
Iowa (annualized gain)	0.022	0.016
	(1.660)	(1.160)
Kentucky (annualized gain)	0.030	0.034
	(2.240)	(2.470)
Louisiana (annualized gain)	0.019	0.021
	(1.470)	(1.530)
Maine (annualized gain)	0.027	0.017
	(1.880)	(1.100)
Maryland (annualized gain)	0.037	0.037
	(2.710)	(2.530)
Massachusetts (annualized gain)	0.014	0.008
	(1.000)	(0.500)
Michigan (annualized gain)	0.049	0.049
	(3.720)	(3.520)
Minnesota (annualized gain)	0.040	0.039
	(3.050)	(2.870)
Mississippi (annualized gain)	0.018	0.020
	(1.270)	(1.240)
Missouri (annualized gain)	0.013	0.007
	(0.950)	(0.490)
Nebraska (annualized gain)	0.035	0.033
	(2.620)	(2.340)
New Jersey (annualized gain)	0.026	0.014
	(1.240)	(0.620)
New Mexico (annualized gain)	0.024	0.019
	(1.780)	(1.310)

Table G.5—Continued

	Random Model	Fixed Model
New York (annualized gain)	0.034	0.035
	(2.570)	(2.550)
North Carolina (annualized gain)	0.056	0.057
	(4.280)	(4.180)
North Dakota (annualized gain)	0.019	0.013
	(1.470)	(0.970)
Pennsylvania (annualized gain)	0.009	0.010
	(0.460)	(0.440)
Rhode Island (annualized gain)	0.021	0.027
	(1.630)	(1.980)
South Carolina (annualized gain)	0.028	0.023
	(1.940)	(1.490)
Tennessee (annualized gain)	0.016	0.018
	(1.130)	(1.230)
Texas (annualized gain)	0.055	0.047
	(4.090)	(3.380)
Utah (annualized gain)	0.003	0.007
	(0.210)	(0.440)
Virginia (annualized gain)	0.015	0.011
	(1.110)	(0.790)
West Virginia (annualized gain)	0.027	0.027
	(2.070)	(1.970)
Wisconsin (annualized gain)	0.033	0.025
	(2.370)	(1.710)
Wyoming (annualized gain)	0.014	0.013
	(1.060)	(0.940)
R^2	NA	0.655

Table G.6

Regression Results for Estimating the Annualized State Trends for Seven Tests— Census-NAEP Family Variable (t-statistics in parentheses)

	Random Model	Fixed Model
Number of observations	242	242
Dependent variable	Score	Score
Intercept	−0.411	3.271
	(−0.480)	(2.130)
Dummy—8th	−0.209	−0.653
	(−0.370)	(−1.040)
Dummy—4th-grade reading	1.341	1.330
	(2.230)	(2.240)
Mobility—8th grade	−0.001	0.001
	(−0.280)	(0.280)
Mobility—4th-grade reading	−0.004	−0.004
	(−1.250)	(−1.210)
Income—4th-grade reading	−0.007	−0.009
	(−1.590)	(−1.890)
Income—8th grade	0.001	0.003
	(0.240)	(0.630)
Single parent—4th-grade reading	0.003	0.005
	(0.280)	(0.430)
Single parent—8th grade	0.004	0.007
	(0.400)	(0.700)
Black—4th-grade reading	−0.003	−0.003
	(−1.460)	(−1.480)
Hispanic—4th-grade reading	−0.006	−0.006
	(−2.870)	(−2.890)
High school—4th-grade reading	−0.010	−0.010
	(−1.500)	(−1.620)
High school+—4th-grade reading	−0.012	−0.012
	(−2.410)	(−2.450)
College—4th-grade reading	−0.003	−0.002
	(−0.460)	(−0.320)
Black—8th grade	−0.001	−0.002
	(−0.420)	(−0.660)

Table G.6—Continued

	Random Model	Fixed Model
Hispanic—8th grade	0.001	0.002
	(0.570)	(0.820)
High school—8th grade	0.001	0.002
	(0.220)	(0.290)
High school +—8th grade	0.007	0.012
	(1.560)	(2.200)
College—8th grade	0.000	−0.002
	(0.040)	(−0.350)
Income	0.001	0.013
	(0.140)	(0.610)
Single parent	−0.011	−0.012
	(−1.150)	(−1.230)
Black	−0.009	−0.009
	(−3.060)	(−1.630)
Hispanic	−0.007	−0.018
	(−2.120)	(−3.140)
High school	0.014	−0.027
	(1.390)	(−1.350)
High school+	0.005	−0.050
	(0.700)	(−3.000)
College	0.026	−0.007
	(2.640)	(−0.390)
Mobility	−0.006	−0.008
	(−1.710)	(−2.110)
participation	−0.001	−0.001
	(−0.560)	(−0.360)
Alabama (annualized gain)	0.024	0.028
	(2.030)	(2.300)
Arizona (annualized gain)	0.021	0.022
	(1.730)	(1.780)
Arkansas (annualized gain)	0.019	0.023
	(1.420)	(1.680)
California (annualized gain)	0.037	0.037
	(2.990)	(2.980)
Colorado (annualized gain)	0.029	0.035
	(2.380)	(2.900)

Table G.6—Continued

	Random Model	Fixed Model
Connecticut (annualized gain)	0.039	0.040
	(3.310)	(3.360)
Delaware (annualized gain)	0.018	0.015
	(1.480)	(1.270)
Florida (annualized gain)	0.038	0.042
	(3.120)	(3.450)
Georgia (annualized gain)	0.010	0.009
	(0.820)	(0.720)
Indiana (annualized gain)	0.043	0.044
	(3.600)	(3.670)
Iowa (annualized gain)	0.021	0.017
	(1.720)	(1.410)
Kentucky (annualized gain)	0.042	0.044
	(3.530)	(3.670)
Louisiana (annualized gain)	0.022	0.028
	(1.800)	(2.380)
Maine (annualized gain)	0.028	0.035
	(2.090)	(2.500)
Maryland (annualized gain)	0.042	0.046
	(3.300)	(3.510)
Massachusetts (annualized gain)	0.019	0.014
	(1.490)	(1.070)
Michigan (annualized gain)	0.048	0.043
	(3.950)	(3.620)
Minnesota (annualized gain)	0.038	0.035
	(3.200)	(2.970)
Mississippi (annualized gain)	0.014	0.021
	(1.040)	(1.480)
Missouri (annualized gain)	0.015	0.014
	(1.140)	(1.090)
Nebraska (annualized gain)	0.035	0.035
	(2.910)	(2.850)
New Jersey (annualized gain)	0.024	0.019
	(1.210)	(0.900)
New Mexico (annualized gain)	0.015	0.015
	(1.180)	(1.190)

Table G.6—Continued

	Random Model	Fixed Model
New York (annualized gain)	0.032	0.030
	(2.730)	(2.540)
North Carolina (annualized gain)	0.058	0.060
	(4.910)	(5.040)
North Dakota (annualized gain)	0.019	0.016
	(1.560)	(1.330)
Pennsylvania (annualized gain)	0.014	0.015
	(0.730)	(0.810)
Rhode Island (annualized gain)	0.032	0.037
	(2.700)	(3.120)
South Carolina (annualized gain)	0.025	0.018
	(1.820)	(1.270)
Tennessee (annualized gain)	0.027	0.028
	(2.050)	(2.050)
Texas (annualized gain)	0.055	0.052
	(4.540)	(4.340)
Utah (annualized gain)	0.016	0.030
	(1.220)	(2.190)
Virginia (annualized gain)	0.018	0.018
	(1.560)	(1.530)
West Virginia (annualized gain)	0.037	0.042
	(3.070)	(3.490)
Wisconsin (annualized gain)	0.031	0.030
	(2.490)	(2.360)
Wyoming (annualized gain)	0.015	0.009
	(1.170)	(0.660)
R^2	NA	0.78

Table G.7

Correlation Matrix Among State Trends Results from Different Models in Tables G.4, G.5, and G.6

	Random SES	Fixed SES	Random SES-FE	Fixed SES-FE	Random Cen-NAEP	Fixed Cen-NAEP
SES_RDM	1.000					
SES_FXD	0.950	1.000				
SES-FE_RDM	0.996	0.939	1.000			
SES-FXD	0.949	0.981	0.942	1.000		
CN_RDM	0.927	0.947	0.919	0.943	1.000	
CN_FXD	0.821	0.868	0.799	0.878	0.940	1.000

Table G.8

**Regression Results for Estimating the
Annualized State Trends for the Five Math
Tests Using the SES Family Variable
(t-statistics in parentheses)**

	Random Model	Fixed Model
Family variable	SES	SES
Number of observations	171	171
Dependent variable	Score	Score
Intercept	–0.143	–0.146
	(–0.650)	(–0.590)
Dummy—8th grade	0.151	0.198
	(0.890)	(1.110)
Mobility—8th grade	–0.002	–0.002
	(–0.890)	(–1.000)
SES—8th	0.269	0.288
	(2.770)	(2.680)
SES	1.536	1.231
	(9.300)	(2.570)
Mobility	0.003	0.001
	(1.190)	(0.400)
Participation	0.000	0.001
	(–0.090)	(0.490)
Alabama (annualized gain)	0.030	0.032
	(2.620)	(2.620)
Arizona (annualized gain)	0.032	0.033
	(2.740)	(2.660)
Arkansas (annualized gain)	0.029	0.036
	(2.050)	(2.330)
California (annualized gain)	0.037	0.038
	(3.260)	(3.100)
Colorado (annualized gain)	0.039	0.040
	(3.480)	(3.330)
Connecticut (annualized gain)	0.038	0.039
	(3.480)	(3.320)
Delaware (annualized gain)	0.016	0.015
	(1.470)	(1.300)

Table G.8—Continued

	Random Model	Fixed Model
Florida (annualized gain)	0.040	0.039
	(3.580)	(3.250)
Georgia (annualized gain)	0.014	0.009
	(1.220)	(0.720)
Indiana (annualized gain)	0.050	0.049
	(4.540)	(4.160)
Iowa (annualized gain)	0.024	0.021
	(2.050)	(1.710)
Kentucky (annualized gain)	0.038	0.042
	(3.450)	(3.570)
Louisiana (annualized gain)	0.031	0.031
	(2.770)	(2.700)
Maine (annualized gain)	0.024	0.014
	(1.830)	(0.950)
Maryland (annualized gain)	0.046	0.047
	(3.890)	(3.640)
Massachusetts (annualized gain)	0.022	0.022
	(1.740)	(1.610)
Michigan (annualized gain)	0.057	0.058
	(5.050)	(4.870)
Minnesota (annualized gain)	0.041	0.040
	(3.650)	(3.380)
Mississippi (annualized gain)	0.026	0.028
	(2.000)	(1.910)
Missouri (annualized gain)	0.022	0.018
	(1.780)	(1.320)
Nebraska (annualized gain)	0.036	0.031
	(3.120)	(2.540)
New Jersey (annualized gain)	0.038	0.036
	(1.970)	(1.650)
New Mexico (annualized gain)	0.032	0.027
	(2.840)	(2.210)
New York (annualized gain)	0.036	0.038
	(3.270)	(3.230)
North Carolina (annualized gain)	0.070	0.072
	(6.300)	(6.130)

Table G.8—Continued

	Random Model	Fixed Model
North Dakota (annualized gain)	0.021	0.017
	(1.860)	(1.440)
Pennsylvania (annualized gain)	0.024	0.026
	(1.340)	(1.370)
Rhode Island (annualized gain)	0.037	0.043
	(3.340)	(3.650)
South Carolina (annualized gain)	0.035	0.031
	(2.590)	(2.100)
Tennessee (annualized gain)	0.030	0.034
	(2.420)	(2.470)
Texas (annualized gain)	0.061	0.056
	(5.430)	(4.660)
Utah (annualized gain)	0.018	0.021
	(1.370)	(1.520)
Virginia (annualized gain)	0.026	0.025
	(2.390)	(2.110)
West Virginia (annualized gain)	0.042	0.044
	(3.770)	(3.750)
Wisconsin (annualized gain)	0.038	0.036
	(3.120)	(2.730)
Wyoming (annualized gain)	−0.005	−0.008
	(−0.310)	(−0.450)
R^2	NA	0.784

Table G.9—Continued

	Random Model	Fixed Model
North Carolina (annualized gain)	0.070	0.072
	(6.340)	(6.180)
North Dakota (annualized gain)	0.020	0.017
	(1.790)	(1.430)
Pennsylvania (annualized gain)	0.024	0.025
	(1.340)	(1.360)
Rhode Island (annualized gain)	0.037	0.043
	(3.340)	(3.640)
South Carolina (annualized gain)	0.035	0.031
	(2.650)	(2.100)
Tennessee (annualized gain)	0.030	0.034
	(2.410)	(2.490)
Texas (annualized gain)	0.061	0.056
	(5.440)	(4.680)
Utah (annualized gain)	0.016	0.020
	(1.260)	(1.460)
Virginia (annualized gain)	0.027	0.025
	(2.440)	(2.110)
West Virginia (annualized gain)	0.041	0.044
	(3.730)	(3.750)
Wisconsin (annualized gain)	0.038	0.036
	(3.120)	(2.720)
Wyoming (annualized gain)	−0.005	−0.007
	(−0.290)	(−0.410)
R^2	NA	0.787

Table G.10

**Regression Results for Estimating the
Annualized State Trends Using Only Math
Tests and Census-NAEP Family Variable
(t-statistics in parentheses)**

	Random Model	Fixed Model
Family variable	Cen–NAEP	Cen–NAEP
Number of observations	171	171
Dependent variable	Score	Score
Intercept	−1.662	2.054
	(−1.920)	(1.360)
Dummy—8th grade	−0.309	−0.753
	(−0.630)	(−1.360)
Mobility—8th grade	−0.001	0.000
	(−0.330)	(−0.040)
Income—8th grade	0.002	0.006
	(0.680)	(1.500)
Single parent—8th grade	−0.014	−0.017
	(−1.520)	(−1.810)
Black—8th grade	0.002	0.003
	(1.040)	(1.350)
Hispanic—8th grade	0.002	0.002
	(0.970)	(1.180)
High school—8th grade	0.005	0.007
	(1.050)	(1.380)
High school +—8th grade	0.009	0.014
	(2.100)	(3.070)
College—8th grade	0.001	0.002
	(0.200)	(0.340)
Income—8th grade	−0.001	−0.023
	(−0.160)	(−1.040)
Single parent	0.016	0.024
	(1.650)	(2.230)
Black	−0.012	−0.013
	(−4.150)	(−2.070)
Hispanic	−0.005	−0.013
	(−1.610)	(−2.050)

Table G.10—Continued

	Random Model	Fixed Model
High school	0.012	−0.018
	(1.260)	(−0.910)
High school+	0.010	−0.030
	(1.270)	(−1.890)
College	0.027	−0.005
	(2.880)	(−0.310)
Mobility	0.004	0.004
	(1.090)	(1.070)
Participation	0.000	0.001
	(0.230)	(0.400)
Alabama (annualized gain)	0.031	0.034
	(2.840)	(3.030)
Arizona (annualized gain)	0.035	0.038
	(3.030)	(3.210)
Arkansas (annualized gain)	0.032	0.037
	(2.350)	(2.610)
California (annualized gain)	0.040	0.038
	(3.590)	(3.380)
Colorado (annualized gain)	0.040	0.045
	(3.650)	(4.090)
Connecticut (annualized gain)	0.042	0.043
	(3.920)	(4.100)
Delaware (annualized gain)	0.019	0.016
	(1.730)	(1.520)
Florida (annualized gain)	0.040	0.040
	(3.590)	(3.490)
Georgia (annualized gain)	0.016	0.014
	(1.430)	(1.250)
Indiana (annualized gain)	0.050	0.051
	(4.640)	(4.670)
Iowa (annualized gain)	0.022	0.017
	(1.950)	(1.450)
Kentucky (annualized gain)	0.041	0.041
	(3.760)	(3.830)
Louisiana (annualized gain)	0.032	0.036
	2.930	3.350

Table G.10—Continued

	Random Model	Fixed Model
Maine (annualized gain)	0.024	0.026
	(1.800)	(1.810)
Maryland (annualized gain)	0.052	0.054
	(4.290)	(4.300)
Massachusetts (annualized gain)	0.027	0.026
	(2.190)	(2.030)
Michigan (annualized gain)	0.060	0.060
	(5.360)	(5.360)
Minnesota (annualized gain)	0.040	0.038
	(3.710)	(3.520)
Mississippi (annualized gain)	0.029	0.037
	(2.230)	(2.650)
Missouri (annualized gain)	0.023	0.022
	(1.860)	(1.720)
Nebraska (annualized gain)	0.033	0.030
	(2.810)	(2.490)
New Jersey (annualized gain)	0.044	0.039
	(2.160)	(1.810)
New Mexico (annualized gain)	0.028	0.030
	(2.470)	(2.590)
New York (annualized gain)	0.038	0.038
	(3.540)	(3.540)
North Carolina (annualized gain)	0.073	0.076
	(6.730)	(6.890)
North Dakota (annualized gain)	0.018	0.014
	(1.660)	(1.270)
Pennsylvania (annualized gain)	0.022	0.024
	(1.250)	(1.380)
Rhode Island (annualized gain)	0.041	0.046
	(3.780)	(4.240)
South Carolina (annualized gain)	0.038	0.032
	(2.780)	(2.220)
Tennessee (annualized gain)	0.038	0.043
	(2.980)	(3.130)
Texas (annualized gain)	0.062	0.058
	(5.640)	(5.270)

Table G.10—Continued

	Random Model	Fixed Model
Utah (annualized gain)	0.016	0.025
	(1.260)	(1.860)
Virginia (annualized gain)	0.029	0.028
	(2.720)	(2.650)
West Virginia (annualized gain)	0.043	0.046
	(3.940)	(4.240)
Wisconsin (annualized gain)	0.038	0.038
	(3.200)	(3.130)
Wyoming (annualized gain)	−0.004	−0.008
	(−0.230)	(−0.510)
R^2	NA	0.847

Table G.11

Correlation Matrix Among State Math Trends from Different Models

	Random SES	Fixed SES	Random SES-FE	Fixed SES-FE	Random Census-NAEP	Fixed Census-NAEP
SES-RDM	1.000					
SES-FXD	0.972	1.000				
SES-FE-RDM	0.999	0.970	1.000			
SES-FE-FXD	0.972	1.000	0.970	1.000		
CN-RDM	0.983	0.975	0.986	0.974	1.000	
CN-FXD	0.950	0.975	0.949	0.975	0.971	1.000

Table G.12

Hausman Results for Differences Between Random- and Fixed-Effect Coefficients for Regressions in Tables G.1, G.2, and G.3

Value Added Model	Hausman Statistic	Statistical Significance
Table G.1—SES	3.12	
Table G.2—SES-FE	7.24	
Table G.3—Census-NAEP	243.90	1

Hypothesis: The difference in coefficients is not systematic ($\beta\_Fixed = \beta\_Random$).

Table G.13

Hausman Results for Differences Between Random- and Fixed-Effect Coefficients for Regressions in Tables G.4, G.5, and G.6

Trend Model: Total	Hausman Statistic	Statistical Significance
Table G.4—SES	85.03	1
Table G.5—SES-FE	180.28	1
Table G.6—Census-NAEP	44.23	

Hypothesis: The difference in coefficients is not systematic ($\beta\_Fixed = \beta\_Random$).

Table G.14

Hausman Results for Differences Between Random- and Fixed-Effect Coefficients for Regressions in Tables G.8, G.9, and G.10

Trend Model: Math	Hausman Statistic	Statistical Significance
Table G.8—SES	51.82	
Table G.9—SES-FE	58.24	5
Table G.1—Census-NAEP	412.20	1

Hypothesis: The difference in coefficients is not systematic ($\beta\_Fixed = \beta\_Random$).

STATISTICAL RESULTS FOR ESTIMATING SCORE DIFFERENCES FOR STUDENTS FROM SIMILAR FAMILIES ACROSS STATES

We estimated the score differences for students from similar families using random- and fixed-effect models that include family variables, participation rates, and national gain scores for each test. These results are described in Chapter Six. The regression results used for the estimations used to generate Table 6.1 have already been provided in Appendix G (Tables G.1, G.2, and G.3). However, the state-specific random and fixed effects are not provided in these tables. Table H.1 summarizes the estimated state-specific random and fixed effects and their statistical significance from the estimations in Tables G.1, G.2, and G.3.

Table H.2 provides the correlation matrix for the random- and fixed-effect state residuals from the six models. The Census-NAEP results generally have the lowest correlation with the other results because of the presence of "wrong signs" in the family variables. The results of this model would imply that higher parental education—other things being equal—would lead to lower achievement. The coefficients of the racial and/or ethnic variables are also much more negative than the results from the individual-level models. For instance, the coefficient for the Hispanic dummy implies that—other things equal—Hispanics would score 1.8 standard deviation below white students. Estimates from individual-level models are in the range of 0.2 to 0.3 standard deviation.

The problem in fixed-effect modeling of panel data with limited time-series variation is that the fixed dummies remove much of the cross-sectional variation that is often necessary for obtaining good coefficient estimates for the independent variables. If there is little

Table H.1

Summary of Estimated Score Differences for Students from Similar Families Across Models

	Random Effects							Fixed Effects			
	Avg.	SES	Sig	SES-FE	Sig	Census-NAEP	Sig	SES	Sig	SES-FE	Sig
Texas	0.166	0.200	1	0.191	1	0.212	1	0.138	1	0.088	1
Wisconsin	0.142	0.140	1	0.138	1	0.105	1	0.161	1	0.163	1
Montana	0.122	0.108	1	0.095	1	0.098	5	0.151	5	0.158	1
Iowa	0.113	0.103	1	0.097	1	0.071	5	0.140	5	0.151	1
Maine	0.099	0.084	10	0.080	5	0.060	10	0.128	10	0.143	5
North Dakota	0.081	0.053	10	0.037		0.083	5	0.107	10	0.124	10
Indiana	0.074	0.083	5	0.084	1	0.055	10	0.077	10	0.069	5
New Jersey	0.061	0.052	10	0.074	1	0.037		0.063	10	0.079	5
Nebraska	0.056	0.045	10	0.037		0.038		0.075	10	0.085	10
Missouri	0.055	0.064	5	0.065	5	0.044	5	0.056		0.048	
Connecticut	0.052	0.024		0.050	10	0.038	10	0.057		0.091	5
Oklahoma	0.040	0.055	10	0.044		0.042		0.039		0.018	
Georgia	0.039	0.079	10	0.085	1	0.071	5	0.003	5	-0.041	
Virginia	0.037	0.036		0.049	10	0.060	5	0.022	5	0.020	
Wyoming	0.034	0.029		0.022		-0.001		0.054		0.064	
Minnesota	0.031	0.010		0.012		-0.003		0.055		0.080	
Massachusetts	0.020	-0.013		0.000		0.044		0.020		0.047	

Table H.1—Continued

		Random Effects						Fixed Effects			
	Avg.	SES	Sig	SES-FE	Sig	Census-NAEP	Sig	SES	Sig	SES-FE	Sig
Michigan	0.014	0.017		0.020		0.025		0.006		0.000	
Pennsylvania	0.005	0.015		0.020		-0.023		0.009		0.005	
Arizona	0.003	0.029		0.020		0.039		-0.020		-0.053	
New Hampshire	-0.001	-0.032		0.024		-0.035		0.025		0.063	
Colorado	-0.006	-0.018		-0.016		-0.014		0.000		0.015	
North Carolina	-0.010	0.016		0.016		0.041		-0.044		-0.079	
Washington	-0.014	-0.027		-0.024		-0.015		-0.010		0.008	
Idaho	-0.015	-0.022		-0.031		-0.035		0.002		0.012	
Ohio	-0.016	-0.007		-0.004		-0.019		-0.023		-0.031	
New Mexico	-0.019	0.039		0.018		-0.017		-0.038		-0.095	10
South Carolina	-0.026	0.024	10	0.020		0.033		-0.073		-0.133	10
Florida	-0.034	-0.002		0.002		-0.019		-0.062		-0.091	10
Oregon	-0.038	-0.054		-0.057		-0.024		-0.035		-0.018	
New York	-0.038	-0.029		-0.023		0.005		-0.063		-0.080	5
Maryland	-0.055	-0.051	1	-0.026		-0.053		-0.074	5	-0.069	5
Delaware	-0.064	-0.050	10	-0.037	10	-0.050		-0.086	10	-0.095	5
Utah	-0.074	-0.091		-0.094	1	-0.115	1	-0.050		-0.021	
Tennessee	-0.077	-0.051		-0.051	10	-0.043		-0.106	10	-0.135	1
Kentucky	-0.086	-0.063		-0.068	5	-0.068	10	-0.104	5	-0.129	1

Table H.1—Continued

	Random Effects							Fixed Effects			
	Avg.	SES	Sig	SES-FE	Sig	Census-NAEP	Sig	SES	Sig	SES-FE	Sig
Arkansas	-0.087	-0.039		-0.048	10	-0.073	5	-0.114	5	-0.162	1
Vermont	-0.106	-0.121	1	-0.117	1	-0.096	5	-0.112		-0.085	
Rhode Island	-0.117	-0.128	1	-0.121	1	-0.084	5	-0.131	1	-0.123	5
Alabama	-0.133	-0.090	5	-0.094	1	-0.075	5	-0.179	5	-0.229	1
West Virginia	-0.135	-0.108	1	-0.117	1	-0.140	1	-0.144	5	-0.167	1
Mississippi	-0.137	-0.067		-0.082	5	0.006		-0.222	10	-0.319	1
Louisiana	-0.156	-0.089	10	-0.096	1	-0.089	5	-0.216	5	-0.289	1
California	-0.174	-0.153	1	-0.148	1	-0.117	1	-0.216	1	-0.238	1

Table H.2

Correlation Matrix Among Unexplained State Residuals from Different Models

	Random Model	Fixed Model	Random Model	Fixed Model	Random Model	Fixed Model
	SES	SES	SES-FE	SES-FE	Cen-NAEP	Cen-NAEP
SES-RDM	1.000					
SES-FXD	0.870	1.000				
SES-FE-RDM	0.990	0.880	1.000			
SES-FE-FXD	0.741	0.975	0.766	1.000		
CN_RDM	0.933	0.791	0.931	0.668	1.000	
CN_FXD	0.541	0.675	0.511	0.668	0.540	1.000

time-series variation in the data or if differences exist in time-series and cross-sectional effects, the model may fail to provide credible coefficients. With our small data set, the fixed-effect models reduce the degrees of freedom significantly, and the Census-NAEP model has the fewest degrees of freedom, since it has several family variables (as opposed to one family variable in SES and SES-FE) that are fully interacted. We believe that the weakness in the results partially reflects the limited degrees of freedom and the lack of cross-sectional variation.

If we eliminate these results, the correlation among the state residuals is 0.67 or higher. The correlation among the results of the random-effect models is 0.93 or higher, and the correlation between the two fixed-effect results is 0.98. Thus, the lower correlation in the results occurs between random- and fixed-effect models.

The primary difference between fixed- and random-effect models is the assumption in random-effect models that there is no correlation between the random effects and the set of independent family variables. The fixed-effect models allow the correlation between residuals and family variables to affect the coefficients of family variables, giving the family variables less influence. When the family variables have less influence, the residual rankings tend more toward the raw scores. For instance, if no family variables were introduced, the unexplained state residuals would be the differences in raw scores. The fixed-effect models introduce some influence of family variables and move states with less advantageous family characteristics higher in the rankings of residuals. The random-effect models allow the most family influence and give states with less-advantageous family characteristics the highest rankings in the residuals. However, these movements in the residuals are relatively small, as indicated by the high correlation among the residuals from the various models.

STATISTICAL RESULTS FOR ESTIMATING EFFECTS OF STATE POLICY AND EDUCATIONAL CHARACTERISTICS

Tables I.1, I.2, and I.3 provide the regression results for equations involving the state policy and educational characteristics variables that are described in Chapter Seven. Tables I.1, I.2, and I.3 provide the results used in Tables 7.1, 7.2, and 7.3. Tables I.1, I.2, and I.3 provide the random- and fixed-effect model results using the SES, SES-FE, and Census-NAEP family variables, respectively. The results using three model specifications for resource variables are shown in each table. The columns correspond to the following models:

Model 1:   Per-pupil expenditure

Model 2:   Prekindergarten, pupil-teacher ratio, teacher salary, and teacher resources

Model 3:   Prekindergarten, pupil-teacher ratio, teacher resources, teacher education, and teacher experience.

The results generally show that the coefficients of the policy and characteristics variables are fairly stable across the models, but the statistical significance of some of these variables falls to insignificance in the fixed-effect models because of the removal of the cross-sectional variation.

Tables I.4 and I.5 provide the results introducing a family interaction and a squared pup-tchr term using the random-effect model with SES-FE. These results are used in Table 7.4. Table I.5 tests for the interaction of prekindergarten and family, and the data are used in Table 7.5.

Tables I.6, I.7, and I.8 show the Hausman test results for the policy models for SES, SES-FE, and Census-NAEP, respectively. The results show that the hypothesis that there are no systematic differences between fixed and random coefficients is accepted for seven of the nine models.

Table I.1

Regression Results for Policy Variables Using SES (t-statistics in parentheses0)

Model	Random			Fixed		
	Model 1	Model 2	Model 3	Model 1	Model 2	Model 3
Number obs	271	271	271	271	271	271
Depvar	Score	Score	Score	Score	Score	Score
Intercept	-0.519 (-2.130)	0.502 (1.630)	-0.012 (-0.030)	-0.705 (-2.520)	0.345 (0.930)	0.072 (0.150)
South	0.039 (0.650)	0.010 (0.170)	-0.006 (-0.120)			
Midwest	0.121 (2.620)	0.104 (2.310)	0.090 (2.000)			
West	0.050 (0.840)	0.074 (1.100)	0.049 (0.760)			
Urban	0.001 (0.850)	0.000 (0.200)	0.000 (0.260)			
Rural	0.001 (1.280)	0.000 (0.030)	0.000 (-0.300)			
Dummy–8th	0.214 (1.090)	-0.043 (-0.160)	-0.086 (-0.310)	0.173 (0.920)	-0.083 (-0.360)	-0.103 (-0.450)
Dummy–4thR	-0.284 (-2.670)	-0.294 (-2.860)	-0.289 (-2.840)	-0.282 (-2.120)	-0.287 (-2.140)	-0.292 (-2.150)

Table I.1—Continued

Model	Random			Fixed		
	Model 1	Model 2	Model 3	Model 1	Model 2	Model 3
Gain 90–92 8mth	0.091 (8.740)	0.103 (8.510)	0.104 (7.830)	0.075 (4.390)	0.093 (5.650)	0.093 (5.510)
Gain 92–96 8mth	0.198 (10.780)	0.210 (10.850)	0.213 (8.350)	0.174 (6.390)	0.204 (8.250)	0.196 (6.680)
Gain 92–94 4rd	-0.089 (-6.520)	-0.099 (-6.880)	-0.104 (-7.170)	-0.094 (-5.550)	-0.099 (-5.410)	-0.109 (-5.420)
Gain 92–96 4mth	0.096 (5.500)	0.072 (3.710)	0.064 (3.030)	0.092 (5.720)	0.079 (3.970)	0.057 (2.270)
Mobility x 8th	-0.003 (-1.260)	-0.002 (-0.660)	-0.001 (-0.560)	-0.002 (-1.080)	-0.001 (-0.480)	-0.001 (-0.410)
Mobility x 4thR	0.004 (2.670)	0.005 (2.860)	0.005 (2.840)	0.004 (2.130)	0.005 (2.150)	0.005 (2.160)
SES X 8th	0.341 (3.780)	0.267 (2.920)	0.270 (2.870)	0.350 (3.710)	0.289 (2.890)	0.288 (2.890)
SES x 4thR	-0.101 (-1.020)	-0.110 (-1.120)	-0.095 (-0.920)	-0.177 (-1.490)	-0.195 (-1.610)	-0.185 (-1.520)
SES	1.165 (9.950)	1.175 (12.230)	1.132 (10.850)	0.755 (2.380)	0.753 (2.350)	0.739 (2.310)
Mobility	0.004 (1.690)	0.003 (1.360)	0.004 (1.600)	0.004 (1.240)	0.004 (1.190)	0.005 (1.320)

Table I.1—Continued

Model	Random			Fixed		
	Model 1	Model 2	Model 3	Model 1	Model 2	Model 3
Participation	-0.001 (-0.990)	-0.001 (-1.260)	-0.001 (-1.240)	-0.001 (-0.980)	-0.001 (-1.160)	-0.001 (-1.100)
Per-pupil exp.	0.047 (3.360)			0.098 (3.470)		
Prekindergarten		0.004 (1.760)	0.003 (1.760)		0.003 (1.550)	0.003 (1.440)
Missing prekindergarten		-0.032 (-1.190)	-0.029 (-1.150)		-0.031 (-1.010)	-0.034 (-1.090)
Pupil-teacher (1–40)		-0.021 (-2.720)	-0.020 (-2.710)		-0.026 (-2.600)	-0.028 (-2.640)
Pupil-teacher (5–80)		0.006 (0.820)	0.007 (0.870)		0.007 (1.790)	0.007 (1.780)
Salary		0.001 (0.120)			0.005 (1.110)	
Tchr res—low		-0.003 (-1.670)	-0.003 (-1.850)		-0.002 (-1.160)	-0.002 (-1.140)
Tchr res—med		-0.003 (-1.380)	-0.002 (-1.180)		-0.002 (-1.440)	-0.002 (-1.110)
% teacher BA			0.001 (1.350)			0.000 (0.150)

Table I.1—Continued

Model	Random			Fixed		
	Model 1	Model 2	Model 3	Model 1	Model 2	Model 3
Teacher exp (3–90)			0.008 (2.190)			0.005 (1.380)
Teacher exp (10–190)			0.003 (1.060)			0.003 (0.820)
Teacher exp (20+0)					0.005 (1.650)	0.006 (1.710)
R-squared	NA	NA	NA	0.725	0.73	0.735

Table I.2

Regression Results for Policy Variables Using SES-FE (t-statistics in parentheses)

Model	Random			Fixed		
	Model 1	Model 2	Model 3	Model 1	Model 2	Model 3
Number of observations	271	271	271	271	271	271
Depvar	Score	Score	Score	Score	Score	Score
Intcpt	-0.497	0.555	0.018	-0.725	0.343	0.036
	(-2.030)	(1.830)	(0.050)	(-2.580)	(0.920)	(0.070)
South	0.030	0.000	-0.010			
	(0.500)	(0.000)	(-0.200)			
Mdwest	0.114	0.095	0.084			
	(2.450)	(2.170)	(1.880)			
West	0.035	0.057	0.039			
	(0.580)	(0.870)	(0.620)			
Urban	0.001	0.000	0.000			
	(0.660)	(-0.060)	(0.010)			
Rural	0.001	0.000	-0.001			
	(0.850)	(-0.410)	(-0.730)			
dummy—8th	0.217	-0.009	-0.054	0.173	-0.072	-0.092
	(1.110)	(-0.030)	(-0.190)	(0.910)	(-0.310)	(-0.400)
dummy—4thR	-0.334	-0.346	-0.341	-0.294	-0.299	-0.302
	(-3.080)	(-3.290)	(-3.250)	(-2.220)	(-2.230)	(-2.240)
gain 90–92 8mth	0.091	0.104	0.105	0.075	0.093	0.093
	(8.770)	(8.640)	(7.960)	(4.390)	(5.650)	(5.500)
gain 92–96 8mth	0.197	0.210	0.212	0.175	0.204	0.196
	(10.620)	(10.690)	(8.290)	(6.400)	(8.230)	(6.670)
gain 92–94 4rd	-0.092	-0.104	-0.108	-0.098	-0.104	-0.114
	(-6.700)	(-7.100)	(-7.400)	(-5.830)	(-5.750)	(-5.690)

Table I.2—Continued

Model	Random			Fixed		
	Model 1	Model 2	Model 3	Model 1	Model 2	Model 3
gain 92–96 4mth	0.096	0.070	0.063	0.089	0.074	0.054
	(5.470)	(3.680)	(2.990)	(5.530)	(3.720)	(2.120)
mobility x 8th	-0.003	-0.002	-0.002	-0.003	-0.001	-0.001
	(-1.300)	(-0.800)	(-0.670)	(-1.160)	(-0.590)	(-0.520)
mobility x 4thR	0.005	0.005	0.005	0.005	0.005	0.005
	(3.070)	(3.280)	(3.240)	(2.230)	(2.240)	(2.240)
SES-FE x 8th	0.479	0.383	0.384	0.509	0.431	0.429
	(3.980)	(3.170)	(3.090)	(4.060)	(3.250)	(3.240)
SES-FE x 4thR	-0.203	-0.215	-0.195	-0.307	-0.336	-0.322
	(-1.580)	(-1.650)	(-1.430)	(-2.090)	(-2.250)	(-2.150)
SES-FE	1.495	1.531	1.472	0.664	0.624	0.606
	(9.410)	(11.520)	(10.270)	(1.590)	(1.480)	(1.440)
mobility	0.004	0.003	0.004	0.005	0.005	0.006
	(1.740)	(1.450)	(1.640)	(1.440)	(1.420)	(1.530)
partic	-0.001	-0.001	-0.001	-0.001	-0.001	-0.001
	(-1.010)	(-1.310)	(-1.270)	(-1.100)	(-1.310)	(-1.230)
per pup exp	0.047			0.096		
	(3.390)			(3.360)		
pre kindgtn		0.004	0.003		0.004	0.003
		(1.860)	(1.870)		(1.590)	(1.490)
missing prekindergarten		-0.031	-0.029		-0.034	-0.037
		(-1.200)	(-1.150)		(-1.090)	(-1.180)
pup-tchr (1–4)		-0.020	-0.020		-0.026	-0.028
		(-2.710)	(-2.670)		(-2.600)	(-2.640)
pup-tchr (5–8)		0.006	0.006		0.007	0.007
		(0.710)	(0.750)		(1.710)	(1.690)

Table I.2—Continued

Model	Random			Fixed		
	Model 1	Model 2	Model 3	Model 1	Model 2	Model 3
salary		0.000 (-0.020)			0.004 (0.910)	
tchr res–low		-0.003 (-1.790)	-0.003 (-1.960)		-0.002 (-1.230)	-0.002 (-1.210)
tchr res–med		-0.003 (-1.410)	-0.002 (-1.230)		-0.002 (-1.440)	-0.002 (-1.130)
% tchr BA			0.001 (1.300)			0.000 (0.200)
tchr exp (3–9)			0.008 (2.080)			0.005 (1.330)
tchr exp (10–19)			0.003 (1.120)			0.003 (0.860)
tchr exp (20+)			0.005 (1.720)			0.006 (1.70)
R-sq	NA	NA	NA	0.722	0.728	0.733

Table I.3
Regression Results for Policy Variables using Cen-NAEP (t-statistics in parentheses)

Model	Random			Fixed		
	Model 1	Model 2	Model 3	Model 1	Model 2	Model 3
# obs	271	271	271	271	271	271
Depvar	Score	Score	Score	Score	Score	Score
intcpt	-1.049	0.000	-0.645	-0.016	1.331	0.914
	(-0.940)	(0.000)	(-0.770)	(-0.010)	(1.060)	(0.690)
south	0.035	-0.043	-0.036			
	(0.500)	(-0.750)	(-0.770)			
mdwest	0.139	0.068	0.078			
	(2.500)	(1.480)	(1.710)			
west	0.048	0.038	0.049			
	(0.630)	(0.480)	(0.640)			
urban	0.002	0.001	0.001			
	(1.400)	(0.850)	(1.230)			
rural	0.001	0.000	0.000			
	(1.410)	(-0.190)	(0.120)			
dummy—8th	-0.151	-0.434	-0.527	0.190	-0.312	-0.30
	(-0.220)	(-0.940)	(-1.180)	(0.360)	(-0.570)	(-0.540)
dummy—4thR	0.562	0.712	0.738	0.506	0.633	0.667
	(1.010)	(1.270)	(1.290)	(1.010)	(1.260)	(1.320)
gain 90–92 8mth	0.116	0.127	0.125	0.103	0.118	0.117
	(8.160)	(7.790)	(7.360)	(5.790)	(6.890)	(6.600)
gain 92–96 8mth	0.214	0.225	0.228	0.192	0.222	0.213
	(9.760)	(9.690)	(7.820)	(6.820)	(9.010)	(7.370)
gain 92–94 4rd	-0.067	-0.077	-0.079	-0.065	-0.068	-0.075
	(-4.430)	(-5.020)	(-4.800)	(-3.640)	(-3.560)	(-3.620)

Table I.3—Continued

Model	Random			Fixed		
	Model 1	Model 2	Model 3	Model 1	Model 2	Model 3
mobility X 4thR	0.001	0.000	0.000	0.001	0.000	0.000
	(0.600)	(0.050)	(-0.070)	(0.480)	(0.110)	(0.120)
income X 4thR	-0.011	-0.012	-0.011	-0.011	-0.011	-0.011
	(-3.300)	(-3.460)	(-3.350)	(-3.060)	(-3.100)	(-3.050)
income X 8th	0.000	-0.002	0.000	0.000	-0.002	-0.002
	(0.060)	(-0.470)	(-0.120)	(0.130)	(-0.720)	(-0.540)
sngl par X 4thR	0.014	0.008	0.008	0.013	0.008	0.010
	(1.370)	(0.790)	(0.850)	(1.540)	(0.990)	(1.150)
sngl par X 8th	-0.001	-0.006	-0.005	-0.003	-0.004	-0.002
	(-0.150)	(-0.710)	(-0.630)	(-0.410)	(-0.480)	(-0.300)
black X 4thR	-0.003	-0.003	-0.003	-0.003	-0.002	-0.003
	(-1.420)	(-1.130)	(-1.230)	(-1.550)	(-1.190)	(-1.510)
Hispanic X 4thR	-0.003	-0.003	-0.003	-0.003	-0.003	-0.003
	(-1.460)	(-1.410)	(-1.450)	(-1.620)	(-1.580)	(-1.750)
Hgh Schl X 4thR	-0.007	-0.006	-0.006	-0.006	-0.006	-0.006
	(-1.000)	(-0.790)	(-0.780)	(-1.200)	(-1.050)	(-1.170)
Hgh Schl+ X 4thR	-0.009	-0.010	-0.010	-0.008	-0.009	-0.009
	(-1.500)	(-1.600)	(-1.540)	(-1.920)	(-2.030)	(-2.150)
college X 4thR	0.003	0.004	0.004	0.003	0.003	0.003
	(0.650)	(0.780)	(0.710)	(0.530)	(0.640)	(0.490)
black X 8th	-0.001	0.001	0.000	-0.002	0.000	-0.001
	(-0.640)	(0.310)	(0.140)	(-0.920)	(-0.270)	(-0.560)

Table I.3—Continued

Model	Random			Fixed		
	Model 1	Model 2	Model 3	Model 1	Model 2	Model 3
Hispanic X 8th	0.001	0.002	0.002	0.001	0.002	0.002
	(0.770)	(2.070)	(1.940)	(0.350)	(1.280)	(1.020)
Hgh Schl X 8th	0.002	0.005	0.006	0.000	0.002	0.002
	(0.330)	(0.870)	(1.010)	(−0.060)	(0.420)	(0.400)
Hgh Schl+ X 8th	0.005	0.007	0.007	0.005	0.007	0.007
	(0.910)	(1.430)	(1.340)	(1.090)	(1.560)	(1.430)
college X 8th	0.002	0.004	0.004	−0.001	0.003	0.002
	(0.260)	(0.640)	(0.580)	(−0.150)	(0.570)	(0.440)
income	0.006	0.006	0.008	0.014	0.022	0.022
	(1.120)	(1.330)	(1.570)	(0.880)	(1.280)	(1.290)
sngl par	−0.014	−0.007	−0.006	−0.011	−0.008	−0.009
	(−1.610)	(−1.010)	(−0.900)	(−1.410)	(−1.030)	(−1.170)
black	−0.005	−0.006	−0.006	−0.009	−0.011	−0.011
	(−2.010)	(−2.740)	(−2.590)	(−2.430)	(−2.680)	(−2.720)
hisp	−0.003	−0.005	−0.005	−0.013	−0.014	−0.013
	(−1.040)	(−1.760)	(−1.930)	(−3.000)	(−3.390)	(−3.130)
Hgh Schl	0.010	0.009	0.009	0.011	0.002	0.004
	(0.840)	(1.000)	(0.990)	(0.680)	(0.130)	(0.230)
Hgh Schl+	0.004	0.007	0.005	−0.022	−0.026	−0.025
	(0.440)	(0.900)	(0.640)	(−1.620)	(−1.940)	(−1.900)
colleg	0.017	0.013	0.011	−0.003	−0.012	−0.012
	(1.670)	(1.620)	(1.360)	(−0.190)	(−0.960)	(−0.890)
mobility	0.000	0.000	0.001	0.001	0.002	0.002
	(−0.020)	(0.020)	(0.360)	(0.350)	(0.450)	(0.480)
partic	−0.001	−0.001	−0.001	0.000	−0.001	−0.001
	(−0.660)	(−1.160)	(−1.010)	(−0.440)	(−0.730)	(−0.660)

Table I.3—Continued

Model	Random			Fixed		
	Model 1	Model 2	Model 3	Model 1	Model 2	Model 3
per pup exp	0.042 (3.030)			0.079 (2.670)		
preindergarten		0.005 (2.420)	0.005 (2.410)		0.004 (1.910)	0.004 (1.840)
missing preindergarten		-0.044 (-1.490)	-0.046 (-1.460)		-0.032 (-1.080)	-0.034 (-1.140)
pup/tchr (1–4)		-0.019 (-2.480)	-0.019 (-2.400)		-0.020 (-2.180)	-0.023 (-2.330)
pup/tchr (5–8)		0.006 (0.840)	0.007 (0.980)		0.007 (1.760)	0.007 (1.830)
salary		-0.003 (-0.840)			0.001 (0.130)	
tchr res–low		-0.003 (-1.840)	-0.003 (-2.030)		-0.002 (-1.410)	-0.002 (-1.470)
tchr res–med		-0.002 (-1.230)	-0.002 (-1.160)		-0.002 (-2.030)	-0.002 (-1.240)
% tchr BA			0.001 (1.760)			0.000 (-0.070)
tchr exp (3–9)			0.007 (1.800)			0.005 (1.470)
tchr exp (10–19)			0.003 (1.080)			0.003 (0.940)
tchr exp (20+)			0.004 (1.540)			0.005 (1.220)
R–sq	NA	NA	NA	0.789	0.797	0.802

Table I.4

Regression Results Testing for Significance of Family-Pupil–Teacher Interactions and Thresholds Using Random Effect Model and SES-FE
(t-value in parenthesis)

	Model 1	Model 2	Model 3	Model 4
Number of observations	158	158	158	158
Dependent variable	Score	Score	Score	Score
Intercept	0.908	−0.115	1.163	0.190
Dummy—4th-grade reading	−0.345	−0.338	−0.343	−0.336
	(−3.17)	(−3.17)	(−3.08)	(−3.03)
South	−0.074	−0.102	−0.119	−0.145
	(−1.30)	(−1.79)	(−2.08)	(−2.53)
Midwest	−0.016	−0.048	−0.036	−0.066
	(−0.32)	(−0.94)	(−0.76)	(−1.35)
West	−0.087	−0.112	−0.131	−0.153
	(−1.12)	(−1.43)	(−1.73)	(−2.05)
Urban	0.001	0.001	0.001	0.001
	(0.69)	(0.66)	(0.72)	(0.71)
Rural	0.000	0.000	0.000	0.000
	(−0.30)	(−0.19)	(0.07)	(0.18)
Gain 92–94 4th-grade reading	−0.109	−0.111	−0.105	−0.107
	(−6.54)	(−6.61)	(−6.33)	(−6.44)
Gain 92–96 4th-grade math	0.056	0.054	0.058	0.056
	(2.73)	(2.64)	(2.80)	(2.73)
Mobility—4th-grade reading	0.005	0.005	0.005	0.005
	(3.15)	(3.15)	(3.06)	(3.01)
SES–FE—4th-grade reading	−0.145	−0.117	−0.150	−0.123
	(−1.13)	(−0.90)	(−1.17)	(−0.94)
SES–FE	1.811	1.893	−0.547	−0.432
	(12.47)	(12.64)	(−0.54)	(−0.55)
Mobility	0.002	0.002	0.000	0.001
	(0.53)	(0.72)	(0.00)	(0.20)
Partic	−0.001	−0.001	−0.001	−0.001
	(−1.02)	(−0.82)	(−1.20)	(−1.02)
Prekindergarten	0.005	0.005	0.005	0.005
	(1.96)	(2.01)	(2.20)	(2.23)
Missing prekindergarten	−0.018	−0.020	−0.016	−0.018
	(−0.89)	(−1.04)	(−0.90)	(−1.07)

Table I.4—Continued

	Model 1	Model 2	Model 3	Model 4
Pupil-teacher (1–4)	−0.008	0.097	−0.012	0.087
	(−1.06)	(1.63)	(−1.81)	(2.10)
Salary	−0.008	−0.008	−0.010	−0.010
	(−1.71)	(−1.68)	(−2.19)	(−2.20)
Teacher resources—low	−0.006	−0.006	−0.005	−0.006
	(−2.36)	(−2.68)	(−2.23)	(−2.60)
Teacher resources—medium	−0.004	−0.005	−0.004	−0.005
	(−1.29)	(−1.51)	(−1.22)	(−1.48)
Pupil-teacher squared		−0.003		−0.002
		(−1.68)		(−2.46)
Pupil-teacher —SES–FE			0.125	0.123
			(2.41)	(3.24)
R^2	NA	NA	NA	NA

Table I.5

**Regression Results Testing for Significance of
Family-Prekindergarten Interactions Using
Random Effect Model and SES-FE
(t-value in parenthesis)**

	Random Model	Fixed Model
Number of obs	158	158
Dependent variable	score	score
Intercept	0.840	−0.335
	(2.39)	(−0.51)
Dummy—4th-grade reading	−0.343	−0.329
	(−3.14)	(−2.44)
South	−0.084	
	(−1.44)	
Midwest	−0.006	
	(−0.12)	
West	−0.085	
	(−1.09)	
Urban	0.000	
	(0.28)	
Rural	0.000	
	(−0.28)	
Gain 92–94 4th-grade reading	−0.106	−0.098
	(−6.50)	(−4.39)
Gain 92–96 4mth	0.060	0.081
	(2.92)	(2.93)
Mobility—4th-grade reading	0.005	0.005
	(3.11)	(2.44)
SES-FE—4th-grade reading	−0.199	−0.177
	(−1.59)	(−1.08)
SES-FE	1.992	2.167
	(11.70)	(2.97)
Mobility	0.002	0.000
	(0.51)	(0.03)
Participation	−0.001	−0.001
	(−0.59)	(−0.98)
Prekindergarten	0.003	0.004
	(1.58)	(1.00)

Table I.5—Continued

Model	Random	Fixed
Missing prekindergarten	–0.024	0.042
	(–1.21)	(1.01)
Prekindergarten—SES–FE	–0.042	–0.046
	(–1.81)	(–1.55)
Pupil-teacher (1–4)	–0.009	0.027
	(–1.25)	(.32)
Salary	–0.008	0.012
	(–1.86)	(1.24)
Teacher resources—low	–0.005	–0.006
	(–2.25)	(–1.92)
Teacher resources—medium	–0.003	–0.005
	(–1.08)	(–1.56)
R^2	NA	0.665

Table I.6

Hausman Test Results for Policy Equations Using SES

Policy Model	Hausman Statistic	Statistical Significance
Per-pupil expenditure	7.12	
Prekindergarten, pupil-teacher ratio, teacher salary and resources	83.09	1
Prekindergarten, pupil-teacher ratio, teacher resources, education, and experience	15.08	

Hypothesis: The difference in coefficients is not systematic (β_Fixed = β_Random).

Table I.7

Hausman Test Results for Policy Equations Using SES-FE

Policy Model	Hausman Statistic	Statistical significance
Per-pupil expenditure	9.44	
Prekindergarten, pupil-teacher ratio, teacher salary and resources	22.91	
Prekindergarten, pupil-teacher ratio, teacher resources, education, and experience	16.32	

Hypothesis: The difference in coefficients is not systematic (β_Fixed = β_Random).

Table I.8

Hausman Test Results for Policy Equations Using Census-NAEP

Policy Model	Hausman Statistic	Statistical significance
Per-pupil expenditure	136.38	
Prekindergarten, pupil-teacher ratio, teacher salary and resources	53.00	
Prekindergarten, pupil-teacher ratio, teacher resources, education, and experience	1,508.25	1

Hypothesis: The difference in coefficients is not systematic (β_Fixed = β_Random).

ROBUST REGRESSION RESULTS

Table J.1 shows the results of OLS estimation for the policy model using robust and nonrobust regression. The robust regression weights outliers less to test the sensitivity of results to the effect of outliers. These results use the default options in STATA for determining the weight assigned to outliers. The results are fairly insensitive to weighting outliers less than other points. We also tested the sensitivity of results with a variety of other tests that assign different weights to data points and found the results to be fairly insensitive.

Table J.1

Robust and Nonrobust OLS Regression Results

	Model 1 OLS, Robust	Model 2 OLS, Nonrobust
Number of observations	271	271
Dependent variable	Score	Score
Intercept	0.776	0.837
	(3.110)	(3.330)
Dummy—8th grade	0.353	0.291
	(1.700)	(1.390)
Read4	−0.314	−0.389
	(−1.830)	(−2.260)
South	−0.063	−0.048
	(−2.000)	(−1.520)
Midwest	0.042	0.046
	(1.670)	(1.800)
West	−0.034	−0.021
	(−0.860)	(−0.530)
Urban	0.000	0.000
	(0.660)	(0.370)
Rural	0.000	0.000
	(−0.150)	(−0.400)
1992 8th grade math	0.120	0.122
	(6.110)	(6.190)
1996 8th grade math	0.206	0.208
	(9.040)	(9.050)
1994 4th grade reading	−0.102	−0.111
	(−4.980)	(−5.400)
1996 4th grade math	0.050	0.053
	(2.450)	(2.570)
Change—8th grade	−0.005	−0.005
	(−1.930)	(−1.610)
Change—4th grade reading	0.005	0.006
	(1.840)	(2.260)
SES-FE—8th grade	0.329	0.416
	(2.100)	(2.640)

Table J.1—Continued

	Model 1 OLS, Robust	Model 2 OLS, Nonrobust
SES-FE * 4th grade reading	−0.281	−0.191
	(−1.540)	(−1.040)
Schl	1.749	1.664
	(12.400)	(11.700)
Change	0.002	0.002
	(0.830)	(0.730)
Participation	−0.002	−0.002
	(−2.520)	(−2.090)
Prekindergarten	0.003	0.004
	(2.320)	(3.240)
Noprekindergarten	−0.032	−0.036
	(−2.380)	(−2.620)
Pupil-teacher	−0.011	−0.012
	(−2.840)	(−3.110)
Salary	−0.004	−0.005
	(−1.310)	(−1.570)
Teacher resources—some	−0.005	−0.005
	(−3.410)	(−3.590)
Teacher resources—most	−0.003	−0.003
	(−1.360)	(−1.600)
R^2	0.896	0.892

MAKING COST-EFFECTIVENESS ESTIMATES FROM THE TENNESSEE CLASS-SIZE EXPERIMENT

CLASS-SIZE REDUCTIONS

Implementing a class size of 16 rather than 24 in K–3 raised achievement for those in small classes all four years by 0.25 to 0.40 standard deviation (Krueger, 1999a; Nye et al., 1999a). We used a conservative 0.30 standard for the estimates made here.

These smaller classes increased the number of teachers by 50 percent in K–3. We assumed that K–3 teachers are 4/13 (13 being the total number of grades in K–12) of total K–12 classroom teachers and that classroom instruction-related costs (teacher salary, tuition assistance, instructional supplies, and purchased instructional services) consume about 65 percent of the total budget.[1] Then, the estimated percentage increase in expenditures from the Tennessee class-size reduction is (0.50) x (4/13) x (0.65) = 0.10, or 10 percent of the budget for regular students. The per-pupil expenditure in 1993 through 1994 in Tennessee was approximately $4,400, so the added per-pupil expenditure is estimated at (0.10) x ($4,400) = $440 per pupil. The cost per 0.10 standard deviation gain (the actual gain is estimated at 0.30) is then $150 per pupil in additional expenditures.

---

[1]Table 163, *Digest of Educational Statistics*, provides 1993 to 1994 expenditures for classroom instruction (141.6 billion) and total expenditures (265.3 billion). We have included capital outlays (23.7) and interest on debt (5.3) to allow for classroom construction costs but have excluded "other current expenditures" related to adult education (4.7). This provides an estimate of (141.4 + 23.7 + 5.3)/(265.3 – 5.3) = 0.65. Arguably, one should include operations and maintenance (23.9), which would bring the total to 0.75. However, some slack classroom capacity exists, and operation and maintenance costs should not rise proportionately even if all-new construction is required.

TEACHER AIDES

The estimates for the effects of teacher aides in large classrooms are generally positive but are not statistically significant and are highly variable (Krueger, 1999a). Depending on the equations used, and the grade in which the measurement was made, the effect varies from zero to 33 percent of the class-size effect. We assume here a liberal estimate of 25 percent of the class-size effect, or 0.075 standard deviation.

Adding teacher aides would increase "teachers" by 100 percent in K–3. We assume the salary of an aide is two-thirds of a classroom teacher, with similar fringe benefits. No new classrooms are needed for aides, so we assume that instructional expenditures are 0.60 of total expenditures. Then, the estimated increase in per-pupil expenditures is $(1.0) \times (2/3) \times (4/13) \times (0.60) = 0.13$, or 13 percent of expenditures. The cost in per-pupil expenditures is $(\$4,400) \times 0.13$ or $570 per pupil, for a gain of 0.075 standard deviation. So, the cost per 0.10 standard deviation of gain is $(570) \times (0.10)/0.075 = \$760$ per pupil. This estimate is nearly five times more expensive than class-size reductions, so it is doubtful any set of changed assumptions could make aides nearly as effective as class-size reductions.

REGRESSION COST ESTIMATES

Table L.1 shows the cost regression results used in Chapter Eight, Tables 8.1 and 8.2. The dependent variable is per-pupil expenditures. The regressions are estimated using the random-effect models. An OLS model shows that the adjusted R-squared explained by the regressions is 0.95 or above. Column 2 introduces the SES-FE variable to determine how much of the unexplained variance in state per-pupil spending might be accounted for by SES-FE. The results indicate that certain unexplained expenditures are accounted for by higher SES. The coefficient indicates a range of about $400 in per-pupil expenditures from the lowest to highest SES states that is not accounted for by our variables. Similarly, the score variable is introduced to test whether the unexplained cost is partly explained by higher test scores. The results indicate the existence of excluded cost expenditures across states that are positively correlated with higher achievement. However, the coefficients of the remaining variables do not change much with the introduction of these variables, so the marginal cost estimate in each resource category is not affected by these excluded costs.

Table L.1

Cost Regressions
(t-statistics in parentheses)

	Model 1	Model 2	Model 3	Model 4
Number of observtions	271	271	271	271
Dependent variable	Expend.	Expend.	Expend.	Expend.
Intercept	2.750	2.779	2.347	2.393
	(4.430)	(4.840)	(3.770)	(3.970)
Pupil-teacher ratio (1–80)	–0.196	–0.190	–0.181	–0.178
	(–7.050)	(–7.300)	(–6.730)	(–6.710)
Teacher resources—low	0.005	0.005	0.008	0.008
	(1.790)	(1.660)	(2.970)	(2.800)
Teacher resources—medium	0.005	0.005	0.008	0.008
	(1.520)	(1.300)	(2.360)	(2.160)
Salary	0.148	0.145	0.141	0.140
	(12.720)	(12.040)	(11.860)	(11.490)
Prekindergarten	0.012	0.011	0.011	0.011
	(2.700)	(2.650)	(2.470)	(2.440)
Disabled	0.016	0.018	0.017	0.018
	(1.230)	(1.410)	(1.360)	(1.470)
Limited English	0.004	0.004	0.006	0.006
	(0.310)	(0.340)	(0.560)	(0.560)
Transportation	0.004	0.003	0.004	0.004
	(4.190)	(4.150)	(4.320)	(4.250)
SES–FE		1.101		0.657
		(2.640)		(1.700)
Score			0.383	0.360
			(4.150)	(3.950)
R^2	NA	NA	NA	NA

BIBLIOGRAPHY

Achilles, C. M., B. A. Nye, J. B. Zaharias, and B. D. Fulton, "The Lasting Benefits Study (LBS) in Grades 4 and 5 (1990–1991): A Legacy from Tennessee's Four Year (K–3) Class Size Study (1985–1990), Project STAR," paper presented at the North Carolina Association for Research in Education, Greensboro, N.C., January 14, 1993.

Alexander, K., and D. R. Entwisle, "Isolating the School's Contribution to Achievement: School Year Versus Summer Gains," paper presented at the meeting of the American Association for the Advancement of Science, Philadelphia, PA, February 1998.

Ballou, D., and M. Podgursky, "Recruiting Smarter Teachers," *Journal of Human Resources*, Vol. 30, No. 2, Spring 1995, pp. 326–338.

_____, *Teacher Pay and Teacher Quality*, Kalamazoo, Mich.: W. E. Upjohn Institute for Employment Research, 1997.

Barnett, Steven, "Long-Term Effects of Early Childhood Programs on Cognitive and School Outcomes," *The Future of Children*, Los Altos, CA: The David and Lucile Packard Foundation, Vol. 5, No. 3, Winter 1995.

Becker, Gary, *A Treatise on the Family*, Cambridge, Mass.: Harvard University Press, 1981.

_____, *Human Capital: A Theoretical and Empirical Analysis with Special Reference to Education*, 3rd ed., Chicago: The University of Chicago Press, 1993.

Betts, Julian, and J. Shkolnik, "Estimated Effects of Class Size on Teacher Time Allocation in Middle and High School Math Classes," *Educational Evaluation and Policy Analysis*, Vol. 20, No. 2, Summer 1999.

Boardman, A. E., and R. J. Murnane, "Using Panel Data to Improve Estimates of the Determinants of Educational Achievement," *Sociology of Education*, Vol. 52, April 1991, pp. 113–121.

Boozer, Michael A., A. Krueger, and S. Wolkon, *Race and School Quality Since Brown v. Board of Education*, Brookings Papers on Economic Activity (Microeconomic), Washington, D C.: Brookings Institution, 1992, pp. 269–326.

Boruch, R. F., *Randomized Experiments for Planning and Evaluation*, Thousand Oaks, Calif.: Sage Publications, 1994.

Boruch, R., and E. Foley, "The Honestly Experimental Society: Sites and Other Entities as the Units of Allocation and Analysis in Randomized Trials," in L. Bickman, ed., *Validity and Social Experimentation: Donald T. Cambell's Legacy*, Thousand Oaks, Calif.: Sage, in press.

Brewer, Dominic, C. Krop, B. Gill, and R. Reichardt, "Estimating the Costs of National Class Size Reductions under Alternative Policies," *Educational Evaluation and Policy Analysis*, Vol. 20, No. 2, Summer 1999.

Bryk, Anthony S., and S. Raudenbush, "Toward a More Appropriate Conceptualization of Research on School Effects: A Three-Level Hierarchical Linear Model," *American Journal of Education*, November 1988.

Burtless, Gary, ed., *Does Money Matter? The Effect of School Resources on Student Achievement and Adult Success*, Washington, D.C.: Brookings Institution, 1996.

Campbell, J. R., P. L. Donahue, C. M. Reese, and G. W. Phillips, *NAEP 1994 Reading Report Card for the Nations and the States: Findings from the National Assessment of Educational Progress and Trial State Assessment*, Washington, D.C.: National Center for Education Statistics, 1996.

Card, David, and Alan Krueger, "Labor Market Effects of School Quality," in Burtless (1996), pp. 97–140.

Chambers, Jay, *The Patterns of Teacher Compensation*, Washington, D.C.: National Center for Educational Statistics, NCES 95-829, January 1996.

Clotfelter, Charles T., and Helen Ladd, "Recognizing and Rewarding Success in Public Schools," in Helen Ladd, ed., *Holding Schools Accountable*, Washington, D.C.: Brookings Institution, 1996.

Cohen, David K., "Standards-Based School Reform: Policy, Practice, and Performance," in Helen Ladd, ed., *Holding Schools Accountable*, Washington, D.C.: Brookings Institution, 1996.

Coleman, James S., "Social Capital in the Creation of Human Capital," *American Journal of Sociology*, No. 94, 1988, pp. s95–s120.

_____, *Foundations of Social Theory*, Cambridge, Mass.: Harvard University Press, 1990.

Coleman, James S., Ernest Q. Campbell, Carol J. Hobson, James McPartland, Alexander M. Mood, Frederic D. Weinfeld, and Robert L. York, *Equality of Educational Opportunity*, Washington, D.C.: U.S. Government Printing Office, 1966.

Consortium on Productivity in the Schools, *Using What We Have to Get the Schools We Need*, New York: Teachers College, Columbia University, 1995.

Cook, Michael, and William N. Evans, "Families or Schools? Explaining the Convergence in White and Black Academic Performance," working paper, 1997.

Cook, Thomas D., "Considering the Major Arguments Against Random Assignment: An Analysis of the Intellectual Culture Surrounding Evaluation in American Schools of Education," paper presented at the Harvard Faculty Seminar on Experiments in Education, 1999.

Darling-Hammond, L., *Doing What Matters Most: Investing in Quality Teaching*, New York: National Commission on Teaching and America's Future, 1997.

Dunn, Judy, and Robert Plomin, *Separate Lives: Why Siblings Are So Different*, New York: Basic Books, 1990.

Ehrenberg, Ronald G., and Dominic J. Brewer, "Do School and Teacher Characteristics Matter? Evidence from High School and Beyond," *Economics of Education Review*, Vol. 13, No. 1, 1994, pp. 1–17.

Ehrenberg, Ronald G., and Dominic J. Brewer, "Did Teachers' Race and Verbal Ability Matter in the 1960's? Coleman Revisited," *Economics of Education Review*, Vol. 14, No. 1, 1995, pp. 291–299.

Elmore, Richard F., *Restructuring Schools: The Next Generation of Educational Reform*, San Francisco: `Jossey-Bass, 1990.

Elmore, Richard F., C. H. Abelmann, and S. F. Furman, "The New Accountability in State Education Reform: From Process to Performance," in Helen Ladd, ed., *Holding Schools Accountable*, Washington, D.C.: Brookings Institution, 1996.

Evans, William N., Sheila Murray, and Robert Schwab, "Schoolhouses, Courthouses, and Statehouses after Serrano," *Journal of Policy Analysis and Management*, No. 16, January 1997, pp. 10–31.

_____, "The Impact of Court-Mandated School Finance Reform," in Helen Ladd, Rosemary Chalk, and Janet Hansen, eds., *Equity and Adequacy in Education Finance*, Washington, D.C.: National Research Council, National Academy Press, 1999.

Ferguson, Ronald F., "Paying for Public Education: New Evidence on How and Why Money Matters, " *Harvard Journal on Legislation*, Vol. 28, 1991, pp. 465–497.

Ferguson, Ronald F., "Can Schools Narrow the Black-White Score Gap," C. Jencks and M. Phillips, eds., in *The Black-White Score Gap*, Washington, D.C.: Brookings Institution, 1998a.

Ferguson, Ronald F., "Teachers' Perceptions and Expectations and the Black-White Score Gap" C. Jencks and M. Phillips, eds., in *The Black-White Score Gap*, Washington, D.C.: Brookings Institution, 1998b.

Ferguson, Ronald F., and Helen F. Ladd, "How and Why Money Matters: An Analysis of Alabama Schools," in Helen F. Ladd, ed., *Holding Schools Accountable*, Washington, D.C.: Brookings Institution, 1996.

Feuer, Michael, Senior Analyst and Project Director of the U. S. Office of Technology Assessment, Oversight Hearings of the Report of the National Council on Education Standards and Testing, p. 91.

Finn, Chester, E., Jr., and Theodore Rebarber, eds., *Education Reform in the '90s*, New York: Macmillan, 1992.

Finn, Jeremy D., and Charles M. Achilles, "Answers and Questions About Class Size: A Statewide Experiment," *American Educational Research Journal*, Vol. 27, No. 3, Fall 1990, pp. 557–577.

_____, "Tennessee's Class Size Study: Findings, Implications and Misconceptions," *Educational Evaluation and Policy Analysis*, Vol. 20, No. 2, Summer 1999.

Gamoran, Adam, "Student Achievement in Public Magnet, Public Comprehensive, and Private City High Schools," *Educational Evaluation and Policy Analysis*, Vol. 18, No. 1, Spring 1996, pp. 1–18.

Goertz, Margaret, E., Robert E. Floden, and Jennifer O'Day, *Studies of Education Reform: Systemic Reform, Volume I: Findings and Conclusions*, New Brunswick, N.J.: CPRE, Rutgers University, 1995.

Goldhaber, Dan D., and Dominic J. Brewer, "Why Don't Schools and Teachers Seem to Matter? Assessing the Impact of Unobservables on Educational Productivity," *Journal of Human Resources*, Vol. 32, No. 3, 1997, pp. 505–523.

_____, "Teacher Licensing and Student Achievement," in Marci Kanstoroom and Chester Finn, eds., *Better Teachers, Better Schools*, New York: Thomas B. Fordham Foundation, 1999.

Greenwald, Rob, L. V. Hedges, and R. Laine, "The Effect of School Resources on Student Achievement," *Review of Educational Research*, Vol. 66, No. 3, Fall 1996, pp. 361–396.

Grissmer, David, *Educational Productivity*, Washington, D.C.: Center for Educational Development and Research, 1997.

_____, "Assessing the Evidence on Class Size: Policy Implications and Future Research Agenda," *Educational Evaluation and Policy Analysis*, Vol. 20, No. 2, Summer 1999.

_____, "The Use and Misuse of SAT Scores," *Journal of Psychology, Law and Public Policy*, forthcoming.

Grissmer, David, and Ann Flanagan, "Exploring Rapid Score Gains in Texas and North Carolina," commissioned paper, Washington, D.C.: National Education Goals Panel, 1998.

Grissmer, David W., and Ann Flanagan, "Moving Educational Research Toward Scientific Consensus," in David Grissmer and Michael Ross, eds., *Analytic Issues in the Assessment of Student Achievement*, 2000.

Grissmer, David W., Ann Flanagan, and Jennifer Kawata, *Assessing and Improving the Family Characteristics Collected with the National Assessment of Educational Progress*, unpublished manuscript, Santa Monica, Calif.: RAND, no date.

Grissmer, David, A. Flanagan, and S. Williamson, "Why Did Black Test Scores Rise Rapidly in the 1970s and 1980s?" in Christopher Jencks and Merideth Phillips, eds., *The Black-White Test Score Gap*, Washington, D.C.: Brookings Institution, 1998b.

Grissmer, David, A. Flanagan, and S. Williamson, "Does Money Matter for Minority and Disadvantaged Students: Assessing the New Empirical Evidence," in William Fowler, ed., *Developments in School Finance: 1997*, U.S. Department of Education, NCES 98-212, 1998c.

Grissmer, David, and Sheila Nataraj Kirby, "Teacher Turnover and Teacher Quality," *Teacher's College Record*, Vol. 99, No. 1, Fall 1997.

Grissmer, D. W., S. N. Kirby, M. Berends, and S. Williamson, *Student Achievement and the Changing American Family*, Santa Monica, Calif.: RAND, MR-488-LE, 1994.

_____, *Testing Multiple Risk Hypothesis for Explaining Black Score Gains*, paper presented at the Seventh International Conference on Socioeconomics, April 1995.

Grissmer, David, Stephanie Williamson, Sheila Nataraj Kirby, and Mark Berends, "Exploring the Rapid Rise in Black Achievement Scores in the United States (1970–1990)," in U. Neisser, ed., *The Rising Curve: Long-Term Changes in IQ and Related Measures*, Washington, D.C.: American Psychological Association, 1998a.

Hannaway, Jane, and Martin Carnoy, eds., *Decentralization and School Improvement*, San Francisco: Jossey-Bass, 1993.

Hanushek, Eric A., "The Economics of Schooling: Production and Efficiency in Public Schools," *Journal of Economic Literature*, Vol. 24, 1986, pp. 1141–1176.

_____, "The Impact of Differential Expenditures on School Performance," *Educational Researcher*, Vol. 18, No. 4, pp. 45–51, 1989.

_____, *Making Schools Work: Improving Performance and Controlling Costs*, Washington, D.C.: Brookings Institution, 1994.

_____, "Measuring Investment in Education," *Journal of Economic Perspectives*, Vol. 10, No. 4, Fall 1996a, pp. 9–30.

_____, "Outcomes, Costs and Incentives in Schools," in Eric Hanushek and Dale Jorgenson, eds., *Improving America's Schools: The Role of Incentives*, Washington, D.C.: National Academy Press, 1996b.

_____, "School Resources and Student Performance," in Burtless, (1996), 1996c. , pp. 43-73.

_____, "Assessing the Empirical Evidence on Class Size Reductions from Tennessee and Non-Experimental Research," *Educational Evaluation and Policy Analysis*, Vol. 20, No. 2, Summer 1999.

Hanushek, Eric A., and Dale Jorgenson, *Improving America's Schools: The Role of Incentives*, Washington, D.C.: National Academy Press, 1996.

Hanushek, Eric A., and Steven G. Rivkin, "Understanding the Twentieth-Century Growth in U.S. School Spending," *Journal of Human Resources*, Vol. 32, No. 1, Winter 1997.

Hanushek, Eric A., Steven G. Rivkin, and Lori L. Taylor, "Aggregation and the Estimated Effects of School Resources," *The Review of Economics and Statistics*, Fall 1996, pp. 611–627.

Hanushek, Eric A., and Lori L. Taylor, "Alternative Assessments of the Performance of Schools: Measurement of State Variations in Achievement," *Journal of Human Resources*, No. 25, Spring 1990, pp. 179–201.

Hauser, R. M., "Trends in Black-White Test Score Differentials: Uses and Misuses of NAEP/SAT Data," in U. Neisser, ed., *The Rising Curve: Long-Term Changes in IQ and Related Measures*, Washington, D.C.: American Psychological Association, 1998.

Haveman, Robert, and Barbara Wolfe, *Succeeding Generations: On the Effects of Investments in Children*, New York: Russell Sage Foundation, 1994.

_____, "The Determinants of Children's Attainments: A Review of Methods and Findings," *Journal of Economic Literature*, Vol. 33, December 1995, pp. 1829–1878.

Heckman, James, Anne Layne-Farrar, and Petra Todd, "Does Measured School Quality Really Matter? An Examination of the Earnings-Quality Relationship," in Burtless (1996), pp. 192–289.

Heckman, J. J., and Smith, J., "Assessing the Case for Social Experiments," *Journal of Economic Perspectives*, Vol. 9, No. 2, Spring 1995.

Hedges, Larry V., and Rob Greenwald, "Have Times Changed? The Relation Between School Resources and Student Performance," in Burtless (1996), pp. 74–92.

Hedges, Larry V., Richard D. Laine, and Rob Greenwald, "Does Money Matter: Meta-Analysis of Studies of the Effects of Differential School Inputs on Student Outcomes," *Educational Researcher*, Vol. 23, No. 3, 1994, pp. 5–14.

Hedges, Larry V., and Amy Nowell, "Group Differences in Mental Test Scores: Mean Differences Variability, and Talent," in C. S. Jencks and M. Phillips, eds., *The Black-White Test Score Gap*, Washington, D.C.: Brookings Institution, 1998.

Jencks, Christopher and Meredith Phillips, *The Black-White Test Score Gap*, Washington, D.C.: Brookings Institution, 1998.

Kanstoroom, Marci, and Chester Finn, eds., *Better Teachers, Better Schools*, New York: Thomas B. Fordham Foundation, 1999.

Karoly, Lynn A., Peter W. Greenwood, Susan S. Everingham, Jill Houbé, M. Rebecca Kilburn, C. Peter Rydell, Matthew Sanders, and James Chiesa, *Investing in Our Children: What We Know and Don't Know About the Costs and Benefits of Early Childhood Interventions*, Santa Monica, Calif.: RAND, 1998.

Koretz, D., "State Comparisons Using NAEP: Large Costs, Disappointing Benefits," *Educational Researcher*, Vol. 20., No. 3, April 1991.

Krueger, Alan B., "Reassessing the View That American Schools Are Broken," *Economic Policy Review*, March, 1998, pp. 29–43.

_____, "Experimental Estimates of Education Production Functions," *Quarterly Journal of Economics*, Vol. CXIV, 1999a, pp. 497–532.

_____, An Economist View of Class Size Reductions, Mimeo, Princeton University, 1999b.

Ladd, Helen F., ed., *Holding Schools Accountable*, Washington, D.C.: Brookings Institution, 1996a.

Ladd, Helen F., "Introduction," in H. F. Ladd, ed., *Holding Schools Accountable*, Washington, D.C.: Brookings Institution, 1996b.

Ladd, Helen F., Rosemary Chalk, and Janet S. Hansen, *Equity and Adequacy in Educational Finance: Issues and Perspectives*, Washington, D.C.: National Academy Press, 1999.

Lankford, Hamilton, and James Wyckoff, "The Allocation of Resources to Special Education and Regular Instruction," in Helen F. Ladd, ed., *Holding Schools Accountable*, Washington, D.C.: Brookings Institution, 1996.

Levin, Henry M., *Cost-Effectiveness: A Primer, New Perspectives in Evaluation*, Vol. 4, London: Sage Publications, 1983.

Lyon, Reid G., "Learning Disabilities," *The Future of Children*, Vol. 6, No. 1, Spring 1996.

Manski, C. F., "Learning About Treatment Effects from Experiments with Random Assignment of Treatments," *The Journal of Human Resources*, Vol. 31, No. 4, 1996, pp. 709–733.

Massell, Diane, and Susan Fuhrman, *Ten Years of State Education Reform, 1983–1993*, New Brunswick, N.J.: Consortium for Policy Research in Education, CPRE Research Reports Series RR-028, 1994.

Massell, Diane, Michael Kirst, and Margaret Hoppe, *Persistence and Change: Standards-Based Reform in Nine States*, Philadelphia, PA: Consortium for Policy Research in Education, University of Pennsylvania, Graduate School of Education, 1997.

Masten, A. S., "Resilience in Individual Development: Successful Adaptation Despite Risk and Adversity," in M. C. Wang and E. W. Gordon, eds., *Educational Resilience in Inner City America: Challenges and Prospects*, Hillsdale, N.J.: Lawrence Erlbaum Associates, 1994.

Meyer, Robert H., "Can Schools Be Held Accountable for Good Performance? A Critique of Common Educational Performance Indicators," in Emily P. Hoffman, ed., *Essays on the Economics of Education*, Kalamazoo, Mich.: W. E. Upjohn Institute for Employment Research, 1993, pp. 75–101.

_____, "Value-Added Indicators of School Performance," in Eric Hanushek and Dale Jorgenson, eds., *Improving America's Schools: The Role of Incentives*, Washington, D.C.: National Academy Press, 1996.

Miller, Karen E., Jennifer E. Nelson, and Mary Naifeh, *Cross-State Data Compendium for the NAEP 1994 Grade 4 Reading Assessment*, National Center for Educational Statistics, 1995.

Molnar, Alex et al., "Estimated Achievement and Teacher Time Allocation Effects from a Quasi-Experimental Class Size Reduction in

Wisconsin," *Educational Evaluation and Policy Analysis*, Vol. 20, No. 2, Summer 1999.

Monk, David H., *Educational Finance: An Economic Approach*, New York: McGraw-Hill, 1990.

Monk, D., "Educational Productivity Research: An Update and Assessment of Its Role in Educational Finance Reform," *Educational Evaluation and Policy Analysis*, No. 14, 1992, pp. 307–332.

Mosteller, F., "The Tennessee Study of Class Size in the Early School Grades," *The Future of Children*, Vol. 5, No. 2, 1995, pp. 113–127.

Mullis, I. V. S., Dossey, J. A., Owen, E. H., and Phillips, G. W., *NAEP 1992 Mathematics Report Card for the Nation and the States: Data from the National and Trial State Assessments*, Washington, D.C.: National Center for Educational Statistics, 1993.

Murnane, Richard J., and Frank Levy. "What General Motors Can Teach U.S. Schools about the Proper Role of Markets," *Phi Delta Kappan*, Vol. 77, 1996, pp. 109–114.

Murnane, Richard J., John Willett, and Frank Levy, "The Growing Importance of Cognitive Skills in Wage Determination," *Review of Economics and Statistics*, Vol. 77, 1995, pp. 251–66.

National Center for Educational Statistics, U.S. Department of Education, *Cross–State Data Compendium for the NAEP 1994 Grade 4 Reading Assessment: Findings from the Trial State Assessment in Reading of the National Assessment of Educational Progress*, Washington, D.C.: U.S. Government Printing Office, 1995.

_____, *Private Schools in the United States: A Statistical Profile 1990–91*, Washington, D.C.: U.S. Government Printing Office, NCES 95-330, 1995.

_____, *Digest of Educational Statistics*, Washington, D.C.: U.S. Department of Education, NCES 1999-036, 1986, 1990, 1996, 1998.

National Education Association, *Status of the American Public School Teacher 1995–96*, Washington, D.C., July 1997.

Nye, B. A., C. M. Achilles, J. B. Zaharias, and B. D. Fulton, *Project Challenge Third Year Summary Report: An Initial Evaluation of* the Tennessee Department of Education "At Risk" Student/Teacher Ratio Reduction Project in Seventeen Counties, 1989–1990 Through 1991–92, Nashville, Tenn: Center of Excellence for Research in Basic Skills, College of Education, Tennessee State University, April 1995.

Nye, B. A., L. Hedges, and S. Konstantopoulos, The Effects of Small Class Size on Academic Achievement: The Results of the Tennessee Class Size Experiment, manuscript under review, Department of Education, University of Chicago, 1999a.

Nye, Barbara, Larry V. Hedges, and Spyros Konstantopoulos, "The Long Term Effects of Small Classes: A Five-Year Follow-up of the Tennessee Class Size Experiment," Educational Evaluation and Policy Analysis, Vol. 20, No. 2, Summer 1999b.

O'Day, Jennifer A., and M. S. Smith, "Systemic Reform and Educational Opportunity," in S. Fuhrman, ed., Designing Coherent Education Policy, San Francisco: Jossey-Bass, 1993, p. 251.

Office of Science and Technology Policy, Investing in Our Future: A National Research Initiative for America's Children for the 21st Century, Washington, D.C.: The White House, April 1997.

Peisner-Feinberg, Ellen S., and Margaret R. Burchinal, "Relations Between Preschool Children's Child-Care Experiences and Concurrent Development: The Cost, Quality, and Outcomes Study," Merrill-Palmer Quarterly, Vol. 43, No. 3, July 1997, pp. 451–477.

Plomin, Robert, and D. Daniels, "Why Are Children from the Same Family So Different from Each Other?" Behavioral and Brain Science, Vol. 10, 1987, pp. 1–16.

Powell, Brian, and Lala Carr Steelman, "Bewitched, Bothered and Bewildering: The Use and Misuse of State SAT and ACT Scores," Harvard Educational Review, Vol. 66, Spring 1996, pp. 27–59.

Powell, Irene, and James Cosgrove, "Quality and Cost in Early Childhood Education," The Journal of Human Resources, Vol. XXVII, No. 3.

Ramey, C. T., and S. Ramey, "Early Intervention and Early Experience," *American Psychologist*, Vol. 53, No. 2, 1998, pp. 109–120.

Raudenbush, Stephen W., "Random Effects Models," in H. Cooper and L. V. Hedges, eds., *The Handbook of Research Synthesis*, New York: Russell Sage Foundation, 1994.

Raudenbush, Stephen W., Randall P. Fotiu, and Yuk Fai Cheong, "Inequality of Access to Educational Resources: A National Report Card for Eighth Grade Math," 1998.

Raudenbush, Stephen W., and J. Douglas Wilms, "The Estimation of School Effects," *Journal of Educational and Behavioral Statistics*," Vol. 20, No. 4, Winter 1995, pp. 307–335.

Reese, C. M., K. E. Miller, J. Mazzeo, and J. A. Dossey, *NAEP 1996 Mathematics Report Card for the Nation and the States*, Washington, D.C.: National Center for Educational Statistics, 1997.

Reschly, Daniel J., "Identification and ... Disabilities," ... *Special Education for ... with Disabilities*, Vol. 6, No. 1, Spring 1996.

Rice, Jennifer K., "Estimated Effects of Class Size on Teacher's Time Allocation in High School Mathematics and Science Courses," *Educational Evaluation and Policy Analysis*, Summer 1999.

Rothstein, Richard, and K. H. Miles, *Where's the Money Gone? Changes in the Level and Composition of Education Spending*, Washington, D.C.: Economic Policy Institute, 1995.

Rutter, M., ed., *Studies in Psychosocial Risk: The Power of Longitudinal Data*, Cambridge: Cambridge University Press, 1988.

Salganik, Laura, "Apples and Apples: Comparing Performance Indicators for Places with Similar Demographic Characteristics," *Educational Evaluation and Policy Analysis*, Vol. 16, No. 2, Summer 1994, pp. 125–141.

Sanders, W. L., and S. P. Horn, "Research Findings from the Tennessee Value-Added Assessment System (TVAAS) Database:

Implications for Educational Evaluation and Research," *Journal of Personnel Evaluation in Education*, Vol. 12, 1998, pp. 247–256.

Saranson, Seymour, B., *The Predictable Failure of Educational Reform*, San Francisco: Jossey-Bass, 1990.

SAS Institute, SAS/STAT Software-Changes and Enhancements, Release 6.11, Cary, N.C., 1999.

Shaughnessy, C. A., J. Nelson, and N. Norris, *NAEP 1996 Mathematics Cross State Data Compendium for the Grade 4 and Grade 8 Assessment*, U.S. Department of Education, NCES-98-481, 1998.

Shkolnik, J., and J. R. Betts, *The Effects of Class Size on Teacher Time Allocation and Student Achievement*, unpublished manuscript, San Diego: University of California, Department of Economics, 1998.

Singer, Judith D., "Using SAS PROC MIXED to Fit Multilevel Models, Hierarchical Models and Individual Growth Models," *Journal of Educational and Behavioral Statistics*, Vol. 24, No. 4, Winter 1998, pp. 323–355.

Smith, Marshall, S. and Jennifer O'Day, "Systemic School Reform," in Susan Fuhrman and Betty Malem, eds., *The Politics of Curriculum and Testing: The 1990 Yearbook of the Politics of Education Association*, London: Falmer, 1990, pp. 233–267.

Tyack D., and L. Cuban, *Tinkering Toward Utopia: A Century of Public School Reform*, Cambridge, Mass: Harvard University Press, 1995.

Vinovskis, Maris A., "An Analysis of the Concept and Uses of Systemic Educational Reform," *American Educational Research Journal*, Vol. 33, No. 1, Spring 1996.

Vinovskis, Maris A., "Missing in Practice: Systemic Development and Rigorous Program Evaluation at the U.S. Department of Education," paper presented at Conference on Evaluation of Educational Policies, American Academy of Arts and Sciences, May 1999.

Wilson, K. G., and B. Davis, *Redesigning Education*, New York: Henry Holt and Company, 1994.

Word, E. R., J. Johnston, and H. P. Bain, *Student Teacher Achievement Ratio (STAR): Tennessee's K–3 Class Size Study. Final Summary Report 1985–1990*, Nashville, Tenn: Tennessee Department of Education, 1990.

_____, *The State of Tennessee's Student/Teacher Achievement Ratio (STAR) Project: Technical Report 1985–1990*, Nashville: Tennessee State Department of Education, 1994.

Wright, S. P., S. P. Horn, and W. L. Sanders, "Teacher and Classroom Context Effects on Student Achievement: Implications for Teacher Evaluation," *Journal of Personnel Evaluation in Education*, 11, 1997, pp. 57–67.